SPORT AND THE LAW

SPORT,
CULTURE
& SOCIETY

DAVID K. WIGGINS, SERIES EDITOR

SPORT AND THE LAW

Historical and Cultural Intersections

Edited by
Samuel O. Regalado
and
Sarah K. Fields

FAYETTEVILLE
THE UNIVERSITY OF ARKANSAS PRESS
2014

ISBN: 978- 1-55728-666-6
e-ISBN-13: 978-1-61075-549-8

18   17   16   15   14   5   4   3   2   1

Designer: Ellen Beeler

♾The paper used in this publication meets the minimum requirements of the American
National Standard for Permanence of Paper for Printed Library Materials Z39.48–1984.

Library of Congress Control Number: 2014944822

For Professor LeRoy Ashby
Excellent scholar, inspiring teacher, and proponent for justice.
Thank you for your wisdom and sound guidance.

Contents

Series Editor's Preface

Sport is an extraordinarily important phenomenon that pervades the lives of many people and has enormous impact on society in an assortment of different ways. At its most fundamental level, sport has the power to bring people great joy and satisfy their competitive urges while at once allowing them to form bonds and a sense of community with others from diverse backgrounds and interests and various walks of life. Sport also makes clear, especially at the highest levels of competition, the lengths that people will go to achieve victory as well as how closely connected it is to business, education, politics, economics, religion, law, family, law, family, and other societal institutions. Sport is, moreover, partly about identity development and how individuals and groups, irrespective of race, gender, ethnicity or socioeconomic class, have sought to elevate their status and realize material success and social mobility.

Sport, Culture, and Society seeks to promote a greater understanding of the aforementioned issues and many others. Recognizing sport's powerful influence and ability to change people's lives in significant and important ways, the series focuses on topics ranging from urbanization and community development to biography and intercollegiate athletics. It includes both monographs and anthologies that are characterized by excellent scholarship, accessibility to a wide audience, and interesting and thoughtful design and interpretations. Singular features of the series are authors and editors representing a variety of disciplinary areas and who adopt different methodological approaches. The series also includes works by individuals at various stages of their careers, both sport studies scholars of outstanding talent just beginning to make their mark on the field and more experienced scholars of sport with established reputations.

Sport and the Law includes ten essays written by noted academicians from history, law, and American studies. Edited by Samuel O. Regalado and Sarah K. Fields, two well-known historians of sport with extensive publication records, the book assesses in much detail a number of prominent court cases involving sport and its participants in the post–World War II period. Acknowledging there were a number of important legal decisions regarding sport and its participants prior to this time, Regalado and Fields chose instead to solicit essays concerned with court cases following the "great conflict" since that period has seen a remarkable growth in sport and its close interconnection with such important issues as race, gender, transnationalism, and cold war politics. The result is a fascinating yet easily accessible book that will be of interest to those interested in specific sports-law cases, the historical and social context in which they were adjudicated, and their ultimate legacy to sport and America more generally. Equally important is how the collection of essays uncovers the stories of brave athletes who fought to extend their human rights and the individuals who either supported or opposed those efforts.

DAVID K. WIGGINS

Acknowledgments

I owe my deepest gratitude to Sarah Fields, my friend and colleague, whose professionalism and good cheer helped us endure the many bumps that editors experience in the course of anthology projects. Working with a nationally recognized legal scholar such as she has been one of the most rewarding experiences in my career. The editors at the University of Arkansas Press, Larry Malley, then director of the Press, and David K. Wiggins, the sport history series editor, are also deserving of kudos for taking on our idea and lending constant support and helpful suggestions throughout the entire process. As well, it should be noted that the North American Society for Sport History (NASSH) was an ideal venue that not only brought me together with Sarah and David, but also with many of those who wrote essays for this book. Contributors Richard Crepeau, Ron Briley, Thomas Hunt, Steven Gietschier, Dan Nathan, and Jan Todd are not only respected scholars, but also cherished friends whose help and advice has greatly contributed to my career. Furthermore, outside of the NASSH circle, Arturo Marcano and David Fidler, whose scholarly work and humanitarian legal efforts on behalf of young Latino baseball prospects is commendable, demonstrated great patience and commitment to our anthology. As such, I send my two friends many thanks. Anne DeMartini is another who stayed with us from the beginning, and it is to our good fortune that she did in that her work is a significant contribution to the anthology. Along with the aforementioned people, I received constant backing, as I always do, from my colleagues at the Department of History, California State University, Stanislaus.

SAM REGALADO

I, too, want to thank all of our amazing contributors in addition to our colleagues at NASSH who commented on many of these papers and ideas; all are great scholars and good friends. I share Sam's appreciation for the University of Arkansas Press and the support of then publisher Larry Malley and series editor Dave Wiggins. We are also grateful for the careful editing by Debbie Upton. For me this project spanned two different institutions, and I am grateful for the assistance that came from both places. At the Ohio State University, my colleagues in the former Sport Humanities Program, particularly Mel Adelman and the graduate students, as well as the faculty in the Kinesiology program heard me talk through this project for years. At the

University of Colorado Denver, my new colleagues in the Communication Department were understanding and supportive as we finished this up soon after my arrival. They also directed me to the Auraria Campus Library, where the remarkable research librarians helped me collect last-minute obscure sources. Thanks as well to Dawn Comstock, who has listened patiently to the ebbs and flows of my enthusiasm over the years and has offered helpful advice and support. This anthology, however, would never have existed without Sam Regalado. When we first met years ago at a NASSH conference, I knew I had found a kindred spirit who got as excited about the intersection of sport and legal history as I did. I am deeply grateful to have had the pleasure of working with him and of being his friend.

SARAH FIELDS

CHAPTER ONE

Introduction

In May 1987, during a commemorative speech on the bicentennial of the United States Constitution, associate Supreme Court justice Thurgood Marshall observed, "that the true miracle was not the birth of the Constitution, but its life." He argued that the amendments added in quest of the Constitution's promise has been, in fact, proof of the document's continued heartbeat through the centuries.[1] Additionally, civil war, territorial expansion, evolution of commerce, and a quest for civil liberties and rights, in one manner or another, all contributed to the nation's changing legal profile as Americans strove to achieve the constitutional ideals they held sacred in their democracy.

Within this American democracy, sport, too, played a vital role in the construction of what Marshall called the Constitution's "promising evolution through 200 years of history." As recreation matured beyond that of a simple leisure activity and into a huge commercial institution, athletics and standout athletes were lifted onto a pedestal that magnified a romanticized vision of the nation. In reality, however, sport also mirrored the problems that, too often, blocked the path to true equality on many fronts. With the Constitution well past 150 years in existence by the middle of the twentieth century, Americans still wrestled with the albatross of race and gender discrimination that had plagued the nation since its origins, as well as new legal challenges on such topics as collective bargaining, corporate collusion, and international human rights, among others. For many, by the end of World War II, the promise of a fair shake and opportunity seemed, at the very least, quite unpromising.

In step with Marshall's vision of a "living" document, sport and jurisprudence provided a unique alliance as a participant in the evolutionary process of constitutional law. As seen in US Supreme Court landmark cases, lower-level decisions, events, activism, and commercial practices, sport as a distinct feature in the legal arena helped to change public policies and the often-discriminatory means by which they were practiced. Moreover, legal decisions that involved athletics and their participants contributed to new observations and questions in redefining constitutional interpretations. After 1945, sport and the law were not mutually exclusive, but a joint and powerful tool that helped to raise awareness of societal shortcomings and to advance the quest of reaching the American ideals of equality and justice.

Sport and the Law: Historical and Cultural Intersections is a collection of essays that capture the personalities and events brought together in different lawsuits. The book provides a significant means to observe and analyze how sport and the law helped to create change in American society, but also examines how sport and the law factored into the larger human saga and the manner in which people tackled the issues of their day. The focus on post–World War II cases is the result of the increased dynamics in the relationship between American society and sport. To be sure, there did exist some significant legal cases prior to this period. However, after 1945, with a larger middle class and an explosion of mass media, sport, as never before, grew increasingly tied to such divisive issues as the civil rights movement, the Cold War, Vietnam, feminism, and transnationalism. Moreover with participants and consumers on the rise, the national media exhibited its immense presence and disseminated information on a grand scale. Ultimately, judicial decisions that involved sport or sports figures took on a new level of significance that, beyond the athletic arenas and playing fields, impacted the lives of all in the changing profile of the nation that emerged after World War II.

Essays by scholars in American Studies, History, and Law, are divided into three sections: "The Burger Supreme Court and Sports," "Antitrust Law and Sports," and "The Impact of Sport on Law," which explore some of the cases in which sport and law intersect and the impact the cases had on American society. Note, however, that many of these essays transcend the theme of the section in which they have been placed; almost every essay, in fact, could be placed in multiple sections. For example, the topic of antitrust law appears in Sarah K. Fields's analysis of *Haywood v. NBA* (1971) and Richard C. Crepeau's work on *Flood v. Kuhn* (1972), but these essays are located in "The Burger Supreme Court and Sports," along with Samuel O. Regalado's "*Clay, aka Ali v. U.S.* (1971): Muhammad Ali, Precedent, and the Burger Court" and Steven P. Gietschier's "How the Burger Court Came to Be" largely because all three legal cases were decided by the Supreme Court under Chief Justice Warren Burger.

The section on "Antitrust Law and Sports" includes an essay by Ron Briley examining the Danny Gardella lower-level 1948 court case regarding free agency and baseball and Thomas M. Hunt and Janice S. Todd's examination of *Franz v. United States Powerlifting*, exploring how the lifters' antitrust challenge against a single governing body actually fragmented the sport. Both of these studies are significant in the world of antitrust and sport even though none was adjudicated at the Supreme Court level.

Although all the essays could fit into the third section on "The Impact of Law on Sports," those in this section focus on legal issues, which have immediate implications for the present-day human rights issues. Anne L. DeMartini's analysis of Renée Richards's 1976 lawsuit against the US Tennis Association and its due process ramifications is now timely because of the increasing public discussion of the rights of transgender and transsexual athletes. Human rights issues, found in another essay by Arturo J. Marcano and David P. Fidler, were also the embodiment of transnational business tactics by which Major League Baseball treated its Caribbean recruits as commerce while it danced around reform measures that called into question its dubious behavior with under-aged prospects. Finally, similar calls for reform in the quest for fairness are found in the case of Ed O'Bannon, discussed by Daniel A. Nathan. O'Bannon's lawsuit attempts to regain control of his own image for commercial purposes. Nathan maintains that the lawsuit has lent itself to the larger argument over the validity of the National Collegiate Athletic Association's definition of amateurism. In critically placing the relationship of athletics and jurisprudence in a historical context, *Sport and the Law* argues that lawsuits and sport helped to shape what Justice Marshall described as the Constitution's continued "evolution."

Sport and the Law is intended for both an educated lay and scholarly audience as well as for college programs of study in law, sport, American studies, and history. Although the essays themselves are examples of detailed and thoughtful scholarship, they are written in an accessible, jargon-free manner that assumes no prior knowledge of legal, historical, or jurisprudential theory on the part of the reader. While other books have focused on the effect of law and case law on the field of sport, very few, if any, have placed the sports case law into a detailed historical and cultural context that breathes life to the legal decisions, those that had a profound impact on American sport, law, and society. Each chapter introduces the reader to the legal case or topic in clear detail and explains the legal context of the topic, and then each chapter explores how the topic fits into the broader American social fabric and the multilayered implications of the case. Further, each chapter considers how the specific sports law case did or did not impact the broader legal issues; for example, the Muhammad Ali chapter considers how the case brought into focus the parameters on defining conscientious objector cases, which better protected the rights of petitioners. In all, *Sport and the Law: Historical and Cultural Intersections* provides for the reader the opportunity to see immediately the interconnecting threads that weave the law and American sport and society together.

SECTION I

THE BURGER SUPREME COURT AND SPORT

The Burger Court was a Supreme Court of transition in a time of turmoil, and the Court itself was changing. This change was noteworthy during the Court terms of 1971 and 1972 when the three cases in this section were decided. In 1971, when the *Clay v. United States* and *Haywood v. NBA* decisions were rendered, Warren Burger was the chief justice and the associate justices were William Brennan, Hugo Black, Harry Blackmun, William O. Douglas, John Harlan II, Thurgood Marshall (who did not participate in *Clay* because he had been solicitor general when the case began), Potter Stewart, and Byron White. By the 1972 term, William Rehnquist had replaced Harlan and Lewis Powell had replaced Black. Powell, however, recused himself from *Flood v. Kuhn* because he owned stock in Anheuser-Busch, which owned the St. Louis Cardinals.

The Burger Court as a whole was a transition from trending liberal to trending conservative. The previous chief justice, Earl Warren, had led a Court from 1953 until 1969, which was generally viewed as liberal. The Warren Court was noted for landmark decisions like *Brown v. Board of Education*, one that ended racial segregation in schools, and *Miranda v. Arizona,* a decision that required police to inform arrestees immediately of their Constitutional rights. The new president Richard M. Nixon appointed Warren Burger chief justice in 1969 after Warren's retirement largely because Nixon believed Burger to be a very different jurist than Warren. The Warren Court did not rely on strict construction of the Constitution; that Court had often relied on ethical principles in deciding cases rather than upon narrow interpretations of the law. In his campaign, Nixon had promised to move the Court to the right and to appoint strict constructionists to the bench. Burger was one of the most important of these appointments.

Despite Nixon's expectations, however, the Burger Court did not make a quantum shift and become overtly conservative—that would occur more dramatically after 1986 when another Nixon appointment, William Rehnquist, moved from associate justice to chief justice. The Burger Court legacy included *Roe v. Wade,* which prohibited states from making abortions illegal, and *Swann v. Charlotte-Mecklenburg Board of Education*, which allowed busing to reduce racial segregation in public schools.

The political and social strife in the early Burger Court period was the nation's chaotic landscape with issues of war, race, and age constantly contested. Sport lurked persistently at the edges of many of these dynamic issues. President Nixon's arrival in the Oval Office resulted in an expansion of the Vietnam War and thus an expansion in the vociferousness of its opponents. One of the more dramatic tensions in those protests came in 1970 when Ohio National Guardsmen fired into a crowd of protesting students at Kent State University, killing four. In the midst of the social battle over the war and in part because of the incongruousness of drafting men too young to vote into the military, the Twenty-Sixth Amendment to the US Constitution granting eighteen-year-olds the right to vote was adopted in July 1971. More positively, Nixon during this time was also engaged in developing a relationship with China, part of which was cemented by so-called ping-pong diplomacy with the exchange of table tennis players.

Sport and politics vividly came together in this era at the 1972 Olympics in Munich, Germany. During the second week of the games, terrorists with Black September invaded the Olympic village and took eleven Israeli athletes and coaches hostage, demanding the release of various Palestinian prisoners being held captive in Israel. Two hostages were killed in the initial takeover; the remaining hostages died during an attempted ambush at the Munich airport by the German police. David Berger, born in Cleveland, Ohio, and who had immigrated to Israel after graduate school, was one of the hostages. President Nixon dispatched an air force jet to return his body to Cleveland for internment. Americans learned of the tragic end to the standoff when sports reporter Jim McKay told the nation "they're all gone."[1] Reflecting the contentious world outside of the Supreme Court, the Burger Court decided three cases involving race, youth, war, and freedom.

CHAPTER TWO

Clay, aka Ali v. U.S. (1971)

MUHAMMAD ALI, PRECEDENT, AND THE BURGER COURT

Samuel O. Regalado

By all appearances, April 28, 1967, was not a normal day at the United States Armed Forces Examining and Entrance Station on San Jacinto Street in Houston, Texas. Though protestors to the war in Vietnam stood outside to express their disenchantment with the draft, to the staff working there, this did not seem out of the norm. But on this day, Muhammad Ali, the heavyweight boxing champion of the world, appeared on the sidewalk on his way for apparent induction into the military. "Don't go! Don't go!" chanted some from the gathering crowd.[1] Other protestors shouted, "Draft beer—not Ali!" H. Rap Brown, there for the Student Nonviolent Coordinating Committee, led the cheers and exchanged the black power–raised first sign with the champ.[2]

Ali did not disappoint his supporters. After he entered the building, he calmly followed the instructions given to him that included a physical examination and the filing of applications. By that afternoon, all that remained was for the new recruit to board a bus for formal entry into the armed services. However, when the officer in charge twice barked out the name "Cassius Clay," Ali stood still. Officials led him away and advised the champ that should he continue to balk, a federal prison sentence was his likely end. Aware of his circumstances, Ali wrote a statement: "I refuse to be inducted into the armed forces of the United States because I claim to be exempt as a minister of the religion of Islam."[3]

With these words, Muhammad Ali took the initial legal steps on a path that, four years later, eventually landed at the feet of United States Supreme

Court. Though he faced tremendous odds, the heavyweight champ who was a black Muslim confronted the United States Government with the type of resolve that he always carried into the ring. His claim rested entirely on the grounds that he was a conscientious objector to war. As a result, Ali became a lightning rod during one of the most contentious periods in United States history. Furthermore, by the time his case reached the court of Warren Burger, the very meaning of the term "conscientious objector" had, by virtue of legal precedent, been redefined. Thus, although Ali had gained global recognition for his achievements in boxing and his outspoken comments on race in America, at issue in *Clay, aka Ali v. U.S.* was neither sports nor race, but a matter of law and how it was defined.[4] At the outset of this odyssey the news of Ali's actions in Houston predictably triggered harsh reaction.

Ali's religious convictions and celebrity standing mattered little to his critics. For instance, on the very day that he left the armed forces station in Houston, one flag-waving woman in his path yelled, "You're headin' straight for jail! You get down on your knees and beg forgiveness from God! My son's in Vietnam and you are no better than he is. I hope that you rot in jail."[5] In reality, Ali, who had by then taken a public position against the Vietnam War, saw criticism against him on the rise for several months prior to his date in Houston. Thus, the pro-war protestor he encountered at the induction center was only the latest in a growing avalanche of feelings against him.

A year and a half earlier, Ali's position first appeared on the national media radar screen when he blurted to a reporter that "I ain't got no quarrel with them Vietcong."[6] His perspective, then, was initially driven by his attitudes on race. But as he traveled throughout the country and fielded questions, he learned that the complicated nature of the war was one of much greater depth. As such, throughout 1966, he strove to better understand the many fronts of the Vietnam War and, in doing so, stiffened his political stance against the conflict. United States policymakers, he concluded, acted duplicitously in their attempts to impart democracy in a foreign land while race relations in his own country were tenuous, at best. Moreover, as the intensity of the war and the casualty figures increased, he viewed the war as being immoral. As he toured the country with this message, critics mounted their own campaign against him.

Old-school sportswriters, who saw the Joe Louis prototype as the model for appropriate black behavior for athletes at the level of a heavyweight champion, led the charge. Mocking Ali by describing him only by his birth name, Red Smith wrote, "Cassius makes himself as sorry a spectacle as those unwashed punks who picket and demonstrate against the war."[7] As popular opinion increased against him, even his own attorneys wilted over the pros-

. pects of facing US lawyers on the issue of the draft. "It looks like trouble, Champ," said Hayden C. Covington. "This isn't like any case I've had before. They want to make an example out of you," he warned.[8]

Covington was correct. On the very day of Ali's refusal to be inducted, even though no official charges had been levied against him, the New York Athletic Commission suspended him.[9] Shortly thereafter, the World Boxing Association stripped him of his title. But Ali was unrepentant. In fact, only minutes after his induction episode, he recalled a sense of euphoria: "this is the biggest victory of my life. I've won something that's worth whatever price I have to pay."[10] As spring turned into summer, government attorneys mounted their case against one of the most high-profile figures of that era. As they prepared to take on Ali, the champ had his supporters. Writer Gerald Early recalled, "When he refused, I felt something greater than pride: I felt as though my honor as a black boy had been defended, my honor as a human being."[11] One elderly gentleman, who came upon the champ, told him, "They can take away the television cameras, the bright lights, the money, and ban you from the ring, but they can't destroy your victory. You have taken a stand for the world and now you're the people's champion."[12]

However, for each person who supported Ali, there seemed to be dozens of others whose comments were less than generous. "They gotcha! They gotcha! Sonofabitch!" yelled American Legion members in Chicago when they saw Ali.[13] One dramatic episode took place on a flight to Houston when, after the plane encountered harsh turbulence, a rattled woman seated across from the champ pointed to him and yelled, "God is punishing us because he's on the plane! Forgive us, Jesus! God is punishing us! God wants you off of this plane!"[14]

Following a brief trial, on June 20, government prosecutors won their case against Ali. Bent on preventing a snowball effect, one attorney introduced race as a factor to convict the defendant. "We cannot let this man get loose, because if he gets by, all black people who want to be Muslims will get out for the same reasons," he argued.[15] Convicted of draft evasion, Ali stood in front of federal district judge Joe E. Ingraham and requested immediate sentencing. "I'd appreciate it if the court will do it now, give me my sentence now, instead of waiting and stalling for time," stated the twenty-five-year-old boxer.[16] Ingraham complied; he fined Ali $10,000 and sentenced him to five years in prison—the maximum for draft evasion. Covington, who himself had developed a reputation for having handled Jehovah Witness cases, appealed the ruling and, thus, took the champ onto another step toward the Supreme Court.[17]

Interestingly, as the Ali case made headlines, two years earlier, Daniel Seeger, a little-known atheist and pacifist, had walked out of the United States Supreme Court with a victory that later had important implications to the champ.[18] To be sure, in that era Muhammad Ali was not the only person to take a conscientious objector stance as a claim to sidestep the military. According to historians Lawrence M. Baskir and William A. Strauss's study of the draft in that period, approximately 172,000 of those drafted applied for the status as conscientious objector.[19] But, until 1965, the Selective Service Board had only granted latitude to those who had clearly been in affiliation with recognized religious organizations. Most specifically, Jehovah Witnesses, Quakers, and Mennonites fell into this category.

Of course, resistance to the draft predated the 1960s. As early as 1794, upon hearing President George Washington's call for conscription to quell rebels in the Whisky Rebellion, outbreaks in resistance to that call occurred in western Pennsylvania and Maryland. Ironically, protesters, as a means to send a message to the "father" of the nation, placed poles in varied locales with signs that read "Liberty or Death."[20] Resistance to the draft took a similar turn during the Civil War as President Abraham Lincoln sought to force those loyal to the union into service against the rebellious South. Such was the climate against the draft, that in July 1863, resistors launched a riot in New York City that resulted in several deaths. Even Jefferson Davis, the Confederate president, faced rebellion for his own rebellion when it came to conscription.

However, not until 1918 did the issue of conscription reach the nation's highest court. A year earlier, with great prodding from the Woodrow Wilson administration, Congress passed the Selective Service Act; a law that compelled men whose age ranged from twenty-one to thirty to register for possible induction into the armed services. Before the war came to its conclusion, approximately 2,800,000 entered the military via the draft. There were, of course, challenges to the law. The case on behalf of Joseph F. Arver and Otto H. Wangerin was the most significant. Having refused induction and subsequently convicted of breaking the federal ordinance in 1917, given the wartime environment and a concern of wholesale evasion of the draft, their case quickly moved to the US Supreme Court. Defense attorneys on their behalf largely based their case on the notion that the Selective Service Act of 1917 was tantamount to slavery. Therefore, they claimed, the entire notion of conscription was in violation of the Thirteenth Amendment. The Supreme Court, however, saw otherwise. Basically, they saw no relationship between slavery and conscription. The justices, instead, claimed that the provisions in the Constitution granted the government the authority to, among other things, declare and wage war effectively. To do so, and by extension, waging an effective war in defense of the union included "the authority to draft citizens directly into the national army."[21]

The Selective Service Act of 1917 did include provisions for pacifists and conscientious objectors. As the history of conscientious objection had its roots in the Revolutionary War, the framers of the 1917 act took into consideration that draft boards were likely to encounter several of these claimants. Under that provision, members of a "well-recognized religious sect or organization" were, in lieu of fighting, assigned to noncombatant duties. Though on appearance this option seemed lax, in reality those who exercised this option often endured ridicule and violence from those assigned to manage them. Deemed to be cowards and unpatriotic, conscientious objectors could count on long hours of hard labor and mistreatment. Moreover, further attempts to completely exempt them from military conscription suffered a blow when the Court, in *U.S. v. MacIntosh* (1931), held that the Constitution did not relinquish conscientious objectors from the draft.[22]

Nine years later, President Franklin D. Roosevelt signed into law the Burke-Wadsworth Act, the first peacetime draft. The act better clarified the boundaries by which conscientious objection might be adjudicated. Accordingly, someone "who, by reason of religious training and belief, is conscientiously opposed to war in any form" could be exempt from military service.[23] More important, the provision went on to state that civilian overseers would supervise conscientious objectors. This was a distinct improvement from World War I when conscientious objectors endured hardships under military control.

By the time of the Korean War, the 1940 Burke-Wadsworth Act continued as the guideline for the draft. From 1950 to 1953, the military conscripted approximately 1.5 million men.[24] As the draft continued into the immediate postwar period, protest to its existence appeared. Anthony Sicurella, a Jehovah's Witness, convicted for draft evasion in 1953, saw his case appear before the Supreme Court in 1955. Claiming to be a conscientious objector, he looked to have his conviction overturned. Several of the justices, however, believed Sicurella's claim to be duplicitous. While, for instance, he was unwilling to defend the nation, he was quite willing to fight in defense of his ministry and church. The defense, led by Hayden C. Covington, whom Ali later employed, argued that the petitioner was a "soldier of Jehovah's appointed Commander Jesus Christ," and, as such, "not authorized by his Commander to engage in carnal welfare of this world."[25] The skeptical justices, as it turned out, did not rule on the merits of the case, but found fault in the Department of Justice protocol that had initially led to the conviction.

"The Department of Justice's error of law in its report to the Appeal Board must vitiate the entire proceedings," the Court determined.[26] While the Court's decision did not set a precedent, its actions in 1955 proved, for Ali in 1971, vital to his own case and fate.

As Anthony Sicurella was a religious man in a conventional sense, Daniel Seeger was not. Seeger, a college student in New York, first claimed exemption as a conscientious objector when, in 1957, the government drafted him for duty. Seeger, whose case reached the Supreme Court in 1964, argued that his conviction should be overturned because the bar, which allowed exemption for those who practiced faith only from recognized and established religions, was unfair. Once there, the justices learned that Seeger's position on God did not necessarily mean "a lack of faith in anything whatsoever." Seeger, instead, opted to believe in "goodness and virtue for their own sakes and a religious faith in a purely ethical creed."[27] The justices of the Warren Court agreed and ruled unanimously in his behalf. In doing so, the Court effectively expanded the definition of conscientious objector. The new ruling, thus, gave legitimacy to nontraditional legal considerations of monotheism on an equal basis with the same rights as those from traditional faiths.

In the midst of an era that saw the Vietnam crises continue to get out of control, Seeger's case, and ultimate conclusion, grew in importance. Only a year earlier, the Congress had voted into passage the Gulf of Tonkin Resolution. As a result, troop levels rose significantly. Adopting a plan called "Rolling Thunder," in early 1965 President Lyndon Johnson approved the military request for an additional 100,000 combat troops to South Vietnam. By the end of the year, US troops fighting in that region totaled 500,000. Bent on the idea that US military might lay as the key to success, the president and General William Westmoreland, his commander in that war, aggressively sought to keep a large military presence on the ground. With the Gulf of Tonkin Resolution in his hip pocket, Johnson believed himself to have a carte blanche approval to conduct the war as he saw fit. As the military campaign in Vietnam increased, on the home front major concerns about the war started to mount. For many young men, the draft was at the top of that list.

In the same year that the Court put *Seeger* to rest, the Selective Service System drafted 230,991. In 1966 and 1967, the government inducted 610,273 more men into the armed services.[28] These ambitious efforts in Vietnam that led to the high number of inductees sent a wave of alarm among those of draft age. As a result, with *Seeger* now a precedent, applications for those who declared themselves to be conscientious objectors rose. The avalanche of requests overwhelmed Selective Service System administrators. They, according to Lawrence M. Baskir and William A. Strauss, "had no mechanism for supervising the implementation of new case law, and local boards were not eager to suffer an intrusion upon their discretion."[29] As such, the draft boards continued to induct in a manner based upon the pre-*Seeger* guidelines. By doing so, "many would-be conscientious objectors were wrongfully denied CO status without realizing it."[30] As the Selective Service System's deviation of the law became clear, challenges to draft board decisions started to climb. However, those charged with evasion of the draft still ran the high risk of conviction and stiff sentences. "No matter how egregious the draft board error, courts refused to intervene unless the individual refused induction and sought release from the military through a writ of habeas corpus," claimed Baskir and Strauss.[31]

Nonetheless, justices and their clerks did not live in a vacuum. Outside of the courtrooms, the war, they realized, was increasingly unpopular. Following the 1968 Tet Offensive, the Vietnam conflict took center stage. Television newscasts kept tabs on the growing number of casualties and the ire of the American public turned on Lyndon Johnson. In March, the president could take no more and announced his decision not to seek reelection. As antiwar movements captured attention on the home front, sentiments inside the courtrooms also exhibited some change. "Convictions were met with light sentences," said Baskir and Strauss.[32] Law clerks, many of whom shared sentiments with the antiwar protesters, began to spend their free time enlightening prospective recruits on their legal options. Paul Harris, a San Francisco law clerk, recalled the day he shared a high school stage with an agent from the Selective Service System. "He only told [the students] about their obligations," said Harris. "So, I had to tell them about their rights." Routinely he told students "if you refuse induction, there is a good chance you will not be found guilty because the Selective Service has violated its own regulations when it tried to draft you."[33]

In the meantime, between 1967 and 1970, Muhammad Ali had become a symbol that transcended the ring. In keeping with the mood of the nation, by the late 1960s, sports figures, such as Ali, "instead of using their position to bolster the status quo, these athletes would become agents for freedom and change," observed historian Jeffery Sammons. "Playing the part of the 'good Negro' was no longer acceptable."[34] Not coincidentally, Ali's popularity was greatest among young male black athletes. For many of them, Ali's defiance to the draft, the boxing establishment, and the mainstream press trumpeted a call to arms. "He was," said Sammons, "an inspiration to black youths, especially proud, dissatisfied young athletes."[35] Indeed, in 1968 Harry Edwards, a San Jose State black sociologist successfully convinced many notable black US Olympians to bypass the summer games in

Mexico City. Those who did attend, such as sprinters Tommie Smith and John Carlos, saw the games as a platform to exhibit their criticism of the racial dynamics in the United States. Raised fists and other forms of protest, however, were but topical exhibitions for what was a much deeper problem. No matter how successful black athletes might be, Edwards claimed that any black achievement in sport "would never result in 'proving themselves' in the eyes of white racists."[36] Edwards, in fact, sarcastically pointed out that "the only difference between a black man shining shoes in the ghetto and the champion black sprinter is that the shoe shine man is a nigger, while the sprinter is a fast nigger."[37]

Outside of the sports world, Ali had also captured the attention of both black and white activists and antiwar demonstrators. Among the most high-profile people in the United States, the champ, said Jeffery Sammons, "became the undisputed champion of the antiestablishment crowd."[38] By comparison, Joe Louis had also found an accepting audience among whites. But those white patrons who supported Louis largely did so because of his mild temperament. In short, to them, he was a "good nigger." Ali, Edwards, and the proponents of Black Power challenged that patronizing characterization. As such, for many young rebellious whites, Ali was the perfect tonic for their own frustrations. "Students seemed willing to overlook his positions on integration, intermarriage, drugs, and the counterculture, all of which followed from his Islamic faith," claimed Sammons.[39]

In the meantime, Richard Nixon won the 1968 presidential election and, upon assuming office, implemented varied strategies that inevitably polarized the US public along ideological and racial lines. Antiwar advocates, to be sure, were at the top of Nixon's "enemies list." To that end, his administration employed various government agencies, among them the Central Intelligence Agency, Federal Bureau of Investigation, and even the Internal Revenue Service, to maintain surveillance on those who opposed the dictates of his presidency. Moreover, like his predecessor, Nixon was determined to achieve a military victory in Vietnam. Though the president announced and employed his "Vietnamization" program, one that called for a slow withdrawal of US troops in 1969, there appeared to be little evidence that the conflict in Vietnam was coming to an end. As such, with vigor, the draft continued and little mercy came to those who attempted to evade it.

Federal judges under Nixon were relentless in their convictions of draft evaders. "By 1969, Selective Service cases had become the fourth largest category on the criminal docket," claimed historians Lawrence M. Baskir and William A. Strauss. "They were a common topic of discussion at judicial conferences and sentencing institutes."[40] In a year in which 283,586 men were inducted, approximately 100,000 continued to resist. And Muhammad Ali was one of them.

Since his 1967 conviction, Ali remained outside of prison due to effective counsel and his financial resources. Two years later, Ali appealed his case to the Supreme Court. But the Court did not initially take the case. Instead, it remanded it back to the original district court so that it might review the protocol of the conviction. In short, the Court wanted to see if any evidence against Ali had been obtained as a result of illegal wiretaps. After extensive review, the district court concluded that the evidence was legally obtained and, as such, returned Ali's case to the Court of Warren Burger.

Ali's appeal to the Supreme Court seemed to come at an inopportune time. Richard Nixon took his 1968 victory to be a mandate for the "silent majority" of law-abiding Americans. To that end, he welcomed the thought that soon he would have the opportunity to select members of the Supreme Court. The president's opportunity arrived when the venerable Earl Warren, a longtime bane to conservatives, stepped down from his post as chief justice. By then, Nixon's choice to replace Warren was a fait accompli. Burger's conservative principles on justice were, by then, well known. In a 1967 speech, for instance, the Minneapolis native, according to journalists Bob Woodward and Scott Armstrong, "had charged that criminal trials were too often long delayed and subsequently encumbered with too many appeals, retrials, and other procedural protections for the accused that had been devised by the courts."[41] By 1969, Burger's reputation remained intact. Thus, "Burger was chosen because of his judicial experience, his opposition to Warren Court criminal procedure decisions, his criticism of judicial activism, and because his career was free of ethical blemishes," stated legal historian Kermit L. Hall.[42]

This, of course, did not bode well for the Ali legal team. In the midst of the Nixon "Southern Strategy," the odds for any kind of victory seemed unlikely. However, though the connotations of a "Burger Court" gave rise to the notion of a rigidly conservative Court, in 1969, the ideological profile of the associate justices painted a different picture. William Brennan, Hugo Black, William O. Douglas, and Thurgood Marshall were well-known liberals. Byron White, a moderate, was a John F. Kennedy selection. And though John Harlan and Potter Stewart were appointees of Dwight Eisenhower, they were hardly rigid conservatives in their judicial temperament. The Warren Court carry-overs were, according to legal historian Alpheus Thomas Mason, "grounded in American ideological and constitutional taproots."[43] Also, by the time that *Clay, aka Ali v. U.S.* made it to the Court, Harry Blackmun, like Burger, also from the Twin Cities, had joined the justices.

Clay, aka Ali v. U.S. brought to the Supreme Court one of the, if not *the* most, well-known figures of that time. Since his conviction in 1967, Muhammad Ali's image, as a result of his global exposure and continued stance against the war, considerably grew. "The hero and the villain of the late sixties became more thoroughly heroic in the seventies, yet without being reduced to a single dominant image," observed Michael Oriard.[44] In spite of Ali's celebrity, there seemed to be no indication from the justices that sport clouded their vision. But the Court had its fair share of sports enthusiasts. Harry Blackmun was an avid sports fan, as was Chief Justice Burger. William O. Douglas, too, enjoyed recreation and was an avid hiker. Finally, Byron "Whizzer" White, as a result of his distinguished college and professional football career, was the most notable name on the High Court with a relationship to sport. Nor did personal military bias seem to come into play. Only Potter Stewart and White served. Burger, himself, never wore a military uniform.

The Vietnam War, however, had affected the Court. For instance, six of the justices, Douglas, Stewart, Black, Harlan, White, and Brennan, all were on the bench when *Seeger* had visited the Court in 1965. And two members of the Court, Black and Douglas, adjudicated the 1955 *Sicurella* case. Douglas's observations and comments on the *Seeger* case are particularly worth noting. Driven by his convictions regarding the issue of religious freedom, the left-leaning veteran justice, in agreement with the majority opinion, added that "any person opposed to war on the basis of a sincere belief, which in [Seeger's] life fills the same place as a belief in God fills in the life of an orthodox religionist, is entitled to exemption under the statute."[45] Hardly a fan of the Vietnam War, Douglas's comments on *Seeger* did not reveal the depth of his disgust for US policy leaders who supported it. Unlike his colleagues who saw the war as defined only in the political arena, Douglas believed that the "extremely sensitive and delicate questions" regarding the legal appropriateness of the war "was a matter for judicial resolution." Douglas, claimed his biographer Bruce Allen Murphy, "single-handedly tried to either stop the war or keep people from being forced to serve against their will."[46]

Hugo Black, like Douglas, was not shy on his feelings about the Vietnam War. "Vietnam is the worst thing that has ever happened to this country": "It's insanity."[47] But, by the time Ali's case had arrived to the High Court in 1969, Black's chief concern was that the fallout of the war had created domestic chaos. On the heels of the *Tinker v. Des Moines Independent Community School District* (1969) case, one in which the Supreme Court ruled on First Amendment grounds that a school ban to prevent students from wearing black armbands in protest of the war was unconstitutional, Black, in dissent, lashed out: "Uncontrolled and uncontrollable liberty is an enemy to domestic peace."[48]

Clearly, the sitting justices did not ignore the disturbing events and rising tensions that the war had prompted. As they reviewed *Clay, aka Ali v. U.S.*, Gallup Polls indicated that a paltry 28 percent of the public supported the war in Vietnam.[49] Indeed, within the year prior to oral arguments, anxieties increased. With such events as the National Guard opening fire and killing four students at Kent State University in May 1970 and Lieutenant William Calley's conviction of the My Lai massacre in March 1971, the voices of doubt regarding the morale justification of the US role in Vietnam gained considerable traction at all levels of American society.

Liberal leanings alone, however, did not give Ali an edge. Indeed, nor did race. Thurgood Marshall was the lone black on the Court and his propensity to vote as a liberal was well known. But his fame as a great pioneer for civil rights did not equate to a favorable attitude toward those parties to whom the heavyweight champ was affiliated. Since his ascendancy to the Lyndon Johnson administration as solicitor general and later, his 1967 appointment to the High Court, Black militants and those in the Nation of Islam targeted Marshall for harsh criticism. Seen "as a middle-class lawyer with strong ties to the black elite and white establishment," young black radicals followed the lead of their angry leaders who routinely referred to Marshall as "a half-white nigger."[50] Not to be outdone, Marshall won no friends among that crowd after labeling the Nation of Islam as a "bunch of thugs organized from prisons and jails."[51]

While the Supreme Court justices contained a mixed bag of social positions, *Clay, aka Ali v. U.S.* was not the only case that challenged the Selective Service System that appeared on their dockets. Since the 1965 *Seeger* case, the Court found itself expanding its definition of religion as it related to the judicial criteria of conscientious objectors. In *Seeger*, the Court granted conscientious objection status to those outside orthodox religion. The Court, five years later, then held in *Welsh v. U.S.* (1970) that one could be exempt from the draft solely on philosophical or moral objections to war. On March 8, 1971, the justices rendered a decision in *Gillette v. U.S.*, a case by which the petitioner hoped to avoid the draft solely for having been against the Vietnam War. In an eight-to-one decision, the majority drew a boundary for conscription. "We conclude not only that the affirmative purposes underlying [the law] are neutral and secular, but also that valid reasons exist for limiting the exemption to objectors to all war, and that the section therefore cannot be said to reflect a religious preference," stated Justice Thurgood Marshall for the majority.[52] With pacifism and boundaries defined and precedent established, the stage was thus set for *Clay, aka Ali v. U.S.* to visit the Supreme Court.

On April 19, only weeks after the Court's decision on the *Gillette* case, Chauncey Eskridge stood before the justices on behalf of Muhammad Ali. Eskridge was well known in the civil rights movement. He had served as legal counsel for Dr. Martin Luther King Jr. and the Southern Christian Leadership Conference. Moreover, he had been with King at the time of his assassination. The other members of the champ's legal team also had civil rights connections. They included Jack Greenberg, a veteran from the National Association for the Advancement of Colored People (NAACP) Legal Defense Fund who played an instrumental role in the 1954 *Brown v. School Board of Topeka, Kansas*, case, and James M. Nabrit III, whose distinguished father also participated in that monumental case. Nabrit, in fact, returned the next day on behalf of the petitioner to hear the Court's decision in the *Swann v. Charlotte-Mecklenberg School Board* busing case.

Solicitor General Erwin Griswold, who first served in that capacity under Lyndon Johnson, and continued under Richard Nixon, argued on behalf of the government. Griswold's connection to the civil rights movement was also interesting. He served as an expert witness for Thurgood Marshall (who recused himself when *Clay aka Ali v. U.S.* reached the High Court because he was solicitor general when the case first appeared at the federal level) in several cases leading up to *Brown*. And, in the mid-1960s, he worked on Johnson's Civil Rights Commission. By 1971, after having served as the government's counsel on the *Welsh* and *Gillette* cases, he was well versed in conscientious objector arguments.

In the *Clay, aka Ali* case, Griswold made a sound argument that the champ's aversion to war had been, among other things, a selective one. Doing so, of course, was in keeping with the boundaries the Court had established in the *Gillette* case. Indeed, on several public occasions, and based on Federal Bureau of Investigation tapes of Elijah Muhammad, Griswold reminded the justices that Nation of Islam members were not opposed to holy war.[53] On that ground alone, Griswold's argument seemed to carry the day and, with it, an apparent jail sentence for the champ. Chief Justice Burger handed John Harlan the responsibility to write the majority opinion, but Harlan's clerks were not sold on the notion that a holy war was relevant to the principles of the qualifiers for evading the draft. As recounted by historian Jeffery Sammons, "The holy war was really Armageddon, the war of good against evil, the same war that Jehovah's Witnesses would fight—and they were accepted as conscientious objectors."[54]

Another issue included the level of sincerity brought by the petitioner in the objection to war. The "sincerity" gauge, along with the criteria of being opposed to war in any form, and opposition based on religious training and belief, was part of the triad that the justices used to adjudicate the *Ali* case. Convinced of the Armageddon position that his clerks had reinforced, and having determined that Ali's position as a minister of the Nation of Islam gave him the appropriate credentials for religious training and belief, Harlan faced only the "sincerity" criteria to determine the champ's fate. On that count, Harlan's clerks again came to the rescue. As a means to enlighten the justice, they gave him copies of the *Autobiography of Malcom X* and Elijah Muhammad's *Message to the Black Man*. The books made an apparent impact on the justice's thinking and, according to Sammons, "Harlan returned to work a changed man."[55] Harlan, when back at the conference table, determined that the government had mischaracterized Ali as being a racist and the pacifist principles of his defense. Harlan's shift, thus, created a deadlock among the justices and the prospects of a decision against the champ without comment. "It would be as if the Court had never taken the case," reflected Bob Woodward and Scott Armstrong.[56]

At this point, Justice Potter Stewart stepped in and offered an alternative plan. Turning to *Sicurella* for guidance, Stewart carefully studied the case from its origins and found that the Draft Appeal Board gave only vague reasons for its denial of Ali's claim. Not to include specific reasons for such a denial, based on the *Sicurella* decision, was grounds for reversal of the conviction. "Since the Appeal Board gave no reasons for its denial of the petitioner's claim, there is absolutely no way of knowing upon which of the three grounds offered in the Department's letter it relied," read Justice Harlan when rendering the Court's decision.[57] The Court also considered, and incorporated, *Welsh v. United States*, a case decided in 1970. As Jeffrey Sammons points out, in that case the Court "had ruled that moral and ethical objection to war was as valid as religious objection, thus broadening the qualifications."[58] As the Court neared the end of its term, all but Burger had been won over with Stewart's position. Faced with the uncomfortable prospect of being the lone dissenter, which, according to Woodward and Armstrong, "might be interpreted as a racist vote," the chief justice relented. In doing so, he put the final stamp on a decision *per curium*.[59] In Chicago when the decision was announced on June 28, the champ beamed. "I thank Allah and I thank the Supreme Court for recognizing the sincerity of the religious teaching that I've accepted," he told reporters.[60] Four years after he had, in 1967, entered the judicial ring, Ali's victory was complete.

In 1973, President Nixon called an end to the draft. Thus, *Clay, aka Ali v. U.S.*, and its predecessors, was put to rest. Its importance, however, cannot be understated. Since first introduced to the Supreme Court in 1918, the series of conscientious objector decisions was the picture of a claim under constant flux. Claimant Joseph F. Arver, who argued that his World War I conscription was akin to slavery, had little in his defense that resembled Ali's claim nearly fifty years later. And, in between, resistance to the draft on religious grounds left the justices with the unenviable burden of defining religion. In *Clay, aka Ali v. U.S.*, the Court, for the first time, took into consideration variables of all prior conscientious objector decisions and streamlined them into a three-part evaluation. In doing so, it widened the bar for petitioners to make their claims and also gave the justices a needed guide for which to adjudicate cases of this nature. Precedent also played a paramount role in this realm. Since the 1965 *Seeger* decision, the Justice Department and Draft Appeals Board rejection of claimants were often loosely defined. In the Vietnam War years, the federal government's appetite to conscript prospective troops overshadowed the need to follow proper protocol when challenges to the draft occurred. "The 1971 *Clay* (Muhammad Ali) case confirmed what many had argued, that the Selective Service had misread or ignored *Seeger*, and that many accused draft offenders had been wrongly denied conscientious objector exemptions in the late 1960s," observed Lawrence M. Baskir and William A. Strauss.[61]

On legal grounds alone, *Clay, aka Ali v. U.S.* was paramount. Muhammad Ali helped to shape and define the meaning of conscientious objector. In doing so, he also became a symbol who sought justice in the face of overwhelming criticism and tremendous legal odds. Reflecting on the champ, basketball icon Kareem Abdul-Jabbar stated, "He gave so many people courage to test the system."[62] The champ never wavered in his principles. As such, the commitment to his cause forced the justices of the Burger Court to fine tune a designation in the draft that, for too long, continued to exist with critical loose ends that victimized the claimants. With so much on the line for himself, Muhammad Ali's victory in the arena of the Supreme Court was, indeed, his greatest of all.

Though no hard data exists, Ali likely lost millions of dollars as a result of his refusal to be inducted into the military in 1967. When he fought his last bout prior to his ban against Zora Folley on March 22, 1967, he was all of twenty-five years old. He did not resume his career until October 26, 1970, when he climbed into the ring against Jerry Quarry. By then, he was twenty-eight and had lost some of his prime years while fighting in the court of law. While he twice recaptured the heavyweight crown, perhaps in an effort to recoup his earlier losses, the champ continued to fight seven more years after his legendary 1974 victory over George Foremen in Zaire. Well past his prime, Ali was thirty-nine when he retired.

As to his notable Supreme Court victory, when the draft came to an end in 1973, so, too, did the need to test the viability and strength of *Clay, aka Ali v. U.S.* Even though, since that 1971 decision, the United States fought in two wars in Afghanistan and Iraq, the country had little appetite to revisit conscription. As such, *Clay, aka Ali v. U.S.* remains the final say on the matter of religion and the draft and the first one the justices will engage on this issue should Americans again be called into service. Only this time, thanks to Ali, the parameters will be much more clear. Taking the position that *Clay* set a precedent on conscientious objector cases, law professor Michael I. Spak observed, "I have never seen another case of a recognized religion being prosecuted."[63]

In the years past his exit from the ring, Ali, no longer the outspoken individual he once was in the late sixties and early seventies and struggling with Parkinson's disease, drifted out of mainstream attention while granting only occasional interviews and public appearances. In 1996, however, the champ momentarily returned to the center stage when he lit the Olympic Flame in the Opening Ceremonies of that year's games in Atlanta. On that July 19 evening, 83,000 fans cheered wildly as his figure adorned the big screen monitors throughout the arena and broadcasters spoke affectionately of him to worldwide audiences.[64] To be sure, the public's opinion of Ali had clearly softened and his historical legacy built upon his athletic achievements and personal convictions increased. "When Ali put everything he achieved on the line in deference to his religion and political principles that got attention around the world," said sociologist Harry Edwards. "People eventually came to believe Ali was sincere and over time there developed a tremendous degree of unquestioned integrity about him."[65] By 2012, given the mark he had made in the ring and in the courtroom, in the eyes of many he was still the champ.

CHAPTER THREE

Odd Bedfellows

SPENCER HAYWOOD AND JUSTICE WILLIAM O. DOUGLAS

Sarah K. Fields

At first glance, a professional basketball player and a United States Supreme Court justice would seem to have little in common. Spencer Haywood and William O. Douglas, however, traveled very similar paths in their lives, and the intersection of those lives would change the face of professional basketball in America. Although separated by region, age, and race, Haywood and Douglas came from similarly humble beginnings. Both were raised by strong single mothers after their fathers' untimely deaths. Both faced and overcame poverty to achieve, in different ways, national attention, one in basketball and the other in law. In 1971, although they had never met in person, Justice Douglas changed Spencer Haywood's life when he ruled that the National Basketball Association (NBA) must allow Haywood to play in the league.

Haywood v. National Basketball Association is not, from a jurisprudential perspective, a terribly important case. In a brief three-page decision, Justice Douglas, writing as a circuit justice, reinstated a district court injunction that allowed Haywood to play in the NBA while his antitrust lawsuit against the league proceeded. Haywood was challenging the NBA's rule that no player could enter the league until four years after his high school class had graduated. Douglas ruled that the NBA was not exempt from the antitrust laws, that the question of whether the age rule was a violation was an important one, and that excluding Haywood during the litigation process was too serious a detriment to Haywood to be allowed to stand.[1] In legal terms, Douglas's decision was relatively unimportant. No law review article ever focused on the case, nor was it discussed in any of Douglas's biographical and autobiographical writings, perhaps because *Haywood* was, after all, a simple and brief decision by the circuit justice and not the entire Supreme Court. For the basketball world as well as for Haywood the individual, however, the case was monumental. *Haywood* inevitably opened the doors of the NBA to the likes of Michael Jordan, Kobe Bryant, and LeBron James.

Intriguingly, although Douglas supported Haywood's legal claim with just a few paragraphs, the case was significant not just for the world of professional basketball but also because it marked the intersection of two parallel lives. The two men began in similar places and reached remarkable heights with remarkable costs, and in one lawsuit, they crossed paths and changed American sport.

Haywood's Life before Douglas

Spencer Haywood was born in Silver City, Mississippi, in 1949, just three weeks after his father had died. Haywood was two months premature and his survival was in question, but with his mother's careful nurturing, he lived. He grew up in abject poverty scavenging for money with his brothers and sisters (Haywood had six half-siblings and four full-siblings; Haywood was number nine in the birth order of the eleven children). His mother worked in a variety of domestic jobs when she was not laboring in the cotton fields with her children, but the money was never sufficient and Haywood described the family as being "poorer than dirt," on the lowest rung of a social ladder that placed black families well below the white average. Despite the family's lack of money, in his autobiography Haywood emphasized their love and devotion to each other, and he noted that he was particularly special to his mother, writing "I was so close to Mama that if my leg was hurting, she would tell me."[2] The family's bond notwithstanding, Mississippi in the 1950s and early 1960s was a difficult place to be a rural black boy. Haywood described being shot at by passengers in passing pickup trucks and of living in a world that was uninvolved in the civil rights movement.[3] Between racism and class discrimination, Haywood developed a healthy skepticism for those more privileged than himself.

Although Haywood was initially physically small and frail, he grew very tall very quickly. By the age of thirteen, his height was six feet six inches, and he caught the attention of the high school basketball coach who insisted that he try out for the team. Haywood's physique matured, and the coach taught him the fundamentals of the game as Haywood grew into his height and developed his coordination and talent. Following his tenth-grade year, Haywood left Mississippi and moved north to live with his brother. After spending the summer in Chicago, another older brother, Leroy, who was attending Bowling Green State University on a basketball scholarship, encouraged Haywood to come with him to Ohio to try to find a high school team. For several weeks, Haywood lived in the dorm rooms of different players, most of whom were white, and the players smuggled him food and practiced ball with him. Finally Leroy found Haywood a high school coach in Detroit who in turn placed Haywood in a foster family who gave him a home, an education, and stability. In 1967 he led his high school basketball team to the Michigan state championship.[4]

After graduating from high school, Haywood spent the summer in Knoxville, Tennessee, where he had committed to being the first black player at the University of Tennessee (UT) and, in fact, the first black basketball player in the Southeastern Conference (SEC). Although he had not passed UT's entrance examinations, the coach promised Haywood he would not need to attend junior college but could enroll and start practicing with the team as a freshman. At the end of the summer, however, Haywood was told that he would need to go to junior college for a year in Chattanooga before he could enroll at UT and join the team. Frustrated and feeling betrayed, Haywood left the state and, upon the suggestion of his old high school coach, enrolled at Trinidad Junior College in Colorado. While there, he averaged over twenty-eight points and twenty-two rebounds per game.[5]

In part because of his proximity to the Olympic Training Center at Colorado Springs and in part because some of the other great college centers and power forwards (including Lew Alcindor aka Kareem Abdul-Jabbar, Elvin Hayes, and Wes Unseld) chose not to try out for the team, Haywood landed a spot on the roster of the US Olympic basketball team bound for the 1968 games in Mexico City. Haywood claimed the Olympic selection committee's choice to cut Pete Maravich from the team gave him the opportunity to be the leader on that gold medal winning team.[6] After his success in Mexico City, Haywood enrolled at the University of Detroit where, as a sophomore, he led the nation in rebounding (over twenty-one boards per game) and also scored an average of over thirty-two points per game.[7] Despite his success, Haywood was frustrated with the University of Detroit, disliked the new coach who was hired after his sophomore year, and decided that he was ready to play professionally.[8]

In 1969, two professional basketball leagues competed in the United States, the NBA and the American Basketball Association (ABA). Although both had strict rules prohibiting teams from drafting players who were not four years past their high school graduation, the ABA wanted to sign the best college players before the NBA did, so they enacted the hardship rule, which said in essence that if a player was the breadwinner of a family, they could enter the ABA. Spencer Haywood was the first ABA hardship case when he signed with the Denver Rockets.[9]

By the 1969–1970 ABA season, Haywood was twenty years old and two years out of high school; he stood six feet nine inches tall and weighed about 225 pounds. He was just as successful in the ABA as he had been at every previous level, winning the Rookie of the Year and Most Valuable Player awards after leading the league in scoring and rebounding.[10] At the end of the season, Haywood took a closer look at his initial contract, which paid him $50,000 for three seasons of basketball with the Rockets and promised to pay him an annuity of $15,000 a year when he was between the ages of forty and sixty. After Haywood's success as a rookie, the Rockets reworked his contract, which they announced was for $1.9 million over six years. Upon closer inspection, Haywood discovered that only about $510,000 of the contract was guaranteed and that the language surrounding the remainder was vague and unclear as to how the contract could be fulfilled. Attempts to renegotiate stalled, and, frustrated by the Denver tactics, Haywood called Sam Schulman, owner of the NBA Seattle SuperSonics, to discuss the possibility of jumping leagues. Schulman agreed to a contract worth a guaranteed $1.5 million for six seasons and committed to paying for all court and attorney fees to fight to make Haywood a SuperSonic. Haywood was twenty-one years old and three years out of high school.[11]

The Lawsuits

When the NBA learned of Haywood's contract with Seattle, Commissioner Walter Kennedy rescinded the contract, ruling Haywood ineligible to play in the NBA because he was not four years beyond his high school graduation. He also threatened the team with various sanctions. Haywood sued the NBA, arguing that the four-year rule and the draft rule (which prohibited drafting players not four years out of school) were violations of Section One of the Sherman Antitrust Act, which prohibits the restraint of trade. Haywood argued that the NBA was excluding an entire class of people (a group boycott) who were not four years beyond high school and that the group boycott was illegal per se and should be overturned by the courts.[12]

As the legal system moves slowly and a resolution of the case on its merits prior to the end of the 1970–1971 NBA season seemed unlikely, Haywood, as is typical in cases where time is of the essence, filed for an injunction to allow him to play until a court decision could be reached. An injunction is granted if it seems likely that one side will prevail on the merits of the case when it is finally adjudicated and when failure to allow that party to perform as if successful would irreparably harm that party without adversely affecting the opposing party.[13]

The trial court granted Haywood the injunction, allowing him to play with the SuperSonics until a verdict was rendered and prohibiting the league from sanctioning the team. That federal district court ruled that without being allowed to play, Haywood would suffer irreparable injury "in that a substantial part of his playing career [would] have been dissipated, his physical condition, skills and coordination [would] deteriorate from a lack of high-level competition, his public acceptance as a super star [would] diminish to the detriment of his career, his self-esteem and his pride will have been injured and a great injustice [would have been] perpetrated on him."[14] Presumably allowing Haywood to play would not harm the NBA because if he was later ruled to be ineligible, the SuperSonics could forfeit all of the games in which he had played. That would be the team's risk and they were willing to take it. By granting the injunction, the federal district court also seemed to suggest that it believed that the NBA four-year rule could well be a violation of the antitrust laws, but at this point the court did not make a ruling on the merits of the case.

The NBA, not surprisingly, appealed the injunction, arguing that the trial court was in error because Haywood had no likelihood of success on the merits of the case because no antitrust violations had occurred. The Court of Appeals for the Ninth Circuit agreed with the NBA and ordered the injunction stayed—that is, placed on hold. That court concluded essentially that the NBA had always excluded young players under the four-year rule (they referred to the status quo of the league) and added that if Haywood was allowed to play, the NBA and the public would be harmed because of the lack of "orderly regulation" of the league.[15] Haywood appealed the stay of the injunction to the United States Supreme Court.

Again, time was important in this case because the NBA season was moving along and the playoffs were about to begin. The NBA wanted to make sure Haywood did not play in them, and the SuperSonics and Haywood were equally determined to make sure that he did play. The full Supreme Court only hears cases that have been fully adjudicated, which can take years. Fairly frequently, however, appeals on parts of a case or an injunction need to be decided quickly, and to accommodate that need, each member of the Supreme Court serves as a circuit justice, deciding the merits of the appeal individually and quickly for a specific court of appeals circuit. Justice Douglas was the circuit justice in February 1971 for the Ninth Circuit Court of Appeals, and thus he was asked to decide if the district court's injunction should be reinstated or if the court of appeals stay should stand.

Douglas before *Haywood*

William O. Douglas, despite being white and raised in Washington State, had a similar background to Spencer Haywood.[16] Raised by strong but financially challenged women, both were close to their mothers, and each man would rise above his origins to great public heights because of his talent and drive. Both were independent, restless, and sometimes unpopular. Given his background and Douglas's fact-based approach to adjudicating cases, his decision in the *Haywood* case was, in many ways, unsurprising.

Douglas was born in 1898 in Minnesota and was a sickly young child, suffering from eye and stomach problems. When he was nearly two years old, he developed what biographer James F. Simon called infantile paralysis or polio,[17] and his mother, who called him "Treasure," massaged his legs with warm salt water every two hours for six weeks in an attempt to coax him back to health. Although Douglas recovered, his father became ill and died in 1904 after moving the family to the west coast. After the funeral, his mother moved her family of three children to Yakima, Washington, where she struggled to stay afloat financially. The children, including Douglas, held odd jobs after school and, according to tax rolls, because of their efforts and their mother's investments, over the course of Douglas's childhood the family moved from lower class to middle class. The children, however, always believed they were close to destitute.[18]

Douglas was a remarkably bright child and one who was particularly in love with the mountains of western Washington. After his father's death, Douglas wrote in his autobiography that he left the funeral feeling alone and afraid and that he found solace and comfort in the majesty of Mount Adams: "suddenly the mountain seemed to be a friend, a force for me to tie to, a symbol of stability and strength."[19] His biographers all agree that Douglas would feel that tie to the land for the rest of his life, and as a child he used hiking in those mountains to build the leg strength that had been weakened by his childhood illnesses.[20]

After graduating from Whitman College, which he attended on an academic scholarship, and teaching high school for a few years, Douglas left Washington to enroll at Columbia Law School. Like Haywood, Douglas was never quite satisfied with his position in life. After law school he worked in a New York City law firm but he missed the mountains of the west coast and moved back. He found it difficult to make as much money as he felt his family needed in Washington so he returned to New York. After a brief stint teaching at Columbia Law, he became a professor at the Yale School of Law in 1928 and drew close ties with the legal realists. Proponents of this philosophy argued that law should be based less on formalistic legal doctrines (like precedent) and that judges instead should base their decisions on the real-world effects of the laws themselves. The tenants of this doctrine remained with him for the remainder of his career. In his years at Yale, he worked extensively on corporation law, commercial litigation, and bankruptcy law, meeting and becoming friendly with political power broker Joe Kennedy. In 1934, Douglas left Yale to become first a member and then the chair of the US Securities and Exchange Commission. In 1939, at the age of forty, he became one of the youngest men ever named to the Supreme Court.

Ultimately Douglas spent thirty-six years on the Court and was its longest serving and most prolific writer, publishing more opinions and dissents than any other justice. Appointed by President Franklin D. Roosevelt, Douglas over time grew to be one of the more liberal justices ever, albeit always independent and something of a loner. Many of his biographers refer to his statement that the only soul he needed to worry about saving was his own as evidence of his choice to work alone. He was not a consensus builder on the Court, which may be why in part he wrote so many separate opinions.[21] Subsequent legal scholars have critiqued Douglas's lack of jurisprudential consistency (which they blame on his legal realist background) and note that his opinions were not always well substantiated with precedent because he focused more on the facts of the case than other justices.[22] Scholar G. Edward White called Douglas an "anti-judge" who "believed the law was, fundamentally, nothing more than politics."[23]

Regardless of his jurisprudential philosophy, Douglas played a major role in American law and society in his public life. As chair of the Securities and Exchange Commission he had helped to limit fraud and corrupt practices by the Wall Street stock exchange traders. He drafted the first Supreme Court decision that articulated an individual's right of privacy.[24] He was a committed environmentalist who opposed the Vietnam War and firmly believed in the importance of international travel and communication. He supported education and individuality. In addition to his numerous judicial opinions, Douglas wrote prolifically on the topics that concerned him, leaving an extensive written legacy.

Douglas was, however, a controversial justice. Four seems to have been a personally significant number for him as that was the number of times that he married and the number of times the House of Representatives introduced articles for his impeachment. The two became linked in the final impeachment attempt. Unlike many justices, Douglas was never independently wealthy, and his alimony payments to his ex-wives toward the end of his career cost him most of his salary as a justice. To augment his income, he published his writing commercially. When Albert Parvin read Douglas's tract on the importance of international educational exchanges, Parvin was impressed and created the Parvin Foundation to promote international relations through educational exchange programs. Douglas agreed to be president of the foundation and received a stipend for his work; these positions were not unusual for justices at the time. Unfortunately for Douglas, Parvin had made his fortune in Las Vegas hotels and casinos and had some questionable business associations.[25]

In 1970, politics and the Court intersected with Douglas and his financial insecurity. President Richard M. Nixon had campaigned for the presidency in 1968 in part on a platform of appointing more conservative judges. He got his chance in 1969 after Justice Abe Fortas resigned amid allegations of financial impropriety. In 1970, while Nixon's nominee to replace Fortas was under siege in the Senate confirmation hearings, Nixon suggested that Douglas, the icon of liberalism, needed to be removed. He sent his staff to House Majority Leader Gerald Ford, who, on April 15, 1970, called for Douglas's impeachment. Fortunately for Douglas, however, the administration had not collected any real, hard evidence of improper behavior, and Douglas had important, powerful legal friends who conducted his defense free of charge. The defense was made easier because Douglas had kept copious notes of his meetings and engagements and never disposed of receipts, all of which supported his position that he had done nothing wrong. Additionally, politics, which had played a role in the discussion to impeach Douglas, also played a role in ending the matter. The House was considering a bill to allow eighteen-year-olds to vote, a bill Nixon did not support. In the end, the administration agreed to end the attacks on Douglas in exchange for the House Democrats burying the voting bill in committee.[26] The next year, Douglas would rule on *Haywood v. NBA*.

Haywood v. NBA

On March 1, 1971, Justice Douglas released his decision. It was quite brief, only three pages; Douglas was known for his terse decisions. After summarizing the facts of the case and the prior history of the lawsuit, he quickly ordered the injunction reinstated, allowing Haywood to play. In just three paragraphs he explained that the integrity of the playoffs affected his decision. On the one hand, if Haywood were not allowed to play and he won his lawsuit, then he and the SuperSonics would be irreparably harmed because everyone seemed to agree that without Haywood the SuperSonics would not qualify for the playoffs. On the other hand, if Haywood were allowed to play and the district court ruled against Haywood, the NBA league office could then decide how to deal with the Seattle victories and could order that Seattle forfeit any of the games in which Haywood played. The league could then prevent Seattle from participating in the playoffs based on the revised win-loss records of the teams. Douglas added that if Haywood played in the playoffs before a final ruling from the district court and the SuperSonics were to do well in them, the district court could fashion an equitable remedy for the NBA.[27] Not surprisingly given his history as a legal realist, Douglas focused on the facts of the case and the implication of his decision in the real world, but he also had an opinion on the legal issues in the case.

Douglas had grown to oppose baseball's antitrust exemption, and in 1972 would dissent in *Flood v. Kuhn*.[28] His opposition to that exemption would be consistent with his work as a young man on the SEC where he helped to control big business and monopolies and also with his tendency to grow more liberal in his decisions as he aged on the Court. In the *Haywood* case he specifically noted that basketball did not share baseball's favored status and that "this group boycott issue [referring to the four-year rule in the NBA bylaws] in professional sports is a significant one." He then concluded his brief opinion with a rather sarcastic response to the appellate court's desire to preserve the status quo, writing: "The status quo provided by the Court of Appeals is the status quo before [Haywood] signed with Seattle. The District Court preserved the status quo prior to the NBA's action against Seattle and Haywood. That is the course I deem most worthy of this interim protection."[29] Perhaps it is not surprising that a justice who was proud of the fact that he had risen from a small town in Washington State to a US Supreme Court justice in Washington, DC, was not impressed by arguments about maintaining the status quo.[30] Douglas never cared about maintaining the status quo; when doctrine or legal precedent blocked what he believed to be the morally right decision, he simply ignored doctrine and precedent and relied on the facts.[31]

Eight days later the entire court upheld Justice Douglas's decision without comment. Only Justices Potter Stewart and Harry Blackmun agreed with the appellate court and would have vacated the stay, but they did so without writing a dissenting opinion.[32]

On March 22, 1971, Judge Warren J. Ferguson, of the Federal District Court in Central California, awarded Spencer Haywood summary judgment on his claim that the NBA violated the antitrust laws. Judge Ferguson noted that the NBA was not exempt from the antitrust laws. He said that the harm to Haywood and those who were less than four years from their high school graduation was threefold. First, they were victims of exclusion. Second, the competition in the arena in which the victims wished to play (to sell their services) was diminished in that the best players might be excluded by the four-year rule. Third, the NBA was acting as "their own private government" and their members possessed a "shared monopoly."[33]

In response to the NBA's argument that the four-year rule was not a group boycott or a restraint of trade, Ferguson considered the facts of the case and the antitrust laws. He concluded that because the league at the time had teams in seventeen different cities with games and media agreements in multiple states, the business of the NBA was interstate commerce. He also noted that the league and its members had agreed not to do business with players who were not four years beyond high school, which was a group boycott.[34] The fact that the league had no policy or procedure for consider-ing exceptions to the rule emphasized the degree of the group boycott and made it illegal. He dismissed the NBA's argument that the rule was designed solely to encourage players to earn their college degrees as commendable but beyond the scope of the NBA's power. While he apparently found Haywood's argument that the four-year rule was intended to make the college teams a farm system to train players to be likely, Ferguson nevertheless was not convinced that was entirely the case, but he did not consider it sufficient justification for a group boycott of the college players.[35] Haywood and other young players, he ruled, could enter the NBA system.

The *Haywood* case then disappeared from the legal record. Haywood in his autobiography writes that the Seattle owner, Sam Schulman, agreed to pay the league $200,000 in fines for violating league rules but lost no draft picks nor suffered any other repercussions. The Seattle owner, in exchange, agreed to drop his pending lawsuit, which argued that the NBA draft system was a violation of the antitrust laws. The lawsuits cost him about $500,000 in legal fees beyond the NBA fine.[36]

Haywood's and Douglas's Lives after the Lawsuit

In some ways, both Haywood's and Douglas's public lives peaked before the 1971 Supreme Court decision. Haywood's shift to the NBA was not particu-larly smooth—while he played under the injunction, the media, the players, and the fans (especially outside of Seattle) were not welcoming. He faced criticism from sports columnists, boos from the fans, and coldness from the players, all of which surprised him. He had expected antagonism from the owners but not from others associated with the sport and as a result felt iso-lated from everyone except his teammates and the city and fans of Seattle.[37] He seemed to be viewed by everyone outside the city as a mercenary who had not earned his way into the NBA.

After the court battles were over, Haywood had a modestly successful career in the NBA. His five years with Seattle were the most stable of his career, when he was named to four NBA All-Star teams and lead the team in his fifth season to the conference semifinals in the playoffs.[38] After that fifth season, however, at the age of twenty-six, he was traded to the New York Knicks, and his move to New York and change in lifestyle would eventually end his career. New York was a more glamorous city than Seattle, and Haywood joined the fast-track socialite world as quickly as he could. He met and married Iman, who in the course of their tumultuous marriage would become a world-famous supermodel. He also began using cocaine. Haywood never really meshed well with his teammates in New York, and the team only made the playoffs once while he was there. In addition to his growing cocaine use, Haywood also battled a series of injuries and what he felt was a lack of respect and support from the New York media. He was traded to New Orleans in 1978 and played well, but when the Jazz announced they were moving to Salt Lake City, Utah, Haywood asked for a trade and the Jazz sent him to the Lakers.[39]

Although Haywood had had high hopes for Los Angeles, his cocaine addiction took over his life and for all practical purposes ruined his career. Haywood wrote in his autobiography that other members of the Lakers also used cocaine, but he admitted that his addiction was out of control and compounded by his use of other drugs. He became paranoid, convinced that the other players were intentionally trying to make him look bad and that coaching staff was out to get him. Years later, Haywood seemed to have realized that the players were not intentionally making difficult passes to him, yet he still seemed to think that the coaching staff of the Lakers, particularly Paul Westhead, did nothing to help him deal with his drug problem. Toward the end of that season, Haywood finally told Westhead and the Lakers staff that he had a drug problem: he was suspended one week before the NBA championship series, which the Lakers won. After the season the players voted to deny him his full share of the playoff money.[40] Haywood spent one season in Italy and then returned for a season with the Washington Bullets in 1982 but his renewed cocaine use finished his career, and he was waived in 1983. After several years, he entered a series of rehabilitation clinics, finally becoming sober in the mid-1980s. His marriage to Iman ended in divorce in 1987.[41]

By 2010, Haywood had remarried and had three additional children; his daughter with Iman was in her late twenties. He divided his time between Las Vegas, Nevada, and suburban Detroit, Michigan, running his construction company and working with USA Basketball.[42] After years of being ostracized by the NBA, he began working as a league ambassador in 1995, traveling the world to promote the league, and he also served as a board member for the NBA Retired Players Association. Although he had hoped to have the eligibility rule named after him that has not yet occurred.[43]

Justice Douglas's career as a jurist was close to ending in 1971 when he ruled Haywood could play in the NBA. He suffered a severe stroke on December 31, 1974, while vacationing with his wife in the Bahamas. President Gerald Ford sent a military jet to transport the justice's personal physician to the Bahamas and to bring them all back to Walter Reed Hospital in Washington, DC. Despite severe mental and physical impairment, Douglas refused to resign, causing his fellow justices to agree to hold over to the next term any case in which he was the deciding vote. Douglas's reluctance to step down seems to have been in part because of his irrepressible will, his reluctance to admit his diminished capacity, and political calculation. Ford was president when Douglas suffered his stroke, and Ford was the last man to try to impeach Douglas. Plus, Ford was a Republican, and Douglas suspected he would likely try to appoint a conservative judge to replace him, one of the most liberal. Douglas finally retired on November 12, 1975, but he would not go quietly. Despite his resignation, he attempted to submit opinions on cases until Chief Justice Warren Burger told the staff at the court to ignore him. He had a slow physical decline, and he died in 1980 at the age of eighty-two.[44]

Conclusion

Douglas changed the NBA when he ruled that Haywood could enter the league at the age of twenty-one. The two men, one black and one white, one from the West and one from the South, and one fifty years older than the other, came from similar places. Each rose from poverty to public prominence. Each was a loner who never felt completely comfortable with the wealthy world in which he lived. Each felt that he had been denied something. In a 2006 newspaper article in the *Denver Post*, columnist Irv Moss wrote that "Haywood believes his court battles overshadowed his achievements on the basketball court. He doesn't hear any response from players of today who have benefited from his hard-fought, long court battles." Moss added that Haywood believed that he would never be admitted to the Basketball Hall of Fame because the NBA still resented his entering the league early.[45] In 2013 and 2014, Haywood was a finalist for the Hall of Fame but was not selected.[46] Just as Haywood was disappointed that he had not been elected to the Hall of Fame, biographer Bruce Allen Murphy argued that Douglas was never satisfied with being a Supreme Court justice: he wanted to be president of the United States.[47]

The case, which brought the two men together, would have profound implications for the NBA. Countless stars would enter the league earlier than the four-year rule would have allowed. Once players began regularly skipping college to enter the league directly, the NBA lobbied for a change. In 2005, the players union agreed that, beginning with the 2006 draft, the minimum age limit for entering players would be nineteen and all players from the United States should be one year beyond their high school graduation. Because the union and the league agreed to this element in the Collective Bargaining Agreement (CBA), scholars have debated whether it is a violation of the antitrust laws.[48]

In 2011 the league and the players association ended a long lockout with a new CBA. Although issues regarding the one-year removed from high school rule were raised during the negotiations, no change was implemented in the new CBA (which either party can opt out of in six years or it expires on its own in ten years). The new CBA did, however, set up a committee to discuss issues involving the draft and the developmental league including eligibility issues.[49]

The impact of the *Haywood* decision, however, was most profound at the 2010 NBA all-star game. Some forty years after the decision to allow players to enter the draft early, twenty-one of the twenty-four all-star players entered the NBA under the changed rules.

Rarely do Supreme Court justices and professional basketball stars get mentioned in the same sentence, and, at first glance, Haywood's and Douglas's link seems fleeting—a brief circuit justice opinion upholding an injunction that has never been important in the grand scheme of Supreme Court decisions. In this instance, however, Haywood and Douglas led surprisingly similar lives in many ways: from their childhood illnesses and single mothers to achieving the pinnacle of their professions and finding that peak was not all they had hoped. Their lives intersected with this decision, which changed Haywood's life and the NBA. Although Douglas may not have considered his brief decision all that significant in terms of jurisprudence, as a justice who cared about facts and people, he would have known that it was important for Haywood, which likely would have made it important for him. The decision tied two seemingly disparate yet so similar men together in one more way.

CHAPTER FOUR

The *Flood* Case, 1972

Richard C. Crepeau

In late 1969 after refusing to accept his trade from the St. Louis Cardinals to the Philadelphia Phillies in a seven-player deal, Curt Flood, for twelve years a St. Louis outfielder, wrote to Bowie Kuhn declaring his intentions. Flood said among other things: "I do not feel that I am a piece of property to be bought and sold irrespective of my wishes. I believe that any system which produces that result violates my basic rights as a citizen and is inconsistent with the laws of the United States and the several states."[1]

The *Flood* case has become a historical marker in baseball as well as the story of one man's courage in the face of the power of the baseball establishment. Others see it as a story of how one man changed baseball history. Upon some reflection, it may be that neither of these characterizations is an accurate one. Or it may be that both are. Baseball historians and Flood's biographers are all over the map on their assessment of the significance of Curt Flood's defiance of baseball's *status quo*.

The centerpiece of the case was the reserve clause that bound a player for his entire career to the club with which he first signed a contract. Flood's lawyers argued that this represented collusion, violated antitrust legislation, and that it violated the Thirteenth Amendment as a form of involuntary servitude. They argued that forcing a veteran player to uproot himself and family produced undo financial and emotional hardship, represented an unfair labor practice under the Wagner Act, and worked against the advancement of fringe players who might be helped by switching clubs.[2]

MLB's defense rested upon two cases, *Federal Baseball* (1922) and the *Toolson* case (1953). *Federal Baseball* was a decision in a case brought by Ned Hanlon, the owner of the Baltimore Federal League team, who charged violation of antitrust law and conspiracy to destroy his business. On May 29,

1922, the Court issued its unanimous opinion written by Justice Holmes upholding the appeals court decision against Hanlon. Holmes noted that baseball exhibitions were a form of business, but they were purely state affairs and therefore did not constitute interstate commerce. Although the players moved between states, the game itself when played was held in one state. Therefore federal antitrust law did not apply to baseball. Baseball is also not commerce, says Holmes, because it is personal effort not related to production. This convoluted ruling set what came to be regarded as the antitrust exemption for baseball.[3]

The following term Holmes wrote another decision in which he defined vaudeville as interstate commerce because the transport of the apparatus for the show in interstate commerce brought antitrust law into play, thus contradicting his ruling in *Federal Baseball*.[4] Clearly baseball was involved in the transport of apparatus (equipment) of the game from place to place.

The Supreme Court did not deal with the issue again until the *Toolson* case. However, after Danny Gardella returned from Mexico in 1946 to find he, along with all those who had played in Mexico, was being blacklisted, he sued Major League Baseball. He lost in trial court but the Second Circuit Court of Appeals found in his favor. The court pointed out that radio and television put baseball into interstate commerce, and therefore the sport was covered by the Sherman Antitrust Act. The decision described the reserve clause as "shockingly repugnant to moral principals that . . . have been basic in America . . . [since] the Thirteenth Amendment . . . condemning 'involuntary servitude' . . . for the 'reserve clause' . . . results in something resembling peonage of the baseball player."[5]

Gardella was awarded damages and the 1922 decision seemed to have been reversed. Baseball appealed the case and then announced amnesty for all those who had gone to Mexico. Before the case was heard at the Supreme Court MLB settled with Gardella. It was a near thing for baseball that might have lost its antitrust exemption if the case had gone all the way to the Supreme Court.

The Court next dealt with this matter in 1953 when it heard the *Toolson* case involving the reassignment of a minor league player. George Toolson refused to accept his demotion to Class A ball from Triple A. Blacklisted from the game, Toolson then decided to challenge the reserve clause in federal court. Two lower courts ruled against him, relying on *Federal Baseball*.

The Supreme Court agreed to hear his appeal. Toolson's lawyers argued that the coming of radio, television, and air travel, along with the expansion of the minor leagues clearly represented new conditions that placed baseball within the realm of interstate commerce. Here the Supreme Court simply accepted the 1922 precedent of *Federal Baseball*. It added in its ruling a short statement saying that Congress had not acted to change baseball's monopoly status following congressional hearing in 1951; that baseball had been operating under *Federal Baseball* for thirty years relying on the assumption that it was a legal monopoly; and that any future action on baseball's antitrust exemption should be done by the Congress. Then in one additional sentence concluding the *Toolson* ruling, the Court noted that *Federal Baseball* had found that "Congress had no intention of including the business of baseball within the scope of federal antitrust laws."[6] However, according to Brad Snyder, Holmes had said nothing about congressional intent in his ruling, and that it was Chief Justice Earl Warren who added this notation. The impact was to transform the meaning of *Federal Baseball* and effectively grant the antitrust exemption of baseball. What Warren had hoped to do was simply to suggest that Congress had the right to regulate baseball if it desired to do so.[7]

The oddity here is that the House of Representatives, after hearings were conducted by Emanuel Celler's subcommittee on the Study of Monopoly Power into Major League Baseball in 1951, decided not to act on the antitrust exemption preferring to await the Court's decision in this case. So Congress did not act because it believed the Court would, and the Court did not act because Congress didn't.[8]

When Curt Flood decided to move forward with his suit, the Major League Baseball Players Association agreed to back him financially. Former Supreme Court justice Arthur Goldberg represented Flood, a choice now regarded as a major mistake by a number of participants and historians.

The trial court and the US Court of Appeals rejected Flood's claims invoking the precedents of *Federal Baseball* and *Toolson*. The appeals court refused to grant a preliminary injunction against baseball and in that opinion Judge Irving Ben Cooper illustrated one of the problems facing Flood. Many judges had difficulty separating the business of baseball from the game of baseball that many people loved. At one point Judge Cooper called for a "seventh-inning stretch" rather than a recess. At the end of the hearings the judge decided to postpone his decision until additional briefs were filed. He then said that the ball had now been thrown to him, and he hoped he would not "muff it," and compared himself to an umpire promising to call them as he sees them.[9]

In his final ruling denying Flood's request for a preliminary injunction, Judge Cooper wrote:

> Baseball's status in the life of the nation is so pervasive that it would not strain credulity to say the Court can take judicial notice that baseball is everybody's business. To put it mildly and with restraint, it would be

unfortunate indeed if a fine sport and profession, which brings surcease from daily travail and as escape from the ordinary to most inhabitants of the land, were to suffer in the least because of undue concentration by any one or any group on commercial and profit consideration. The game is on higher ground; it behooves us to keep it there.[10]

What followed was a recommendation by Cooper that the case needed a full trial to resolve the issues surrounding the reserve clause, and Cooper shortly thereafter was assigned the case by the chief judge of the district court.[11] Cooper also decided there would be an early trial.

When that trial opened some six weeks later, Arthur Goldberg was now a candidate for governor and was distracted from the details of the case. There had been little preparation by Goldberg and no rehearsal of testimony with Flood. Flood's testimony turned into a fiasco. In addition the entire strategy of Goldberg's team has been questioned with the implication that the interests of Flood and the MLBPA may not have coincided. There were, however, two extremely effective witnesses. Jackie Robinson, now nearing the end of his life, gray, going blind, and a victim of diabetes, spoke against the reserve clause and on behalf of Flood. The courtroom and the judge were transfixed by his testimony. Judge Cooper, again playing the fan, called Robinson into his chambers to seek an autograph. Hank Greenberg followed Robinson to the stand and he too was effective as a witness for the plaintiff.[12]

Many others were called on both sides, but in the end Judge Cooper's decision was probably inevitable and certainly predictable. In his forty-seven-page opinion he upheld *Toolson* and baseball's antitrust exemption. Cooper did not accept the argument that Flood was the victim of involuntary servitude, and on the reserve clause Cooper could find no evidence of abuse resulting from it. He concluded by predicting that the solution to the lawsuit would be found not in the courts, but at the collective bargaining table, refusing to accept the argument that the owners would not bargain in good faith.[13]

It was also very clear that the Second Circuit Court of Appeals would not reverse Cooper's decision, and that this case would be appealed to the Supreme Court. When these proceedings ended, the Supreme Court agreed to hear the *Flood* case. Briefs were filed with Flood's lawyers arguing that *Federal Baseball* and *Toolson* were out of date and not relevant to this case. As a backup position they argued that if the Court agreed that baseball was not interstate commerce, then Flood should be able to seek redress under state antitrust law. MLB's lawyers argued that both cases were in fact relevant, and that baseball had relied on the exemption for thirty years and that should not be changed. In addition the Court had put responsibility for any change on Congress, and Congress had not acted. The exemption clearly rested on the principle of *stare decisis* and the inaction of Congress. The owners also pointed out that the players had agreed to the reserve clause in contract negotiations, and therefore under labor law were not allowed to bring an antitrust suit.[14]

Oral arguments were presented on March 20, 1972. Once again former Supreme Court justice Goldberg turned in a disastrous performance. He embarrassed himself and his former colleagues on the Court by bumbling his way through his unprepared presentation, and when asked questions by the justices he could not remember basic facts. In addition he ran over his allowed time.[15]

Initial discussions indicated that there was a five-to-four majority against Flood and after Justice Powell withdrew from the case it was five-to-three. In the initial vote Justice Burger voted with the minority while Justice Marshall voted with the majority. In the end they would both change sides. Marshall's change came first and so for a short time it can be said the vote was split at four-to-four, still a vote against Flood. Then Burger's change made it five-to-three for baseball. Justice Stewart was charged with choosing the justice to write the majority opinion, which was against Flood, and after a few weeks assigned that task to Justice Harry Blackmun, an avid baseball fan, who in Stewart's view was the only one in the majority who was wavering in his position on the case. Stewart also asked Blackmun to write a one-paragraph decision similar to what had been done in *Toolson*.[16]

In its final form Justice Blackmun's opinion was anything but brief. Justices Stewart and Rehnquist joined Blackmun's opinion, and Justices Burger and White joined in all but part I of the opinion. Justices Douglas and Marshall filed dissenting opinions that were joined by Brennan.

Justice Blackmun's majority opinion was in point of law an affirmation of both *Federal Baseball* and *Toolson,* and indeed Blackmun quoted from *Toolson,* saying that Congress had no intention of including baseball in the federal antitrust legislation. This was always a strange argument as the issue never came up in preparation of and debate on the Sherman Act in Congress.

Part I of the decision, which Burger and White did not care to be associated with, was bizarre. A short history of baseball, a listing of the great players of the game, and praising baseball's place in American culture, citing "Casey at the Bat" and "Tinkers to Evers to Chance," was conveyed in some really "corn ball" prose. It was at the very best embarrassing, and at worst a sign that Justice Blackmun was a crazed Society for American Baseball Research (SABR) member who somehow got appointed by President Nixon to the Supreme Court.

Blackmun did, however, call the antitrust exemption an "aberration" and an "anomaly" while Burger said he had "grave reservations" about the reserve system. The dissenters were stronger in their views.

As you sift through the case you find a number of interesting little notes. Burger in his concurrence notes his sympathy for Douglas's dissent. He says that the errors of *Toolson* have been followed for so long that too many people's affairs rest on that precedent so he would not vote for Flood. Burger seems to be saying that if you compound your errors long enough and screw up enough people's lives, it is good policy and good law to continue doing so, a view echoing *Toolson*.

The decision turned on some odd points. According to Bob Woodward and Scott Armstrong in *The Brethren*, the court was split on *Flood* and the case could have gone either way. There were two possible scenarios that governed the outcome. In one there was some indication that Justice White might be willing to join Marshall's dissent if Marshall would make some changes in his dissent. Marshall refused and did not believe that White would have changed his vote.

The other scenario involved the abortion cases before the court. Chief Justice Burger was looking for a way to carry these cases over to the next term for rehearing, hoping that somehow the minority would become the majority. This was not impossible given the probability of death or resignation overtaking some of the senior judges. This would open the way for more Nixon appointments and a majority against what became *Roe v. Wade* could then materialize.[17]

According to Woodward and Armstrong, Burger visited Blackmun for a long discussion that led to speculation of vote trading. Burger, it was said, agreed to give his vote to Blackmun against Flood. In return Blackmun would agree to postpone the abortion decision, which he did. Justice Douglas was infuriated by Burger's dealing, referring at one point to Nixon's Minnesota Twins and saying, "The Russians once gave two votes to its Chief Justice; but that was too strong even for the Russians."[18]

This scenario is rejected by Brad Snyder, who argues that there is no evidence to support this claim. Snyder points out that as early as January 18 Blackmun had requested that the abortion cases be reargued before a Court with full membership. In addition Blackmun believed that the country could not stand to have the death penalty and abortion declared unconstitutional on the same day.[19]

There was also some speculation that a deal was being cut by Major League Baseball promising that if the case was won, Washington, DC, would get a replacement for the team that had just left for Texas. There is no hard evidence to support the claim, but this was all being discussed in the Washington rumor mill.[20]

Woodward and Armstrong also report that during the writing of the *Flood* opinion, it became a game among the clerks to call Blackmun's office to complain that such and such a player or group of players had not been included on Blackmun's list of greats. Blackmun took all of these seriously and either added players to the list or sent back a defense of the exclusion. Blackmun apparently spent hours pouring over the *Baseball Encyclopedia* and other baseball histories. In a strange prequel Judge Leonard P. Moore had cited a similar roll call of baseball heroes in his concurring opinion in the appeals court decision.[21] This addition of names continued even after the case had been decided but not yet announced. Blackmun added two more players, Jimmie Foxx and Moe Berg, to the list of greats. Even with these additions Blackmun overlooked a name he wanted on the list. He was mortified when he found that the final printed version of the decision did not contain Mel Ott's name. Blackmun had been certain he had included Ott, and on his personal copy of the *Flood* decision he wrote Mel Ott's name in the margin adjacent to the list. One of his law clerks later gave Blackmun a gift of a Louisville Slugger, a Mel Ott model, which became one of Blackmun's prized possessions.[22] Blackmun too seems to have lacked the ability to separate his position as a justice from his personal status as a fan.

What then is the significance of the *Flood* case? A number of historians including Ben Rader and David Voigt see *Flood v. Kuhn* as a significant moment in galvanizing the players to further action on the reserve clause.[23] Charles Alexander and Robert Burk make no firm judgment on the matter, although Burk sees it playing into later attacks on the reserve clause. John Thorn refers to the case as "momentous," seeing it as setting the tone for the labor strife of the 1970s. G. Edward White sees it as part of a general pattern of events leading to the demise of the reserve clause.[24]

Lee Lowenfish argues that there was an impact on the press and public opinion turning both against the reserve clause, a point on which Brad Snyder agrees. Marvin Miller also seems to concur, saying that it "raised consciousness" among both the public and the writers.[25] Chuck Korr sees the case as a deceptive victory for owners who then hardened their position vis-á-vis the Players Association. Leonard Koppett has a similar but more complex view of the case and its consequences. Koppett believed that in the long run the *Flood* case would be a turning point against the reserve clause because it did two important things: It educated the players and the public and it forced the owners to bargain on the reserve clause.[26] Korr also notes: "While Blackmun had said that baseball had a unique status, he also had said that there was every reason to change that." Jules Tygiel in a conference presentation at Frostburg State University argued the *Flood* case accelerated the march to free agency and that Flood's example encouraged other players to challenge the world according to the owners. In his view this moved the end.of free agency ahead several years.[27]

Bowie Kuhn says that the case was not a victory for the owners and that it opened the way for renewed collective bargaining on the reserve clause, although some doubt that Kuhn had a real commitment to that process. He tried to get the baseball owners to understand that, in his words, "Change was in the wind." He sought to convince them that they needed to seek compromise and accommodation with the Major League Baseball Players Association. However, Commissioner Kuhn discovered that a majority of owners had no interest in negotiating on the issues of free agency and the reserve system and misread the *Flood* decision as a victory over the players.[28]

Miller also made an interesting comment on the case in relation to the players. Not one player showed up in court to support Flood, and "*some* of them should have been there." Miller went on to say that this behavior "highlighted the 'me-first' attitude that, regrettably, has always been a part of the game and perhaps a major element in our society as well."[29] In other words the players didn't seem to care about Flood. As for Flood, it was a huge disappointment that not one major league player showed up to support him in the courtroom.[30]

In his book Brad Snyder sees the significance of Flood's actions in very strong terms. For Snyder the legacy is not about congressional actions or court precedents, but rather that Flood started the fight for free agency in baseball, and in the end Flood "changed all of professional sports. Flood's lawsuit sounded the alarm about the player's lack of economic freedom. Curt may not have won a single player free agency, but he exposed baseball's system of perpetual player-ownership as exploitative and un-American." In Snyder's view it gave players greater control over their careers and allowed them to share in the profits generated by modern professional sport. In his evaluation of Curt Flood, "'Curt Flood Stood Up For Us All,'" Michael Lomax takes a wider view of Flood's significance as a hero of the civil rights movement as well as a catalyst for change within baseball.[31]

My own historical judgment is that Flood should be honored for a courageous act, that his case might well have succeeded but for several odd turns within the court including Goldberg's bungled presentation. The case probably did not alter the course that history was already running. The owners and players were on a collision course over the reserve clause and other matters, with or without *Flood*. Curt Flood did, however, give the movement of history a good nudge forward.

In the end Andy Messersmith and Dave McNally had a more profound impact on the course of events, but did the *Flood* case have any bearing on that arbitration ruling? In his decision Peter Seitz said that *Messersmith/McNally* was not a blow against the reserve system on constitutional or moral grounds, and that it is not designed to achieve the objective of the *Flood* case. Neil Flynn on the contrary says that without the loss of *Flood v. Kuhn* the era of free agency would not have come in 1975.[32]

Where does that leave us?

Andrew Zimbalist says that since 1990 there have been four cases addressing aspects of the antitrust exemption. In these cases one state court and one federal court has ruled that the antitrust exemption applies only to the reserve clause, while one state court and one federal court has ruled that it applies broadly to the business of baseball.[33]

The only thing that came out of Congress is the Curt Flood Act of 1998 that may or may not have clarified anything. What it did do was to lift base-ball's antitrust exemption as related to labor issues.[34] The Curt Flood Act has not clarified the continuation of other aspects of the exemption. Some think the entire exemption is gone; others believe that the exemption con-tinues outside the labor issues. This legislation may have been symbolic, but as Neil Flynn says it did contain a phrase that vindicates Curt Flood some thirty years after his trade to Philadelphia, saying that major league baseball players "'will have the same rights under the antitrust laws as do other pro-fessional athletes.'"[35]

What continues to be protected, among other things, are the amateur draft and the control of the minor leagues, the coming of any rival leagues and their battle with MLB, various broadcasting issues including pay per view, special packages, cable, franchise relocation and contraction, and restrictions of municipal ownership.[36]

Flood's legacy then is not entirely clear. What is clear is that this case and subsequent developments were part of a larger story of significant and long-range change in labor-management relations in baseball, and to some degree in all of professional sport in America.

CHAPTER FIVE

How the Burger Court Came to Be

Steven P. Gietschier

This essay is an expanded version of a commentary presented after a round-table discussion at the 2006 convention of the North American Society for Sport History in Glenwood Springs, Colorado. The session was called "Law and Order: Sport and the Warren Burger Court, 1971–1972." Its focus was three cases decided by the United States Supreme Court early in the tenure of Warren E. Burger, chief justice of the United States from 1969 to 1986. The three cases are *Clay, aka Ali v. U.S.*, 403 U.S. 698 (1971) in which boxer Muhammad Ali, denied status as a conscientious objector based on his religious beliefs and affiliation, appealed his conviction under the Selective Service Act for refusing induction into the army; *Haywood v. National Basketball Association*, 401 U.S. 1204 (1971) in which basketball player Spencer Haywood sought an injunction against the National Basketball Association, contending that the league's annual draft, restricted to players four years removed from high school, was a violation of the Sherman Antitrust Act; and *Flood v. Kuhn*, 407 U.S. 258 (1972) in which baseball player Curt Flood sought monetary damages and injunctive relief as a challenge to the reserve clause in the Uniform Players Contract, calling it a violation of antitrust law. The commentary focused on recent Supreme Court history, explaining, in brief, why the chief justice when the Court heard these three cases was Warren Burger and not Abe Fortas.

Were it not for an ill-advised financial arrangement involving $15,000, then considered a substantial sum of money, there would not have been a Burger Court. Instead, there would have been a Fortas Court, but then again, maybe only for a few months. Fortas's undoing took a while, but it began in 1968, a presidential election year called by one historian "the hard year"[1] and by another, "the most turbulent year."[2] Both were under-statements. Closer to the mark was presidential journalist Theodore White's assessment. He called 1968 "grotesque."[3] Lyndon Johnson was president of the United States, but his administration was ripping apart at the seams. The North Vietnamese launched the Tet offensive. Civil unrest ran rampant in American streets with attendant complaints about "police brutality" and calls for "law and order." Senators Eugene McCarthy and Robert Kennedy became insurgent presidential candidates. Johnson decided not to stand for reelection. Assassins murdered Dr. Martin Luther King and Kennedy. By the fall, it appeared likely that Richard Nixon, a Republican, would be elected president over two opponents, Democrat Hubert Humphrey, and George Wallace, a segregationist.

In the midst of this tumultuous year, Earl Warren, chief justice since 1953, added to the turbulence by submitting his resignation to President Johnson. "Pursuant to the provisions of 28 USC, section 371 (b)," he wrote in a one-sentence letter on June 13, "I hereby advise you of my intention to retire as Chief Justice of the United States effective at your pleasure."[4] Warren's arrival at the Court had been tinged with controversy, and his depar-ture would be more deeply colored. Following the sudden death of Chief Justice Fred Vinson on September 8, 1953, President Dwight Eisenhower had named Warren to the Court with a recess appointment on October 2.[5] The former general and the governor of California shared common political beliefs, and Warren had campaigned to help Eisenhower win the 1952 pres-idential election by recommending to Western voters the Republican can-didate who, he said, shared their concerns about hydroelectric power, soil conservation, and other land-use issues.[6] Nevertheless, exactly how Warren became chief justice is a matter of some dispute. In Eisenhower's memoirs, he recalled a postelection conversation with Warren during which "I told the governor that I was considering the possibility of appointing him to the Supreme Court and that I was definitely inclined to do so if, in the future, a vacancy should occur. However, neither he nor I was thinking of the special post of chief justice, nor was I definitely committed to any appointment."[7] In this version of events, Eisenhower settled on Warren as Vinson's replacement only after considering several other potential nominees and then receiving a favorable report from Attorney General Herbert Brownell "on the governor's record of attainments as a lawyer, as district attorney, and as attorney general of California."[8]

In his own memoirs, Warren, admitting that "the general's recollection and mine do not fully agree,"[9] offered a more nuanced account subsequently supported by a brace of biographers. Warren wrote that shortly after the election Eisenhower telephoned him and said, "I want you to know that I intend to offer you the first vacancy on the Supreme Court."[10] Presidential biographer Stephen Ambrose argued that "when Eisenhower made that promise he did not expect that the vacancy would be that of the chief justice himself."[11] The president, in fact, later offered Warren the position of solicitor general, planning to elevate him to the court subsequently as an associate justice, and Warren had accepted in August 1953. Vinson's death changed all that, infusing the phrase "first vacancy" with new and immediate meaning. In the words of Warren's biographer, Ed Cray, Eisenhower, "apparently did not feel himself bound by his pledge," but Warren insisted that this "first vacancy" was rightly his.[12] The president sent Brownell to California to ask Warren to accept the next opening on the court, whenever it might occur, but the governor was adamant. "The president might elevate an associate justice," Cray wrote, "but otherwise, the 'first vacancy' was the chief's position."[13] Eisenhower eventually agreed, and the reaction to his naming Warren was quite favorable. Still, this was a recess appointment, rushed through so that the Court would have a chief in place for the opening of its annual term in October. Warren still needed Senate approval, which came by voice vote on March 1, 1954.[14]

The timing of Warren's retirement announcement and its conditional language proved to be even more controversial than his appointment. Coming as it did just a bit more than four months before the election, Warren's move was criticized for opening the way to a lame-duck nomination; that is, allowing Johnson to name a successor before a new resident would be inaugurated in January 1969. Warren paid no heed to this criticism. In a second letter to the president written on the same day as the first, he asserted that he was leaving the Court "not because of reasons of health or on account of any personal or associational problems, *but solely because of age* [italics in original],"[15] yet most observers concluded that his real motivation was entirely political. Fortas's biographer, Bruce Allen Murphy, wrote that "in a political sense the timing made all the sense in the world."[16] Warren anticipated that Richard Nixon, a man who had written that decisions of the Warren Court had "weakened law and encouraged criminals,"[17] would be elected president, and Warren wanted to deny this man for whom he had no respect the chance to appoint the next chief justice. In addition, Warren feared that Nixon, if given the chance, might nominate Senator Everett Dirksen, a man who, in Warren's words, "has already tried to ruin the Court."[18] Once Warren's intention to retire became public knowledge, Nixon promptly entered the fray, saying that he wanted on the Court only "strict constructionists who saw their duty as interpreting law and not making law."[19] Using some of the coded vocabulary that critics of the Warren Court's decisions had honed over the years, Nixon added that "I would therefore want to select a man who was thoroughly experienced and versed in the criminal law and its problems."[20]

Lyndon Johnson knew that his situation, having the opportunity to appoint a Supreme Court justice in the last months of a presidential term, was far from unique. Cray noted that John Marshall "was confirmed just weeks before President John Adams stepped down" in 1801.[21] Moreover, in the past half century, the Senate had confirmed five justices, including Louis D. Brandeis and Benjamin Cardozo, nominated in the last year of a president's term. Johnson relished politics, of course, but, having announced his intention in March not to seek reelection, he found his power in June to be considerably on the wane. Figuring that Warren's departure would give him one last shot at crafting a legacy and ensuring the survival of Great Society legislation, he decided, first, to accept Warren's resignation "effective at such time as a successor is qualified,"[22] and, second, to appoint not one justice but two. In late June, he nominated Fortas, an associate justice since 1965, to be chief justice and former Texas congressman and Fifth Circuit Court of Appeals judge Homer Thornberry to fill Fortas's seat as an associate. Both men were political allies of the president, Fortas intimately so. He had known Johnson since 1937 when the Texan came to Washington as a congressman and over the years had, in the words of Johnson biographer Robert Dallek, "performed a variety of legal and political tasks for Johnson, usually in secret and with the single-minded goal of serving the President's interests."[23] When Johnson moved to the Senate in 1948, Thornberry assumed his House seat and quickly became Johnson's protégé. "It's just unbelievable how many things he and Mrs. Johnson did to help us when we went to Washington," Thornberry later recalled.[24] President John Kennedy named Thornberry to the federal bench in 1963, and Johnson promoted him to the United States Court of Appeals for the Fifth Circuit two years later. Simultaneously, Fortas continued as an unofficial and often unseen presidential counselor, even after he left private practice and joined the Supreme Court. White House records, according to Murphy, showed "145 LBJ-Fortas meetings between November 23, 1963, and July 2, 1968, and this did not include telephone calls."[25]

Even before announcing his two choices to replace Warren, Johnson negotiated with Dirksen to secure the Minority Leader's crucial support for the tandem. Nevertheless, the president's attempt to "pack" the Court with two "cronies," as the pair would soon be branded, was fraught with enormous difficulties, especially for a president with diminished influence in the

United States Senate. Johnson hoped that he could persuade a number of conservative southern Democratic senators to accept Fortas, with his liberal record, because they would also be getting Thornberry, but this proved to be a hard sell. James Eastland of Mississippi, chairman of the Senate Judiciary Committee and perhaps more unreconstructed than any other senator, warned the president that he "had never seen so much feeling against a man as against Fortas."[26] Arkansan John McClellan asked Eastland to report Fortas's nomination out of committee simply so that he could fight "that SOB"[27] on the floor. Johnson's great friend, Richard Russell of Georgia, initially indicated that he would support Fortas, but Attorney General Ramsey Clark's reluctance to advance another judicial nominee Russell favored killed this deal. Sensing the vulnerability of his position, Fortas agreed, perhaps unwisely, to testify before the Judiciary Committee, charged with the responsibility to pass on his nomination. He thus became the first sitting justice to submit to questioning by a congressional committee, and as such he confronted a barrage of opposition. As the hearings unfolded in July, some senators argued simply that any lame-duck nomination was inappropriate. Others grilled Fortas about his close ties to the president, suggesting that their frequent interactions, an open secret in Washington, violated judicial ethics. Fortas's penchant for verbal sparring with his interrogators did not help either as senators asked pointed questions not only about his own legal beliefs but also about the entire record of the Warren Court to which there was enormous hostility within the committee's membership. To give one example, Democrat Russell Long of Louisiana called Fortas "'one of the dirty five' who sides with the criminal."[28] To give another, South Carolinian Strom Thurmond blamed Fortas for several Warren Court decisions that defined obscenity and pornographic films as speech protected by the First Amendment.[29]

When the committee reconvened in September to hear additional testimony, B. J. Tennery, dean of the Washington College of Law at American University, revealed that Fortas had been paid $15,000 for a teaching a seminar, a series of nine lectures delivered during the summer. The stipend seemed excessive. It far exceeded the pay for comparable academic activity at American, and it represented about 40 percent of the justice's income. But even worse, Tennery revealed that the fee had not been paid from university funds. The money had been raised by Fortas's former law partner, Paul Porter, from five wealthy businessmen.[30] Fortas's critics argued that these five had extensive business interests in companies that could at some time be involved in litigation before the Court. The critics asserted, therefore, that Fortas's consent to this secret arrangement was a serious conflict of interest.

These revelations certainly doomed the nomination, if it wasn't already dead, but the Judiciary Committee nevertheless recommended, 11–6, that the Senate confirm Fortas. But when the nomination reached the floor for debate, it was clear just how much support for Fortas had crumbled. Republicans filibustered, and some Democrats once nominally committed to the nomination changed their minds. The Associated Press estimated that Fortas would not have been confirmed had his nomination come to a vote, but that never happened. A cloture motion, a parliamentary tactic to close debate and force a vote, failed. Cloture required fifty-nine votes, but the motion got only forty-five votes with forty-three against. On October 1, Fortas withdrew his name. He remained on the Court as an associate justice as the 1968 term began, and Warren remained as chief justice, as his letter to Johnson indicated he would. His resignation was still on the table as Nixon was elected president in November and inaugurated in January 1969.[31]

With Johnson no longer in the White House, Fortas could perhaps have expected that his return to the Court might lead to a less busy life. But such was not to be. On May 5, 1969, an article in *Life* magazine entitled "Fortas of the Supreme Court: A Question of Ethics," revealed that the justice, shortly after joining the Court in 1965, had accepted a check for $20,000 from the Wolfson Family Foundation.[32] Financier Louis Wolfson, formerly Fortas's client, was a philanthropist who wanted to ease his friend's transition from private practice to public service. The trouble was that Wolfson had twice been convicted of securities violations and was still under federal investigation when Fortas accepted the check. When the Securities and Exchange Commission concluded its look into two companies in which Wolfson held controlling interests and referred these matters to the Justice Department, Wolfson was indicted again, and Fortas returned the money. But the damage had been done, and William Lambert, the *Life* reporter who wrote the article, had friends at the highest levels of the Nixon administration. Two days after the story appeared, Attorney General John Mitchell showed Warren documents confirming that Fortas's deal with Wolfson was not a one-time gift but a promise of $20,000 a year for life. Under intense pressure wherever he went, Fortas met with his colleagues on the Court on May 13 and submitted his letter of resignation to Warren the following day. To the end he insisted that "there has been no wrongdoing on my part. I have not interceded or taken part in any legal, administrative or judicial matter affecting Mr. Wolfson or anyone associated with him."[33] But his protestations really didn't matter.[34]

On the morning of June 23, 1969, President Nixon did the highly unusual.[35] He took a seat in the audience before the Supreme Court on the last day of its term. Justice Thurgood Marshall opened the session by reading an opinion, and Justice Potter Stewart read two. Then the chief justice turned to the president, who began his remarks in the traditional way, "May it please the Court." Nixon praised Warren's service and his dedication. He acknowledged disagreements over Court decisions, "but standing above those debates," he said, "has been the symbol of the Court as represented by the Chief Justice of the United States: fairness, integrity, dignity."[36] Warren responded in kind. "We serve no majority," he said. "We serve no minority. We serve only the public interest as we see it, guided only by the Constitution and our own consciences."[37] The chief justice recognized the friends who had sat with him for sixteen years, "in spite of the fact that we have disagreed on many occasions,"[38] and then he swore in his successor, Warren Burger, whom Nixon had nominated in May and the Senate had confirmed without controversy.

Born in St. Paul, Minnesota, in 1907, Burger was a solid Republican. Unable to accept a scholarship to Princeton because he had an obligation to help support his family, he took night classes at the University of Minnesota and got his law degree, also at night, from the St. Paul College of Law, graduating *magna cum laude* in 1931. Burger joined a prestigious law firm, practiced widely, and got involved in civic and political life. He organized a Council on Human Relations to fight racial discrimination in St. Paul and served as a trustee of the Mayo Foundation. In 1952, Burger chaired the Minnesota delegation at the Republican convention and cast the votes that gave the nomination to Dwight Eisenhower.[39] In 1953, Eisenhower appointed him assistant US attorney general in the Civil Division and three years later elevated him to a seat on the Circuit Court of Appeals for the District of Columbia, the so-called Little Supreme Court. Burger took a particular interest in international law and in continuing his legal education abroad. Each summer, he traveled to Europe to observe legal proceedings there, and he helped establish the Appellate Judges' Seminar at New York University in 1957. Burger, in fact, became an expert on how the American judicial system functioned, and he often spoke about its shortcomings—court management, case overloads, inefficiencies, judicial education—and the need for reform. When he testified before the Senate Judiciary Committee after being nominated to be chief justice, he said, "The Chief Justice of the United States is assigned many other duties [besides deciding cases], administrative in nature. I would think it was the duty of the Chief Justice . . . to make our system work better. And I would expect to devote every energy and every moment of the rest of my life to that end should I be confirmed."[40]

Burger first sat with the Court in October 1969, and the seat on the Court formerly held by Abe Fortas eventually went to another Minnesotan, Harry Blackmun, nominated by Nixon and confirmed by the Senate after two other nominees, Clement Haynsworth and Harold Carswell, were found wanting. When Justices Hugo Black and John Marshall Harlan retired in 1971, Nixon named Lewis Powell and William Rehnquist to replace them. The Burger Court that decided the three cases discussed in the NASSH round-table thus had the following members: Burger; Black (*Haywood* and *Clay*) followed by Powell (*Flood*); William Douglas; Harlan (*Haywood* and *Clay*) followed by Rehnquist (*Flood*); William Brennan; Stewart; Byron "Whizzer" White; Marshall; and Blackmun. Black and Douglas had been nominated by Franklin Roosevelt; Harlan, Brennan, and Stewart by Eisenhower; White by John Kennedy; and Marshall by Johnson.

Were the Court's decisions in these three cases examples of the strict constructionism that Nixon was seeking? Maybe, although none of them, it should be noted, except perhaps the *Ali* case, bore on the great issues of criminal procedure and civil rights that made the Warren Court so con-troversial. Nixon was more than willing to use public disaffection with the Warren Court as part of a campaign strategy that exploited the fracturing of American society for political purposes. But lest Nixon be accused of an excessive amount of concern in his quest for judicial nominees who would fulfill the promises inherent in his campaign rhetoric, it is good to recall how he came to nominate Rehnquist as an associate justice. Born in Milwaukee in 1924, Rehnquist had graduated first in his class at Stanford Law School in 1951 and gone to Washington to serve as a law clerk for Justice Robert Jackson. He then left Washington to set up a law practice in Phoenix and staked out several conservative political positions that brought him to the attention of other like-minded Republicans. When Nixon tapped Arizonan Richard Kleindienst to be deputy attorney general, Attorney General John Mitchell agreed to bring Rehnquist back to Washington to head the Department of Justice's Office of Legal Counsel.[41] In this position, the con-servative activist screened the president's Supreme Court nominations, including Burger, Haynsworth, Carswell, and Blackmun. When Black and Harlan retired, Nixon advanced the names of Mildred Lillie and Herschel Friday to succeed them, but the American Bar Association's Committee on the Federal Judiciary riled the president by pronouncing both potential nominees "not qualified."[42] Before the dust had settled, Nixon nominated Powell and Rehnquist, suggesting in his announcement that he knew them both and that neither would "place himself above the Constitution or out-side the Constitution."[43] Yet, transcripts of conversations taped in the White House just before Nixon appointed Rehnquist suggest a relationship less based on friendship. In July 1971, the president complained to domestic policy advisor John Ehrlichman about a group, Rehnquist included, that was supposed to be investigating national security leaks. The president said, "You remember the meeting we had when I told that group of clowns we had around here. Renchberg and that group. What's his name?" Ehrlichman replied, "Rehnquist," and Nixon answered, "Yeah, Rehnquist."[44] On other occasions, he called him "Renchberg" or "Rensler," and disparaged the future justice, a Lutheran, by saying, "He looked Jewish."[45]

SECTION II

ANTITRUST LAW AND SPORT

In 1890, the United States Congress passed the Sherman Antitrust Act to break up business trusts and monopolies. The law arose because of "Robber Barons," like John D. Rockefeller of Standard Oil, who wielded the size and power of their companies to devour smaller companies. In the case of Standard Oil, for example, Canadian oil was sent to oil refineries in Ohio. Standard Oil, and thus Rockefeller, owned those refineries; the company then used its might to force the local railroads to not just give Standard Oil an excellent deal on transport but also to give Standard Oil a piece of all the fees that other refineries paid the railroads to transport their own oil. An Ohio state court ordered Standard Oil be dissolved, but Rockefeller simply moved the company to New Jersey. Believing that the federal government was the only entity able to limit large interstate business, Senator John Sherman, a Republican from Ohio, introduced legislation to do just that. The purpose of the law is simple—to promote fair competition—and to be sure that happens, winners of an antitrust lawsuit have their damages trebled.

In 1890 the Sherman Antitrust laws were enacted as a result of the general population's frustration with the powerful trusts controlled by a few individuals, and by many interpretations the laws were intended to protect the consumers by promoting free trade. The law was not necessarily intended to protect businesses. The literal language of the act was short and vague:

> §1: Every contract, combination in the form of trust or otherwise, or conspiracy, in restraint of trade or commerce among the several States, or with foreign nations, is declared to be illegal.

§2: Every person who shall monopolize, or attempt to monopolize, or combine or conspire with any other person or persons, to monopolize any part of the trade or commerce among the several States, or with foreign nations, shall be deemed guilty of a felony.[1]

Legal historian Lawrence Friedman argued that the vagueness of the law indicated that the law's enactment was a political move designed to placate the voters and to let the courts figure out how to deal with the situation.[2] Over time the courts have, in essence, done just that, creating varying tests, particularly when determining if there is a violation of the restraint of trade law. The first basic way to interpret an antitrust issue is as a "per se" violation. Generally courts have determined that certain kinds of agreements between two or more separate entities are blatantly unreasonable and thus are presumed to be violations of the antitrust law without any need to analyze the business's justification for the agreement. An admission or clear evidence of something like price fixing between two companies would be an example of a per se violation. Most sports law issues do not fall under the per se test but rather under something called the "rule of reason" test. In 1918 the Supreme Court gave its first clear articulation of the rule of reason test, writing "the true test of legality is whether the restraint is such as merely regulates, and perhaps thereby promotes, competition, or whether it is such as may suppress or even destroy competition."[3] Very simply, to win an antitrust lawsuit, specifically restraint of trade, the plaintiff must establish that two or more separate entities conspired to unreasonably restrain trade, so that the anticompetitive effects of an agreement outweigh the pro-competitive results for the consumer. The rule of reason test is done on a case-by-case basis and the courts examine the business within its own context. Further, the business itself must involve interstate commerce or the federal antitrust laws do not apply.

When faced with complaints about restraint of trade, sports leagues usually try to argue that (1) they are a single entity (e.g., one NFL with thirty-two teams) because one entity cannot conspire with itself, (2) that the pro-competitive results of the rules outweigh the anticompetitive effects, or (3) that there is no interstate commerce.[4] For example, Jack Molinas, a professional basketball player, was banned from the National Basketball Association (NBA) after the league learned he had gambled on his own games. Molinas argued that the teams in the league had conspired to exclude him, thus restraining trade. But he lost because the league convinced a judge in 1961 that it had a legitimate interest in prohibiting gambling and banning those who violated that rule to assure the public that the games were validly contested, thus the pro-competitive effects of the rule benefited the public more than the rule hindered the sport from the consumer's perspective.[5]

Further, the Sherman Antitrust Act can be essentially waived not just when courts conclude that there is an acceptable reason for doing so but also for statutory and nonstatutory labor exemptions. Statutory exemptions occur when Congress passes a law allowing action that would without that statute be illegal under the Sherman Act. These statutory exemptions often benefit the owners of the teams or the leagues more broadly. For example, the 1961 Sports Broadcasting Act allows sports leagues to pool television rights together to maximize their negotiating power when dealing with media—thus the NBA, for example, can negotiate with a television network for the entire league rather than having each team negotiate their own deal. Just as statutory exemptions can benefit owners and the league, labor law can protect labor and its unions during collective bargaining agreements. Unions can, during collective bargaining, bargain away certain elements that might be considered violations of antitrust law; these become nonstatutory labor exemptions. For example, the NFL has a rule that no player can enter the draft prior to the third year after his high school class graduated. Because the players' union negotiated on this point in a good faith bargaining situation, it is not a violation of the antitrust laws.[6]

The second session of the Sherman Antitrust Act places limits on how an organization can acquire or maintain their position. Large companies are not illegal by definition, rather the courts examine the company's use of exclusionary conduct to gain their size and power. The courts want to protect the public from a company so large and exclusionary that the company can drive up prices because there is no viable competition for the public to approach. In an early antitrust case against Standard Oil, the Supreme Court concluded that the company was an illegal monopoly because it had grown by getting illegal rebates from railroads, industrial spying, and predatory pricing, which showed illegal intent and exclusionary conduct.[7] Thus if a company is large and successful by virtue of better management, better product, or other legal means, that is a natural monopoly and is not illegal under the Antitrust Act.

For sports leagues, the teams face a conundrum. In order to be a smoothly functioning league, the teams must agree to act together to determine rules, scheduling, and other issues to maintain a fair and competitive playing field, which will make the league a better product for the consumers. Further, very few competing professional leagues in the same sport have been simultaneously viable and profitable for very long which means that leagues by themselves often act as monopolies—sometimes naturally by virtue of being the best product and sometimes through more overt, and sometimes unfair, uses of power. On the one hand, if the teams are considered independently, then they are at risk of charges of restraint of trade. On the other hand, if the teams argue that they are actually a single league then the door is open to allegations that the league is a monopoly. Thus, both professional and amateur sport are often vulnerable to antitrust lawsuits in which the courts must balance concerns of the leagues as business entities, the issues of athlete autonomy, as well as the best interests of the consumer.

This section specifically focuses on two cases in two sports addressing antitrust issues: *Gardella v. Chandler*[8] and *Frantz v. United States Powerlifting Federation*.[9] The topic is so pervasive in sport, however, that the *Flood v. Kuhn* and the *Haywood v. NBA* cases of the first section and the *O'Bannon* case of the third section also involve antitrust issues.

CHAPTER SIX

Danny Gardella and Baseball's Reserve Clause

A WORKING-CLASS STIFF BLACKLISTED IN COLD WAR AMERICA

Ron Briley

When former New York Giants outfielder Danny Gardella died at age eighty-five on March 6, 2005, the baseball world paid little attention to his passing. But in the late 1940s, Gardella posed a clear and present danger to the baseball establishment when he challenged the game's reserve clause. In 1946, Gardella failed to sign a contract with the Giants and bolted to the Mexican League. Gardella and other major leaguers enticed south of the border by Mexican entrepreneur Jorge Pasquel and his financially generous contracts were blacklisted for five years by baseball commissioner A. B. "Happy" Chandler and unable to resume their baseball careers in the United States when the Mexican League folded. Denied an opportunity to make a living playing Major League Baseball, Gardella sued the sport, arguing that baseball's reserve clause was in restraint of trade and violated antitrust law.[1]

The vitriolic reply of the baseball establishment was to label Gardella a radical threat to the American way of life embodied in the traditions of the national pastime. Brooklyn Dodgers executive Branch Rickey, who deserves credit for defying baseball's color line by signing Jackie Robinson, was also a staunch anticommunist Republican who interpreted any challenges to management prerogatives as examples of Bolshevism. Speaking in Baltimore on April 13, 1949, Rickey proclaimed that individuals questioning baseball's sacred reserve clause were persons "of avowed communist tendencies who deeply resent the continuance of our national pastime."[2] Commissioner

Chandler also employed rhetorical excess in describing the dire consequences for the American way of life posed by the Gardella lawsuit. Insisting that he tried to reason with Gardella and others who deserted the United States for Mexico during a time of national crisis, Chandler argued, "I tried to get them to live up to their obligations and responsibilities. This was a fight against baseball in the United States. These players joined a group who said they were going to kill baseball in the United States."[3]

Gardella, of course, was no Bolshevik. He was simply a working-class stiff who sought to maintain a job in baseball and obtain a fair salary in return for his labor. Gardella, like many other ball players, perceived the sport's reserve clause as limiting his economic options, constituting an endangerment to his livelihood. Therefore, he sued baseball for banning his return to the Major Leagues after testing the Mexican labor market. Gardella was essentially advocating for a free labor market, while baseball ownership sought to maintain a restricted labor supply. The baseball establishment, however, attempted to portray Gardella as a radical who was challenging traditional American values. The red baiting employed by Major League Baseball was an old tactic going back to nineteenth-century efforts by business to label union organizers as communist agitators. Such rhetoric was even more politically charged during the post–World War II Red Scare in which feminists, liberals, labor unions, and civil rights activists seeking change and reform were characterized as communist sympathizers undermining the American way of life. Danny Gardella wanted a job playing baseball, but he inadvertently became a free speech advocate when baseball ownership attempted to combat his legal challenge with the rhetoric of the blacklist and postwar anticommunist crusade. Thus, an examination of Gardella's lawsuit against Major League Baseball offers insight into the economic structure of the game as well as how business interests sought to use the rhetoric of anticommunism to discredit challenges to monopolistic practices.

History of the Reserve Clause

Baseball and the republic, however, were saved in 1949 when Gardella agreed to a settlement with Organized Baseball, but the reserve clause would be unable to withstand the forces of labor discontent unleashed by Gardella's legal challenge and call for economic justice. The Major League Players' Association backed Curt Flood's unsuccessful Supreme Court case against the reserve clause in 1970, and five years later, arbiter Peter Seitz ruled in favor of players Andy Messersmith and Dave McNally and against baseball ownership by deciding that management could not maintain a player's services indefinitely.

Gardella was proud of the role he played in baseball's labor wars. Blazing a path later followed by Curt Flood, Gardella asserted, "I feel I let the whole world know that the reserve clause was unfair. It had the odor of peonage, even slavery."[4] In an obituary for Gardella, sportswriter Maury Allen observed that the former player should be remembered as a family man with a sense of humor, which prevented him from taking the game too seriously. But Allen concluded that Gardella's role in challenging the reserve clause and baseball ownership should never be forgotten as "he is the guy responsible for the $26 million a year salary of Alex Rodriguez and the millions all the others now get just for playing that little kid's game of baseball."[5]

While Allen may give a bit too much credit to the role played by Gardella in baseball's labor wars, the sacred cornerstone of baseball's monopolistic structure was the reserve clause developed to address the competitive nature of nineteenth-century business. The National Association of Professional Base Ball Players was established in 1871, but this initial professional baseball league collapsed after five years due to raids by wealthy clubs upon the players of teams in smaller markets. Issues of gambling and alcohol consumption among the athletes exacerbated these problems of competitive balance. Accordingly, William Hulbert of Chicago assumed a leading role in the 1876 formation of the National League of Professional Base Ball Clubs with power residing in ownership rather than the players. The new organization sought to restrict competition by limiting the number of franchises, granting territorial rights to clubs, and forbidding the signing of players under contract to rival teams. The agreement to curtail player movement resulted in lower salaries, and by the 1880s the reserve clause was implemented. Under the reserve clause, a club reserved the right to renew a player's contract following each season. Thus, a team could conceivably make the player's contract its property for the remainder of the athlete's career. A player under contract could be traded, but the athlete could not test the market by becoming a free agent. Under the National Agreement of 1883, the reserve clause was extended to the rival American Association, and in 1885 ownership imposed a $2,000 salary cap.[6]

Player opposition to the reserve clause and the low salaries paid by ownership found voice in the Brotherhood of Professional Baseball Players organized by John Montgomery Ward, who attended Columbia University Law School while playing shortstop for the New York Giants. Ward proclaimed, "Players have been bought, sold, and traded as though they were sheep instead of American citizens. Like a fugitive slave law, the reserve clause denies him a harbor and a livelihood, and carries him back, bound and shackled, to the club from which he attempted to escape."[7] The players formed a rival league, but it lasted only a year because its financial backers, deliberately not called "owners," were picked apart by the cunning of Albert Spalding, the most powerful leader of the National League. The revolt was over in 1891, but Ward's eloquent attack upon the reserve system would resonate with Danny Gardella, Curt Flood, and many other ballplayers during the twentieth century.

The next major challenge to the serenity of baseball's economic structure came from the American League in 1901. Under the leadership of Ban Johnson, the newly constituted major league lured more than one hundred players from the National League, and salaries soared as a result of the competition. In an effort to restore stability and impose a restricted owners' rather than players' market, the rival leagues formed the National Agreement of 1903, agreeing to respect each other's reserve system, and a three-man commission was created to oversee baseball.

Player salaries again declined until the Federal League challenge of 1914–1915 when hundreds of athletes jumped to the new league. With competition intense, all major league clubs struggled financially amid considerable litigation over player contracts. In 1915, the Federal League sued the National and American Leagues for restraint of trade in violation of the Sherman Antitrust Act. While awaiting a decision from future baseball commissioner Judge Kenesaw Mountain Landis, a settlement was reached between the Federal League and Major League Baseball. The agreement consisted of absorption of the Federal League franchises into Major League Baseball or a $50,000 buyout. The Federal League club from Baltimore, however, refused the settlement and continued with its antitrust suit.

In April 1921, the District of Columbia Court of Appeals ruled that professional baseball was not subject to antitrust law because the sport failed to constitute interstate commerce. The appeals court concluded that although the travel of players from state to state might appear to be interstate commerce, the game of baseball was "local in its beginning and in its end." The court reasoned that the fact that the owners "produce baseball games as a source of profit, large or small, cannot change the character of the games. They are still sport, not trade."[8] The Supreme Court in the case of *Federal Baseball Club of Baltimore v. National League* upheld the opinion of the appeals court on May 29, 1922.

Writing for a unanimous court, progressive jurist Oliver Wendell Holmes maintained the fiction that professional baseball was a sport rather than a business and was, thus, exempt from antitrust legislation. Holmes wrote that Major League Baseball contracts were "purely state affairs. It is true that, in order to attain for the exhibition the great popularity that they have achieved, competitions must be arranged between clubs from different cities and States. But the fact that in order to give the exhibitions the League must induce free persons to cross state lines and arrange and pay for their doing so is not enough to change the character of the business."[9] In his history of baseball's labor wars, Robert F. Burk asserts that by presenting professional baseball as a sport rather than a business, the court's decision upheld a monopolistic situation in which ownership could continue to exploit players and ignore their grievances. Burk concludes, "With Organized Baseball's power, including the reserve clause, to maintain its monopolies over territory and playing labor now exempted from federal antitrust legislation, the *Federal League* ruling dealt a severe blow to any trade war challenges to the majors, and to the prospects for player economic gain from them."[10]

Jerold J. Duquette suggests, in his work on baseball and antitrust, that the apparent disconnect between the *Federal League* decision and progressivism's goal of maintaining competition through regulation of business is due to the cultural significance many progressives associated with the sport. Concerned with rising immigration from Southern and Eastern Europe, as well as the growth of industry and business threatening traditional American agrarian values, progressivism perceived baseball as a tool through which to shape and transform the emerging industrial order. Duquette writes, "For the leaders and reformers of the Progressive Era, baseball was a tool of reform not the object of reform. Baseball was a game that would be used by these social reformers to inculcate certain values into American society. Fair play, teamwork, sound minds and bodies; these were the buzzwords of a social movement. Baseball was a prop, a metaphor used in the social gospel of progessivism."[11]

Thus, Duquette argues that the *Federal League* decision provides an example of how progressive values were perpetuated during the supposedly reactionary 1920s. Baseball was deserving of an exemption from antitrust practices due to its unique status as a cultural vehicle for the assimilation of immigrants and the new industrial order into the agrarian values of an older, Anglo America. This cultural imperative for the sport identified baseball with the civilizing mission of the nation in a troubled world. In this line of reasoning, Major League Baseball was a cornerstone of American liberty, and an attack upon baseball ownership was perceived as questioning the very principles upon which the nation was founded. Accordingly, it was easy for Branch Rickey to identify opponents of the reserve clause as having "communist tendencies," for the baseball executive was not simply defending business practices but the American way of life. Progressive efforts to maintain the illusion of a classless society were perpetuated in the post–

World War II liberal consensus, which assumed that an expanding capitalist economy would cure all social ills.

For baseball to maintain the fiction that it was a game and not a business, it was imperative that players not voice discontent, while asserting how fortunate they were to be playing baseball. Danny Gardella, who championed the values of economic opportunity for all embraced by Thomas Jefferson's Declaration of Independence, however, shattered this myth of consensus.

Background of Danny Gardella

At first glance, Gardella might seem a strange choice to lead a revolution against the baseball establishment of America, but he was a product of the ethnic and working-class Americans who played an essential role in Franklin Roosevelt's New Deal coalition, while assuring the nation's survival during the Great Depression and World War II. Danny Gardella was born on February 26, 1920, in New York City and was a fan of the New York Giants during his youth. In 1939, the young man began his baseball career in the South with the Class D farm club of the Detroit Tigers in Beckley, West Virginia. During the following two seasons, Danny and his older brother, Albert, played Class D ball in Pine Bluff, Arkansas. Gardella was ineligible for the military draft in World War II due to a punctured eardrum; however, the expanding wartime production offered new economic opportunities. In 1942, Gardella was back in New York City, working in a shipyard and playing semiprofessional baseball. With a shortage of players for major league rosters during the wartime emergency, New York Giants scout Joe Birmingham convinced Gardella to leave the shipyards for a shot at Major League Baseball. Playing briefly during the 1944 baseball campaign, the somewhat stocky Gardella, at five foot-seven inches and 165 pounds, hit six home runs in only 112 at bats. The following season, the left-handed hitting and throwing outfielder enjoyed a solid season, driving in seventy-one runs while hitting eighteen home runs with a .272 batting average.[12]

Although Gardella was living his boyhood dream of playing with the Giants, the twenty-five-year-old athlete was paid less money than he earned at the shipyards. Gardella complained that his baseball salary did not even allow him to buy a decent suit. Nevertheless, the gregarious young man established a reputation for enjoying himself. Gardella asserted that he just loved playing in the Polo Grounds, the home park for the Giants. The outfielder quipped, "I could spit the ball over the fence. I was a good spitter."[13] In addition to making every fly ball an adventure when he was in the field, Gardella was known for his singing and practical jokes. For example, after a day in which he went hitless, Gardella left a suicide note for his roommate,

Cuban infielder Napoleon Reyes. Gardella climbed out his hotel room window and was hanging off the ledge, while a hysterical Reyes was convinced that his teammate had jumped from the open window.[14]

With the end of World War II and the return of veteran players to major league rosters in 1946, Gardella was in no joking mood. He missed the train south to the Giants training camp in Florida and was forced to purchase his own ticket. After arriving in Florida, Gardella got into a dispute with Giants traveling secretary Eddie Brannick over violating a new team rule that players must don a jacket and tie in the team dining area. The angry outfielder refused to sign a $5,000 contract duplicating his salary for the 1945 season. Although talent was diluted during the war years, Gardella believed that his 1945 hitting deserved at least a modest raise. A frustrated Gardella contacted Mexican industrialist Jorge Pasquel, whom the outfielder met at Roon's Gymnasium in New York City during the winter of 1945. Pasquel was surprised to learn that Gardella earned so little playing baseball that it was necessary for him to take an off-season job at the gym. As president of the Mexican League, Pasquel offered Gardella a contract to play baseball south of the border. Still believing that he could secure a berth on the Giants roster, Gardella politely refused Pasquel's proposal. The Mexican baseball official, however, assured the outfielder that the offer was open-ended should Gardella have a change of heart.[15]

Following his failure to reach a salary agreement with the Giants during spring training in 1946, Gardella contacted Pasquel, who sent a representative to accompany the American player to Mexico. Before leaving the Giants training camp, Gardella told reporters, "You may say for me, that I do not intend to let the Giants enrich themselves at my expense by sending me to a minor-league club. They have treated me shabbily, I have decided to take my gifted talents to Mexico."[16] According to Gardella, he was wined and dined in Mexico City, provided with an attractive female escort, and even introduced to Manolite, the famous Spanish matador. Convinced that his Mexican hosts appreciated him, Gardella signed a contract for $8,000, with an option for two more seasons plus a signing bonus of $5,000.[17] In making this agreement, Gardella was not violating his contract with the Giants, for he was an unsigned player. In jumping to the Mexican League, Gardella was, nevertheless, in violation of baseball's sacred reserve clause. But as Gardella made clear with the press in Florida, his motivation for leaving the Giants was not about questioning American values and institutions. It was strictly a question of economics and the ability to earn a decent paycheck for his baseball talents. Upon arriving in Mexico City and meeting officials of the Mexican government, Gardella announced, "They are paying more here, so why shouldn't I play in Mexico?"[18]

Mexican League Challenge

The signing of Gardella was an important opening salvo of a campaign by the five Pasquel brothers, who operated a lucrative import-export business in addition to a brewery, to stock their Mexican League rosters with major league talent in addition to Negro League players, such as Ray Dandridge, already recruited from the United States. Following the Gardella signing, Latinos, such as Dodgers outfielder Luis Olmo and Giants pitcher Adrian Zabala and infielder Nap Reyes, who also suffered racial and cultural discrimination in the United States, joined the Mexican League. The $40,000 contract signed by Olmo, who was scheduled to be the Dodgers fourth outfielder, shocked the American baseball establishment. An exuberant Jorge Pasquel mocked Major League Baseball for offering its players "peon salaries," proclaiming, "I am ready to compete with Organized Ball, dollar for dollar and peso for peso, for the best talent available."[19]

In response to this challenge, baseball commissioner Chandler announced that any players who violated their contracts or reserve status were subject to five-year banishments from Major League Baseball unless they rejoined their teams before opening day. In describing how he arrived at a five-year penalty, Chandler told historian William Marshall that the players would perceive a two-year ban as too lenient. The commissioner concluded, "The first question was having the penalty severe enough so that it would deter fellas who might want to do the same thing for quick money."[20] When Gardella later challenged the reserve clause in court, Chandler publicly responded by adopting the rhetoric of anticommunism and proclaiming that those who jumped to the Mexican League were "disloyal." But it appears that Chandler always understood that the issue was really about money and baseball management's control of its labor supply.

Chandler's threats, nonetheless, failed to intimidate Jorge Pasquel, who attempted to sign such established baseball stars as Bob Feller, Ted Williams, and Stan Musial. While rebuffed by these athletes, who were well paid by the standards of Major League Baseball, the Pasquel brothers were able to lure other veteran players such as Dodger catcher Mickey Owen; pitcher Sal Maglie and infielders Ray Zimmerman and George Hausmann from the Giants; and St. Louis Cardinals pitchers Max Lanier and Fred Martin along with infielder Lou Klein. The Mexican League's biggest coup was St. Louis Browns slugging shortstop Vern Stephens. However, Stephens became quickly disenchanted with Mexico and slipped back across the border on April 5, 1946, returning the Pasquels's money and, with the blessing of Chandler, rejoining the Browns. In all, G. Richard McKelvey writes, "Twenty-three players had made the jump in the hope of improving their financial situations and playing fulltime as 'major leaguers' in another setting."[21]

Despite the lavish promises made by the Pasquel brothers, most of the former major leaguers, including Gardella, eventually became discouraged with life in Mexico. Gardella, however, was initially pleased with conditions in Mexico, noting that former Negro League stars such as Ray Dandridge lived well south of the border. Impressed with Dandridge, Gardella asked, "Man, where did you come from?" Dandridge quipped, "Same country you did."[22] Indicative of his comfort level, Gardella slammed a two-run home run in his first game with the Vera Cruz Blues, leading his club to a 12–5 victory over the Mexico City Reds. He continued to hit well for the first half of the 1946 campaign, slugging two home runs in the Mexican League All-Star Game. But both Gardella and the Blues slumped during the second half of the season. Lonesome, Gardella convinced his girlfriend of two years to join him in Mexico, and the couple married in Mexico City. The American, nevertheless, became disenchanted with baseball and life in Mexico. On the season's final day, Gardella hit a home run, which saved Vera Cruz from finishing in last place. In one hundred games, Gardella batted .275 with thirteen home runs and sixty-four runs batted in, but a disappointed Jorge Pasquel informed Gardella, as well as other Americans, that salaries would be cut for the 1947 season as revenues failed to reach Pasquel's projections. A few hours after his final game in Mexico City, Gardella and his wife, Kate, were on a plane heading home to New York City. While his Mexican adventure was over, Gardella confronted a ban on his return to Major League Baseball, which threatened his financial prospects and ability to begin a family.[23]

Meanwhile, the confrontation between Major League Baseball and the Mexican League also contributed to deteriorating diplomatic relations while the United States was seeking to secure its southern flank in the developing Cold War with the Soviet Union. For example, Branch Rickey pressured outfielder Pete Reiser to resist overtures from Mexico, asserting that the ball player did not "want to be a man without a country."[24] The combative baseball executive also announced that he was seeking an injunction to prevent the Pasquel brothers from interfering with his Brooklyn players. Refusing to be intimidated by Rickey, Bernardo Pasquel proclaimed that he would appeal to the United States Supreme Court "to establish our right to offer better salaries than are now open to players on the American continent."[25] The Pasquel brothers retained the prestigious New York law firm of Harding, Hess, and Elder, which normally handled governmental disputes between Mexico and the United States, suggesting that Mexican officials were lending support to the Mexican League challenge.[26]

In 1946, Miguel Aleman was elected president of Mexico, and Jorge Pasquel raised funds for his cousin and boyhood friend. Pasquel's tweaking of the Americans in the baseball labor wars was considered by many Mexicans as helpful to Aleman's candidacy. After his electoral victory in July 1946, Aleman, however, appeared less supportive of the Pasquels and sought to improve relations with the United States. Seeking to enhance trade and encourage Mexican industrialization, the Truman and Aleman administrations exchanged diplomatic visits. While Aleman was distancing himself from Jorge Pasquel, the Mexican baseball executive was also antagonizing many of his followers by attempting to exercise almost dictatorial control over the Mexican League, interfering in the daily affairs of teams and even the decisions of umpires. The introduction of so many American players also led to an anti-imperialist backlash against perceived domination of Mexican baseball by athletes from the colossus to the north. Mark Winegardner addresses this imperialistic interpretation of the American players in the Mexican League in his novel, *The Veracruz Blues*, which also features Danny Gardella as a major character.[27]

Although Jorge Pasquel's Mexican League continued through the 1948 season, the great experiment of raiding the American baseball market was over following the 1946 baseball season, and most of the Americans who jumped to the Mexican League returned to the United States. Baseball's prodigal sons, however, were hardly welcomed with open arms. Former Dodger catcher Mickey Owen left Mexico before the 1946 season ended and appealed to Commissioner Chandler for immediate reinstatement as Branch Rickey's Dodgers were engaged in a tight pennant with the St. Louis Cardinals. On August 11, 1946, Chandler announced that Owen would have to serve the full five-year term for his disloyalty and defiance of Organized Baseball's rules and traditions. A disappointed Owen retreated to his Missouri farm, and Cubs general manager James Gallagher concluded, "The spectacle of Mickey Owen languishing on a Missouri farm will do more to keep players from jumping this winter than anything Mr. Rickey or the rest of us could do."[28]

Danny Gardella Challenges the Baseball Establishment

Gardella, meanwhile, was playing in 1947 with a barnstorming team organized by former Cardinals pitcher Max Lanier. The team disbanded, however, when Organized Baseball threatened to blacklist any player who competed against the outlawed former major leaguers, and Lanier returned briefly to Mexico. Gardella again took up residence in New York City, where he and his wife were expecting their first child. He caught on with the Gulf Oilers, a semi-pro team on Staten Island. Gardella's presence on the team led to a last-minute cancellation by the Cleveland Buckeyes of the Negro Leagues. According to reports, "The announcer asked the spectators not to hold the action against the players of the Negro National League, because they could not afford to risk the penalty imposed upon players who play against an outlaw."[29] With the entrance of Jackie Robinson into the National League, these black athletes did not want to take the chance that they would be denied the opportunity of following in his footsteps. But the cancellation of the game by the Cleveland Buckeyes triggered a series of events, which would challenge baseball's reserve clause. A disgruntled fan in attendance that night complained to his dentist and baseball fan, Conrad Meibauer. The dentist shared the story with another patient, attorney Frederic Johnson, who then arranged a meeting with Gardella.[30]

Johnson was a lifelong baseball fan and graduate of Harvard Law School, who in 1939 wrote a piece for the *United States Law Review* arguing that the reserve clause would most likely not be able to withstand another legal challenge due to the growth of the sport as an interstate business with new sources of revenue such as selling broadcast rights to games. The attorney was especially interested in Gardella's case as the Giants outfielder was blacklisted for violating the reserve clause rather than a player contract. Accordingly, after a meeting with Johnson on September 17, 1947, Gardella agreed to sue Organized Baseball and signed a 50 percent retainer fee with the lawyer.

The case moved slowly through the court system. In July 1948, Judge Henry Goddard of the US Federal Court in the Southern District of New York dismissed the case as out of the court's jurisdiction. In his remarks, however, Goddard suggested that a reversal of the 1922 *Federal League* decision might be possible because of Major League Baseball's expanding revenues from radio and television rights. Johnson made use of this change in the nature of the baseball business to argue Gardella's case on appeal before the Second Circuit Appellate Federal Court for the Southern District of New York.

The attorney asked the court for $100,000 damages, which would amount to $300,000 under the triple damage provisions of antitrust law; asserting that Chandler's five-year suspension would "destroy the ability of plaintiff as a professional player through the necessary absence from competitive play of the caliber to which he had become accustomed."[31] Johnson argued that Organized Baseball was perpetrating a conspiracy to deny his client an opportunity to pursue his career and livelihood. He insisted that the baseball establishment employed the reserve clause as a weapon "contrary to settled principles of equity and to further a conspiracy in restraint of trade and commerce."[32] Continuing with a rhetorical flourish, Johnson described Major League Baseball as a monopoly "stretching from Hudson's Bay to the Equator" that operated a farm system allowing "players to be signed during infancy without giving to them the common law right to repudiate such contracts upon attaining their majority or to exercise statutory rights for disavowing their contracts upon attaining their majority."[33]

While publicly dismissing the arguments of Johnson and Gardella, baseball officials were privately concerned with the lawsuit. In a 1946 report to baseball ownership after the Pasquel brothers launched their raids upon major league rosters, Chandler warned, "The present reserve clause could not be enforced in an equity court in a suit for specific performance, or as the basis for a restraining order to prevent a player from playing elsewhere, or to prevent outsiders from inducing a player to break his contract."[34] Chandler, thus, believed that baseball's antitrust exemption might be overturned and the powers of the commissioner diminished.[35]

In court, however, baseball's attorney, Mark Hughes, maintained that the 1922 *Federal League* decision was still pertinent to the operations of Major League Baseball. The expansion of television and radio coverage did not fundamentally alter the nature of baseball's 1922 antitrust exemption. Hughes concluded, "If sixteen clubs organized into two leagues are not engaged in interstate commerce, the addition of so-called 'farm clubs,' although increasing the number of clubs does not convert the sport into trade or commerce."[36] The attorney also repeated the refrain that the reserve clause was essential to maintain order within the sport; maintaining that the provision was a tried and true method for "preventing players from disregarding their obligations."[37]

On February 10, 1949, the appellate court ruled 2–1 that Gardella's case be remanded to a lower court for a jury trial. In a dissenting opinion, Judge Harry W. Chase insisted that he perceived no reason to overturn the 1922 opinion of Justice Holmes. Judges Jerome N. Frank and Leonard Hand concluded that baseball's media contracts might bring the sport within the purview of the antitrust laws. In his opinion critiquing the baseball establishment, Frank cited the Thirteenth Amendment and anticipated the later arguments made by Curt Flood before the Supreme Court. Frank described baseball's reserve clause as "holding men in peonage," writing, "Only the totalitarian-minded will believe that high pay excuses virtual slavery."[38] Responding to baseball's claim that the sport could not continue without the reserve clause, the judge concluded, "No court should strive to ingeniously legalize private (even if benevolent) dictatorship."[39] Johnson was enthusiastic about the decision and recognized that he had a sympathetic client in Gardella, who was currently earning $36 a week as an orderly at a Mt. Vernon, New York, hospital. In his response, Gardella proclaimed, "It's just too bad if my case is hurting baseball because I've been hurt pretty bad myself."[40]

Baseball officials reacted with alarm and shock to the suggestion that the sport's reserve clause might be declared in violation of the Sherman and Clayton Antitrust Acts. While baseball ownership was primarily concerned with protecting profit margins, which would be threatened by higher player salaries, Major League Baseball responded with rhetoric proclaiming that the game of professional baseball was an American institution and tradition under attack from forces hostile to the nation's most fundamental values. In a period of political uncertainty and fear exacerbated by Cold War tensions, baseball was joining with Hollywood producers, business executives, university administrators, and conservative politicians who portrayed their critics as in some fashion representative of an alien communist ideology seeking to undermine the American way of life. Historian William Chafe argued that anticommunism damaged the nation by defining as "perilous, unsafe, and out of bounds advocacy of substantial social reform." Chafe wrote,

> Machismo, patriotism, belief in God, opposition to social agitation, hatred of Reds—these were the definitions of true Americanism. In a world where the ultimate power of politics is the power to define what is permissible and impermissible, the crusaders for anticommunism had helped strike from the agenda of acceptable discussion many reforms of greatest significance to social activists.[41]

Similar to Hollywood producers who blacklisted writers and performers for failing to cooperate with the House Committee on Un-American Activities, the baseball establishment sought to impose a blacklist upon those whom the sport characterized as disloyal for challenging the reserve clause.

Branch Rickey's good friend, Senator John W. Bricker of Ohio, proclaimed the identification of baseball with traditional American values. In a January 1949 speech before minor league baseball executives in Columbus, Ohio, Bricker described baseball as essential to the American way of life. The senator extolled baseball officials to combat communism by indoctrinating the nation's youth with American values, concluding as the press paraphrased, "While the marching hordes in China are spreading the doctrine of communism, . . . officials of the national pastime are helping make democracy work in this country by giving every youth a chance to carve out his own career."[42] The editorial pages of the Sporting News echoed the sentiments expressed by

Senator Bricker, rallying true patriots to the defense of baseball's institutions. Describing the Gardella case "as hanging over Organized Ball like the sword of Damocles," the *Sporting News*, nevertheless, congratulated Commissioner Chandler for his strong stand against those Mexican League jumpers who deserted the flag of baseball.[43] The paper concluded that the sport had no reason to be apprehensive, for Organized Baseball was "as American as the laws the courts are called upon to interpret and its integrity unassailable."[44]

Seeking to justify the confidence expressed by the *Sporting News*, baseball commissioner Chandler took aim at Judge Frank's opinion, ridiculing the idea that the reserve clause was the equivalent of modern-day slavery. During a Wilmington, Delaware, speech, the commissioner quipped, "No major league player receives less than $5,000 a year and some of them get close to $100,000. If that's slavery' or servitude, then there's a lot of us who would like to be in the same class."[45] Many journalists supported the sentiments of Chandler. New York sportswriter Dan Daniel asserted that abolishing the reserve clause would bring chaos to Organized Baseball, while Shirley Povich of the *Washington Post* insisted that players were delighted with the high salaries paid by Major League Baseball and wanted no governmental interference with the game. Povich concluded, "If this be peonage let's have more of it."[46] And Representative A. G. Herlong, former president of the Florida State League, questioned Gardella's loyalty to American principles, proclaiming, "Because the well ran dry in Mexico, Gardella came back here, was disciplined, and then brings this unprecedented action."[47]

Acknowledging these charges of disloyalty and his own dire financial circumstances, Mickey Owen presented Commissioner Chandler with a petition for reinstatement, but he was unable to secure Gardella's signature. Expressing sentiments similar to former leftists or communists seeking to have their names taken off the Hollywood blacklist, Owen recanted for his Mexican indiscretion, insisting, "I think Danny is wrong. I would never sue baseball. Baseball didn't make us go to Mexico. I want to play baseball, not destroy it. Baseball must have the reserve clause."[48] The *Sporting News* encouraged Chandler to remain firm with Owen and those who deserted their baseball obligations. The paper editorialized, "There is no second chance any more than there is for an umpire to change his decision. The public would not stand for it."[49]

Chandler denied the petition, and in an address before the third annual Governor's Baseball Dinner in Tampa, Florida, the commissioner employed the language of patriotism, which characterized the anticommunist crusade. Describing those who left Organized Baseball for Mexico as "disloyal," Chandler urged those in attendance to "stand by the flag of

Organized Baseball."[50] Despite the bold stance, baseball officials were concerned that the courts might rule against Organized Baseball. Accordingly, after the US Court of Appeals refused to order the reinstatement of Gardella and Cardinals pitchers Max Lanier and Fred Martin, Chandler, on June 5, 1949, announced that the suspensions of the jumping players were reduced from five to three years and all those who defected were eligible for return to Major League Baseball. Chandler explained that he waited to rescind the ban until he was free from acting under judicial compulsion. In front of an audience composed of reporters, the theatrical commissioner telephoned Owen and told the catcher, "Get your bag packed, boy, and get to your club right away."[51] Far from being magnanimous, William Marshall argues that Chandler's motivation "was designed to take away the players' public support and to defuse and discourage litigation against baseball."[52]

Meanwhile, Gardella and several other disqualified players had discovered more lucrative circumstances in Canada with the Quebec Provincial League. The Drummondville franchise was paying Gardella $7,000, and Gardella's attorney was concerned that his client might now be unable to collect damages because he earned more money playing in Mexico and Canada than during his tenure with the Giants. Johnson, nevertheless, persevered with the case. On September 19, 1949, he interrogated Chandler in a pretrial deposition. The commissioner again attempted to defend baseball by appealing to patriotism and depicting the national pastime as under assault from dissidents. Chandler informed Johnson that in dealing with those who deserted America and baseball, he was simply trying to get them to "live up to their obligations and responsibilities."[53] The players had to be disciplined, Chandler argued, because they "joined a group who said they were going to kill baseball in the United States."[54] It sounded as if Chandler were discussing Soviet subversion in the United States. But Chandler's use of patriotic rhetoric and anticommunist symbolism failed to dissuade Johnson, who continued to hone in on baseball's growing media revenues, undermining the argument that the sport was not part of interstate commerce. Under grueling questioning from Johnson, the commissioner conceded that baseball earned $750,000 from radio rights, while the new television market added $65,000 to baseball's coffers. After a second day of questioning that placed Organized Baseball and Chandler on the defensive, Major League Baseball officials approached Johnson and Gardella with a proposed settlement.[55]

Although Gardella was reluctant to accept a deal, on October 8, 1949, during the World Series between the Yankees and Dodgers, Major League Baseball announced that the case was resolved out of court. Gardella dropped his suit in exchange for an undisclosed cash settlement—an amount later revealed to be $60,000 and half of which went to Johnson. In addition, the St. Louis Cardinals purchased Gardella's contract from the Giants. Despite strong patriotic language, Major League Baseball recognized its legal vulnerability to allegations that the reserve clause was in violation of antitrust law. Accordingly, the *Sporting News*, which had vehemently denounced the jumpers, now praised the Gardella settlement. The paper concluded that Chandler "removed the bitterness from their hearts and put them on the way of winning back all the emoluments and privileges that were theirs before they departed."[56]

Conclusion

Baseball had apparently dodged a bullet as many within the business agreed with the argument of John A. Sprout in an article for the *California Law Review*. Sprout asserted, "It seems probable that the present Supreme Court will find organized baseball subject to the anti-trust laws, and that the Federal Baseball case will be overruled."[57] The baseball establishment, however, was pleasantly surprised in 1953 by the Supreme Court decision in *Toolson v. New York Yankees*.[58] Yankee farmhand George Toolson sued the club rather than accept reassignment, but the court reaffirmed *Federal Baseball*, suggesting that it was the responsibility of Congress to address the issues surrounding baseball and antitrust. Although many bills were introduced in Congress seeking to define baseball's legal status, none passed, and baseball sought to placate congressional critics with territorial expansion. The reserve clause would finally be overthrown through the intransigence of ownership and a strong players' union formed during an era, which encouraged the questioning of institutions and sacred cows such as the reserve clause.

Although the Gardella case failed to overturn the reserve clause, the ball player's challenge to the baseball establishment was significant as it revealed the vulnerability of the sport's ownership. The decision to settle with Gardella reflected fears that increasing radio and television revenues would lay bare the fiction of Justice Holmes's *Federal League* argument that professional baseball constituted a sport rather than interstate commerce. Of course, the *Toolson* ruling demonstrated the court's reluctance to overturn a precedent, preferring that changes in the reserve clause and structure of Organized Baseball come through congressional legislation or collective bargaining. The conservative judicial approach was reaffirmed in the conclusions reached by the court in the 1971 Curt Flood case, and it was an assertive union and a 1975 arbiter's opinion that eventually sounded the death knoll for the reserve clause. Danny Gardella helped pave the way for player emancipation while baseball ownership stubbornly attempted to maintain their exclusive structure that was challenged by a Mexican entrepreneur and players accused of corporate and national disloyalty during the nation's second Red Scare.

As for Danny Gardella, he reported to the St. Louis Cardinals, but his major league career was over. He flied out in his only at bat with the Cardinals. His contract was sold by St. Louis to their Texas League Houston farm club, who, in turn, released Gardella after the 1950 season. The following year Gardella played his final season of professional baseball with the Bushwicks, an independent club in the New York City area. The $30,000, which Gardella received as his part of the settlement with Organized Baseball, was not enough to support a growing family, which eventually included ten children and twenty-seven grandchildren. Gardella worked as a hospital orderly, factory hand, truck driver, and street sweeper in Yonkers, New York. Gardella found happiness in his family, and he never publicly expressed regret for his decision to sue baseball and challenge the reserve clause. Reflecting upon his experiences with the baseball establishment, Gardella remarked, "It was baseball which was wrong—so undemocratic for an institution that was supposed to represent American freedom and democracy."[59] Gardella's lawsuit was initiated to challenge a monopolistic structure, which operated a blacklist and blocked the athlete's efforts to earn a living playing Major League Baseball. Gardella did not perceive himself to be a spokesman for a collective challenge to the baseball establishment. Neither was he a labor agitator nor a free speech advocate questioning the postwar political reaction to liberal reform. He was a working-class stiff trying to maintain his job. Nevertheless, Organized Baseball, concerned about maintaining the sport's position in the postwar economy, employed alarmist Red Scare tactics and rhetoric, which elevated the Gardella's lawsuit into a case that offered important insights into the democratic shortcomings of Major League Baseball and the post–World War II consensus. While baseball officials in the early post–World War II period embraced the patriotic discourse of anticommunism, which perceived any criticism of the reserve clause as an attack upon the national pastime and American way of life, Danny Gardella appealed to the nation's democratic traditions of free speech and equal economic opportunity that were essential to the civil rights movement and labor reform such as outlawing baseball's reserve clause. Organized Baseball and the post–World War II anticommunist crusade attempted to ban such democratic protest as disloyal, but Danny Gardella was a true patriot in the American tradition of equal opportunity, challenging the baseball establishment to maintain his livelihood.

CHAPTER SEVEN

Powerlifting's Watershed

FRANTZ V. UNITED STATES POWERLIFTING, THE LEGAL CASE
THAT CHANGED THE NATURE OF A SPORT

Thomas M. Hunt and Janice S. Todd

Powerlifting once held significant promise as a new and challenging form of
sport. Based on three commonly known movements (squats, bench presses,
and deadlifts), it could be easily understood by any of the millions of people
around the world who lifted weights for recreational or fitness purposes.[1]
Despite the enormity of this potential audience, however, powerlifting has
been relegated to the backwater of international athletics by divisions within
its ranks over the issue of testing for performance-enhancing drugs. With
its roots in the 1970s, this discord is now exemplified by the existence of
approximately twenty-seven separate regional, national, and international
powerlifting governing bodies—each having its own constitution, bylaws,
and regulations.[2] While the early history of the sport's formation, growth,
and breakup has been chronicled, its later story remains largely untold.[3]
As such, powerlifting holds considerable potential for scholars who wish to
work on the cutting edge of a relatively underexamined sport with a fascinating organizational structure. Similarly, the intersection of sport and the law is
an area worthy of greater historical scrutiny. Federal laws such as Title VII of
the Civil Rights Act of 1964 and Title IX of the Educational Amendments of
1972 have, naturally, attracted scholarly attention because of the breadth of
their impact on American culture as well as American sport. However, there
are also dozens of legal disputes heard in courts each year involving athletic
organizations whose impact has escaped scholarly attention.

This article examines just such a case. It explores a federal antitrust case between three sport organizations: the United States Powerlifting Federation (USPF), the International Powerlifting Federation (IPF), and the American Powerlifting Federation (APF).[4] By examining *Frantz v. United States Powerlifting,* some of the complex sets of relationships and issues that make up the "politics" of amateur athletics are revealed. In addition, several unintended consequences of the lawsuit for the sport of powerlifting should give pause to similarly situated individuals and organizations considering analogous courses of action. In a 1933 issue of the *American Sociological Review,* sociologist Robert Merton argued that an "actor's paramount concern with the foreseen immediate consequences excludes the consideration of further or other consequences of the same act." He continued that, "Emotional involvement leads to a distortion of the objective situation and of the probable future course of events; such action predicated upon 'imaginary' conditions must inevitably evoke unexpected consequences."[5] By ignoring these warnings and engaging in conduct that allowed for an antitrust claim to arise, the powerlifting community inadvertently destroyed the great hope of many of its members for widespread acceptance of their sport and, ultimately, a place on the Olympic program. They also, albeit unintentionally, sorely damaged the sport itself by opening the door to a proliferation of powerlifting federations, each of which possesses somewhat different constitutive rules.

Many may believe that powerlifting is so minor a sport and so "unique in the world of amateur [athletics]" as to render it undeserving of serious scholarly attention.[6] These perspectives ignore the potential for explosive growth and participation in the sport that exists within a culture that now recognizes the value of strength training as a part of sport fitness and general fitness and in which many high schools sponsor powerlifting as a varsity sport.[7] As such, lessons should be drawn from its unfulfilled possibilities and applied to the wider arena of athletics. Much can also be learned from powerlifting's development regarding the role that nongovernmental sport organizations play in the international system. With regard to their organizational framework, it is worth noting that amateur sports like powerlifting are traditionally governed in a hierarchal structure in which international federations recognize national sport governing bodies as the official representatives of their respective countries.[8] This structure virtually guarantees that interorganizational policy disagreements will take place. Such was the case in the occurrence of a disagreement between officials of the IPF and the USPF concerning the appropriateness of drug testing. In the end, the antitrust jurisprudence that resulted from the split led to the permanent fragmentation of the sport of powerlifting.

In 1979, the USPF was the sole powerlifting federation in the United States and was subservient only to its international governing body, the IPF. More attuned to the strictures of the Olympic movement than its American counterpart, the IPF began to seriously consider the institution of a viable testing program for performance-enhancing drugs after the International Olympic Committee implemented such a program for steroids at the 1976 Montreal Games.[9] Although not an IOC member, the IPF was affiliated with the General Association of International Sports Federations (GAISF), an organization that sought to coordinate the efforts of all international sport federations (Olympic and non-Olympic), and GAISF urged its member federations to follow the IOC's lead on doping controls. In 1979, the IPF adopted a new bylaw that required "testing procedures for Anabolic Steroids and Amphetamine Supplements for all International Championships" and proposed that it should be implemented at the international level later that year and at the national level in 1980.[10] Ironically, many national Olympic committees refused to implement effective testing programs out of fear that such actions would erode the successes of their athletic teams.[11] The United States Olympic Committee, for instance, worried that doing so would lead to a competitive disadvantage against America's Cold War rivals on the other side of the Iron Curtain.[12]

IPF officials, however, announced that they would test at all subsequent world championships, and they requested that each of their member nations should begin their own testing programs. The IPF's reasons for mandating drug testing were clearly linked to a desire to become part of the Olympic Games; one expert close to the scene also speculated that some IPF members worried that state political bodies might intrude upon the organization's private workings and impose their own policy prescriptions, if the IPF did not act first.[13] In the United States, however, the USPF initially refused to act in accordance with the IPF's new policy and a split arose within the USPF's ranks between those who supported drug testing and those who did not. Longtime powerlifting referee and influential USPF member Roger Gedney lamented that "perhaps men's powerlifting has come to the point where the will to control the use of drugs is nonexistent," a result which he believed was "contributing to the possible personal injury [of competitors] due to known side effects [of anabolic steroids]."[14]

In parallel to the expanding agency of women in the larger society during the 1960s and 1970s, a group of female powerlifters within the USPF became particularly vocal in criticizing their organization's traditional acceptance of performance-enhancing drugs. Seeking to mollify the IPF and a growing faction of its own members who wanted testing, the USPF did, in the end, pass legislation supporting the concept of drug testing. However, the USPF National Committee, composed mostly of men who felt threatened by the potential effects of such a testing program, refused to implement doping controls at any of the national championship meets held in 1978, 1979, and 1980. In November of 1981, a group led by Edmund Bishop ("Brother Bennett"), a USPF official and brother in the Catholic Order of the Sacred Heart, set up a different powerlifting federation called the American Drug Free Powerlifting Association (ADFPA), which promised to conduct drug tests at every contest sanctioned by the organization and not just at the national championships.[15] Outlining the reasons for the creation of the ADPFA, Bishop recalled that "lifters and coaches alike were always coming to me after competitions and pleading, 'Brother, you have to do something about the drug use in this sport.'"[16] "Drugs offend the concept of fairness," Bennett wrote, "[and] [a]thletic competitions are becoming more and more chemical competitions. Does this sound right?? Moral?? Ethical?? . . . If we are to have respect for others, we must first have respect for ourselves. A different world cannot be made by indifferent people."[17] Roger Gedney argued that "Brother Bennett and other drug free athletes are acting out of a frustration probably from either the lack of desire or the inability of the USPF to police and protect its members."[18] Rather than viewing the new splinter group as a competitor, or taking action, however, the USPF saw it as a way to maintain its own anti-testing policies and its president. Conrad Cotter even recommended that the two organizations save money by co-sanctioning competitions.[19]

Mindful of Olympic requirements, however, and angered by the USPF's intractable stance against testing, the largely European-based IPF passed a regulation in November 1983 at their annual Congress obliging all organizations that sent athletes to the world championships to have drug testing at their national meets.[20] As one USPF referee later put it, "We had some less than honest administrators then, and the things that they did turned the Europeans off" with the result that "we found the IPF to be threatening and inconsiderate of basic rights provided under US law, and a bit dictatorial."[21] Disgusted at what they saw as an unwelcome incursion into the politics of American sport, an especially reactionary set of "anti-testers" in the USPF created its own national body later that year with the goal of freedom from international controls.

Started by Ernie Frantz and nine-time world powerlifting champion Larry Pacifico, the American Powerlifting Federation openly accepted the use of steroids and criticized the perceived piousness of the IPF. Ironically, the APF was created as a way to "bring all people together involved in the sport [in the United States] and prevent the organizations from being a threat to each other." Separate records were contemplated by some as a way to "charge up the sport again" by settling the dispute between powerlifting's pro-drug and antidrug factions.[22] Frantz started the APF with this thought in mind, stating in a letter to potential new members that "we will, from the very start, establish our own World Records and American Records."[23] Its founders, in addition, proposed that it serve as a "professional" organization that would draw its members from the "amateur ranks" of the USPF. "Those that are directly involved," its business plan outlined, "should definitely . . . [be those known] for sticking together and planning to create something better for the powerlifter, and not allowing the I.P.F. to dictate to the U.S. lifters."[24]

Some USPF members were convinced by Frantz's logic and supported the idea of separate organizations. In a letter to USPF president Conrad Cotter, Roger Gedney urged "those people who are violating the rules that govern the IPF . . . [to] begin their own organization thereby having the authority to develop and regulate themselves."[25] Maris Sternberg, later a plaintiff in the *Frantz* lawsuit, placed the roots of the movement to secede in the 1981 Master Worlds in Naperville, Illinois, an event during which a variety of new records were disallowed by the IPF. "Ernie obviously was totally upset," she recalled. "Grumbling amongst the lifters began. It grew little by little as it seemed that our USPF officials were more concerned with pleasing the IPF than listening to the American lifter's issues."[26] New APF member Gus Rethwisch concurred that the USPF "[doesn't] have the guts to stand up to the IPF. So, we the lifters are taking things into our own hands and doing your job, USPF!"[27] The USPF's central leadership saw matters differently, of course. Representative of that group's opinion was a suggestion by Cotter that the APF be disbanded in order to satisfy the wishes of the IPF.[28] To the USPF's officers, this seemed the best way to avoid angering their international overseers.

In such a way, members of the APF unwittingly stumbled across an issue that observers of international relations have pondered: the role and significance of international nongovernmental organizations (INGOs) in the global system. Specialists in transnational politics have noticed a tendency among some individuals and groups to view INGOs as threats to the sovereignty of the state.[29] In a slight restructuring of this observation, Frantz extended its logic to include the sanctity of private entities *within* sovereign states. In a 1983 request for new members, for instance, he railed against the encroachments of the IPF and argued, "there are more powerlifters in the US than any other country in the world, yet we are dictated to by a small minority of foreign lifters. The . . . APF will bring the power back where it belongs—to you, the American lifter."[30] Such nationalistic sentiments eventually played a part in causing Frantz to seek legal protections for his new organization. Writing immediately prior to the initiation of his antitrust claim, he stated that "the main issue today is not to let one man [IPF president Heinz Vierthaler] dictate to the US . . . The US provides the majority of the membership and the financing for the IPF. We should be better represented. As Americans, we don't go to other countries and deliberately defy their laws. We must not stand for it in our own country."[31]

Attached to these nationalistic feelings was an overt acceptance of performance-enhancing drugs. The consequent "sportive nationalism," to use a term coined by international doping expert John Hoberman, was, of course, not confined to the United States. A representative to the West German parliament, Wolfgang Schäuble, told the Bundestag in 1977, for example, that "we advocate only the most limited use of these drugs . . . because it is clear that there are [sports] disciplines in which the use of these drugs is necessary to remain competitive at the international level."[32] In a January 28, 1983, proposal for an APF meeting, Frantz similarly declared, "I don't believe in any testing whatsoever at any time. I don't believe it should be brought up at any meeting or with any news media to discredit any [p]owerlifter or to discredit and discourage [p]owerlifting from TV contracts or the like."[33] He further wrote in one of his 1983 advertisements, "Don't be dictated to—Lift the way you want to lift . . . Don't want testing? We won't have any."[34] With regard to the IPF's requirement that all world championship lifts be accompanied with a negative drug-test result, Pacifico stated that "we will also recognize any person who has lost a world title due to drug testing."[35] Spokespersons for the new federation seemed unconcerned that their actions might cost powerlifting its chance of placement on the Olympic program. "If getting into the Olympics is justification for drug testing," argued Rethwisch, "the attitudes of some officials serve to not make the effort worthwhile."[36] Frantz, however, recognized the discord that was likely to ensue with the birth of his new organization. In a letter to the powerlifting community, he stated that "I know one of the pitfalls [for the APF] will be the IPF in the future . . . This will be one of the points we will be discussing at our first planning sessions."[37]

In accordance with Frantz's fears, the IPF informed its members that anyone caught participating in a meet sanctioned by the APF would be punished. In a private letter dated May 11, 1984, IPF secretary Arnold Bostrom outlined his position to Mike Lambert, the influential editor of the sport's chief periodical, *Powerlifting USA*.[38] Bostrom wrote, "Any I.P.F. or U.S.P.F.

member, lifter, or official found to be involved with this meet will be suspended for two years."[39] A worried USPF president Conrad Cotter warned
of "an apparently irresistible temptation to 'starve out' the several powerlifting splinter groups by punishing or threatening to punish USPF members who became in any manner involved in the meets sanctioned by these
groups."[40] However, the IPF threats were intensified after Bostrom learned
that the APF's inaugural event, to be held on September 17, 1984, in Aurora,
Illinois, included a group of South Africans who had already been banned
due to their country's apartheid policies. Frantz countered that the APF "wel-
comes the 33 South African Powerlifting team [members] and officials to
the World Event. . . .This is the first time for South Africa, and we are very
pleased."[41] Despite pressure from the IPF, a few American athletes, including
Maris Sternberg and Felicia Johnson, decided to attend. In a sworn affidavit, Sternberg later stated that she specifically checked with relevant USPF
officials regarding the possibility of a ban if she were to attend the meet and
"was assured [that] no sanctions would be taken."[42]

With an eye toward the potential ramifications that suspensions would
have, the USPF Executive Committee instructed Cotter to take a number of
steps to protect it from any legal action. According to the minutes of a conference call on June 8, 1984, committee member George Zangas asked that
his colleagues on the National Committee be instructed "that while the USPF
does not endorse the A.P.F. or the A.M.P.F. (American Masters Powerlifting
Federation), it will not inflict punishment upon those who are 'involved' in
the meet." In addition, Cotter was directed to "warn all officials 'involved'
in the [APF] meet not to wear a uniform or other symbol identifying him
with the IPF." Finally, legal counsel was to be retained so that Cotter could
respond to Bostrom's position as it was outlined in his letter to Lambert.[43]
Cotter asked Steven Sulzer, a lawyer specializing in antitrust litigation, to
review the IPF's request for sanctions and advise him as to the course of
action that the USPF should take.

In a legal memorandum dated June 29, 1984, Sulzer specified his set of
conclusions. He began by citing a list of IPF bylaws that had the potential for
legal liability, including the exclusive right of the IPF to fees from the broad-
casts of its competitions, the prevention of other organizations from negotiating television contracts, and the preclusion of other groups from holding
meets without an IPF sanction. Although it was not incorporated within the
United States, Sultzer continued, the economic activity of the IPF was of such
a nature as to make it subject to the jurisdiction of the nation's courts. He
believed that "in the present case, the IPF's conduct is so clearly intended to
exclude the AMPF/APF that it should support a finding of specific intent to

monopolize. . . . Many USPF members, lifters, and officials who might otherwise travel to the AMPF/APF meet may forego the opportunity," he pointed out, "with concomitant effects on interstate commerce." More important, he continued, "the loss of the AMPF/APF as a competing organization would have a substantial anticompetitive effect on the relevant markets."[44] The IPF would thus violate the Sherman Act's dictate against those combinations, conspiracies, and contracts "in restraint of trade or commerce among the several States, or with foreign nations."[45] Sulzer concluded with a warning that the USPF was likely to lose in any subsequent lawsuit.[46]

Giving credence to Sulzer's warnings, Cotter drafted a note to Bostrom in which he summarized the USPF's worries. He argued that the threat of suspension "lays the I.P.F. open to both criminal and civil action in U.S. courts. The U.S.P.F. cannot, therefore, be a party to enforcing this rule. Please reconsider."[47] Nevertheless, the IPF Disciplinary Committee met in November 1984 in Dallas, Texas, to deliberate on the issue. A set of handwritten notes from that meeting reveals that "the AMPF/APF championship was discussed *in great detail*."[48] It further recorded that eighteen-month suspensions of the three referees at the APF meet—Ernie Frantz, Ed Jubinville, and Tony Fitton—were justified by their violation of the "rules laid down being explicit[ly] relating to powerlifting outside the jurisdiction of the I.P.F." In addition, all USPF members who lifted at the meet received twelve-month suspensions that were to be instituted at the end of the 1984 Men's World Championships. As Sternberg put it, "the IPF had made threats and now they had to figure out a way to make good on them without looking foolish."[49] On a related issue, the committee expressed "concern" over Larry Pacifico's advertisement of the APF's anti-testing policies in *Powerlifting USA* that it felt "contravenes rules laid down by the I.P.F. relating to anabolic steroids."[50] Pacifico was able to escape penalties only by apologizing to the committee and agreeing to contact those whom his advertisement had reached so that he could retract his statement.[51]

Rather than directly informing the powerlifters of their suspensions, the IPF decided to wait to do so until they attended one of its meets. In so doing, they greatly heightened the anger of the athletes and contributed to the initiation of a lawsuit. Sternberg remembered, "At a closed door meeting . . . , the plan was to deal with our disloyalty. We were never informed of this meeting. We were never given the opportunity to defend ourselves. Basically, we didn't even know the meeting was taking place."[52] According to her affidavit, Sternberg made numerous inquiries as to the nature of her punishment, but was never given any grounds for her banishment.[53] Blaming the USPF, she stated that "despite all of the advance warning, unknown to lifters such as myself, the member nations' officials could have taken action to prevent this from happening when the disciplinary meeting took place."[54] In a letter to IPF president Heinz Vierthaler, Nate Foster, chairman of the USPF's referee's committee, expressed sympathy for the lifters and wrote, "You threaten our citizens, and carry out punishments without a simple hearing permitting the accused the right to present evidence in their behalf."[55] He continued by asking, "Do you want to go down in history as the bullheaded president who forced the USPF to withdraw with half the world powerlifting population, and form a new world Federation, and who lost forever the chance to put this sport in the Olympics[?]"[56]

Sternberg, Diane Frantz, and Felicia Johnson were informed that they would not be allowed to lift in the upcoming IPF Women's World Championship meet when they competed at the Women's Nationals in Boston in February 1985.[57] Usually, Sternberg's and Johnson's first-place victories in Boston would have guaranteed their right to compete in the World Championships as a member of the USPF Women's National Team.[58] At that point, according to Sternberg, she "told the 'powers that be' that I would use every means available to me to be placed on the World team, even if it meant an injunction to stop the meet."[59] Frantz explained his own concerns in a February 4, 1985, note to Cotter in which he linked the IPF penalties to the USPF's unwillingness to protect its lifters. "I am writing in reference to the sanctions taken by the USPF/IPF against the lifters of the APF," he began. "We are still researching this issue but we have a new attorney, one versed in this type of case, and we are sure that we have enough to bring suit."[60] He expressed outrage that Sternberg and Johnson were banned after Cotter had issued a statement in *Powerlifting USA* that no such action was under consideration, the hypocrisy of which offended his sense of the lifters' "civil rights." "Since no one is interested in backing the Constitutional rights of these people as US citizens," he continued, "then I will hold no more USPF sanctioned meets in the state of Illinois."[61] In a final assertion that succinctly captured the damage to sport that can ensue in the wake of legal action, he said, "I hope you can get with your Executive Committee to do the right thing for these girls. If not I will be forced to continue my crusade to fight the USPF until they are no longer a viable organization."[62]

Frantz was—at least initially—particularly upset with Judy Gedney, chairman of the USPF Women's Committee, which by then had become a partially autonomous subunit within the national federation that had jurisdiction over certain aspects of women's powerlifting. Writing to Gedney, he stated that "the men are willing to back us but, as Women's Chairman, it is up to you to come forward and insist that it is illegal for Maris Sternberg and

Felicia Johnson not to be included on the US Women's World Team."[63] As justification for legal action, Frantz asserted that "Olympic recognition will never be achieved" given the current state of the rules and that a comparable punishment for a group of male lifters was never enacted after they were caught using steroids. "The easy way out for the USPFWC," he concluded, "is to do what the committee has done by eliminating Maris and Felicia from the team. In that case the lawsuits have already been prepared and will be brought against you, as USPFWC Chairman and your Committee."[64]

After Cotter and Gedney's receipt of the letters, members of the USPF leadership tried to save their organization from any adverse consequences by distancing themselves from the actions of the IPF. Gedney, for example, wrote Frantz that "I wanted to . . . assure you that neither the USPFWC nor I am in favor of supporting the IPF sanctions. . . . In fact this decision by the IPF is a rather inane rule and should definitely be reconsidered."[65] She also recalled that Cotter had assured her that he had opposed the IPF as far as his powers would allow and pointed out that she herself had recently become a member of the APF. "In short," she continued, "what I'm trying to say is that we are supportive of you and the APF/AMPF."[66] She also agreed with an organizational framework in which parallel federations could best promote the interests of the sport. "When people differ about the rules," she explained, "they can either change the rules, follow the rules or simply say that they are following the rules. You went through a great deal of work to develop an organization with different rules and that's exactly the route that should have been taken."[67] She reasoned that "your efforts to begin an organization with rules differing from the IPF concerning the . . . [d]rug [t]esting process is exactly what should have been done."[68] In addition, Gedney felt that Cotter had deliberately manipulated Frantz's attention toward the women's committee. In a set of handwritten notes she fumed, "someone should set Ernie straight about what a liar Cotter is—we should stuff Cotter in a popcorn ball [and] pour boiling oil on him."[69] Sternberg agreed and later commented that thus "began a program of lies, threats and accusations by the IPF that almost became a joke. Then USPF President [Conrad Cotter] totally sided with the IPF, so there was no help at all."[70]

In the end, the APF lifters used the Men's Senior Nationals held in June 1985 in Chicago as an opportunity to serve USPF and IPF officials the papers that officially commenced a lawsuit.[71] An original complaint was also filed with the Eastern Division of the US District Court for the Northern District of Illinois on July 5, 1985, naming Cotter, the USPF, and the IPF as defendants.[72] Sternberg and Johnson alleged under Sections 1 and 2 of the Sherman Antitrust Act of 1890 that they lost actual and potential employ-

ment opportunities through the USPF and IPF's denial of their right to compete at the World Championships. They further asserted a claim against the
USPF for what they felt was an intentional infliction of mental distress. Ernie
and Diane Frantz asserted that by banning the two aforementioned lifters,
the IPF had "threatened" to ban them as well. Suing as business entities, the
APF and the fitness gym out of which it was run, the Ernie Frantz Health
Studio, claimed that their businesses had suffered economic injury, including lost memberships, by being denied "a fair share of the relevant markets
for sponsoring national and international powerlifting meets."[73] These allegations of "conspiracy to monopolize" and "attempt to monopolize" were
supplemented by the APF's allegation that it had been denied by the IPF its
due share of the market for selling the broadcast rights of its meets. By this
means, the APF joined Sternberg and Johnson as plaintiffs in the case. The
plaintiffs sought several remedies, including monetary relief and an injunction aimed at preventing the IPF from taking similar actions in the future.[74]
All parties to the lawsuit were represented before the US District Court with
the exception of the IPF, which refused to appear before the court due to its
perception of a lack of jurisdiction on the part of an American court over an
international body.

During the course of its proceedings, the federal district court addressed
the IPF's refusal to appear before it. Due to this failure to acknowledge the
jurisdiction of the United States judicial system over its actions in the country, the district court issued a default judgment in favor of the plaintiffs.
While a court in such a procedure does not directly address the accuracy
of an allegation at issue, a claim is, for all practical purposes, taken as true.
The implication in this case was that the antitrust allegations against the
IPF were, in effect, deemed accurate. In a minute order dated February 3,
1987, Judge Harry Leinenweber therefore determined the following monetary damages to be assessed against the IPF for the asserted claims: $20,400
for the APF, $84,375 for the Ernie Frantz Health Studio, and $14,574 for
Sternberg.[75]

In his published opinion and order, Judge Leinenweber then assessed
Sternberg and Johnson's claim of intentional infliction of mental distress on
the part of the USPF. Outlining the state of the law on that type of tort, the
judge explained the requirements for its allegation as including "1) extreme
and outrageous conduct by a defendant; 2) that the defendant engaged in
the conduct knowing that severe emotional distress was certain or substantially certain to follow; and 3) that the plaintiff [actually] suffered severe
emotional distress." The court found that the USPF's involvement in the
affair had not risen to such a level as to offend the first of these points.

Further, Leinenweber declared that Sternberg and Johnson had not actually suffered any severe emotional distress. As such, the USPF's motion to dismiss the allegation was granted due to the fact that the two lifters failed to state a claim upon which relief could be granted.[76]

Regarding the alleged violations of the Sherman Act, Leinenweber likewise found that the USPF's conduct did not offend the statute's stricture that there must be a "'contract, combination . . . or conspiracy' in restraint of trade." The complaint did not, in his opinion, "create the reasonable inference that the USPF shared with the IPF a conscious commitment to monopolize 'the sport of powerlifting,' the market for sponsoring power-lifting meets, or any other relevant market." Moreover, any failure to object to the IPF's punishments did not constitute conspiracy on the part of the USPF because a showing of "intent" was lacking. Further, the court found that there had been no "concerted action" between the USPF and IPF regarding a "refusal to deal or group boycott" of the APF meet. Accordingly, the antitrust claims against the USPF were dismissed. As for Cotter, the court reasoned that "a corporate officer is not capable of conspiring with his corporation to engage in anti-competitive conduct because the corporate officer and the corporation have an identity of interests." This analysis, combined with the complaint's lack of specificity on Cotter's involvement, ensured the USPF president's freedom from liability. The court, therefore, imposed sanctions on the plaintiffs and their attorney, Victor Quilici, under Rule 11 of the Federal Rules of Civil Procedure for naming Cotter in their lawsuit "without any legal or factual basis."[77] Under the rule, Cotter then asked the court to require the plaintiffs to pay $44,700 of his attorneys' fees, the size of which "surprised—[and] shocked—the district judge" so that he vacated that portion of his ruling.[78]

Cotter appealed the district court's denial of his request for attorney fees to the US Court of Appeals for the Seventh Circuit. The USPF also appealed the district judge's rejection of its own request for legal fees. Although he noted precedent that a lower court may deny a request for fees as a sanction if there is an "outrageously large request," appellate judge Frank Easterbrook felt that Cotter's fees were at least potentially reasonable given the amount of time that his lawyers had spent on the case. Proceeding from Rule 11's language that mandates the imposition of sanctions when one is sued without any legal basis, the judge went on to chastise the district court for its lack of intellectual rigor. Easterbrook's point was that while the type of sanction to be imposed under Rule 11 is largely at the district court's discretion, it must use logic in coming to its decision. "Discretionary choices are not left to a court's inclination," he wrote, "but to its judgment; and its judgment is to be guided by sound legal principles."[79] Permitting himself to expound upon this point, Easterbrook went on to say, "the absence of ineluctable answers does not imply the privilege to indulge an unexamined gestalt."[80] Accordingly, the Seventh Circuit reversed the trial court on the issue of Cotter's request and remanded the case, sending it back to district court, "so that the district court may put its reasoning on record—a process that, by inducing critical scrutiny of one's initial reactions, often improves the quality of decisions."[81] Because the trial court failed to conduct a sufficient inquiry as to whether Quilici had properly connected the facts before him to cognizable legal theories (some of which Easterbrook asserted were "half-baked"), the USPF's request for attorney's fees was also remanded.[82]

Characterizing Quilici's allegations against Cotter and the USPF with the words, "neither . . . make[s] much sense," and "not well-grounded in law," Judge Leinenweber, on remand, again declared a violation of Rule 11. Still upset at the enormity of the defendants' requests for monetary sanctions, which had by then increased to $97,000, he admonished, however, "Dealing with a bloated request for attorney's fees is every bit as time consuming, if not more so, than dealing with an obviously deficient complaint."[83] After contemplating what he felt were inappropriate actions on the part of all sides, the judge came up with a compromise: the plaintiffs' attorney was fined $5,666.16 while Steven Sulzer, the defendants' lawyer, was charged $1,416.66.

Although the claims against Cotter and the USPF were dismissed, the lawsuit had a decidedly detrimental impact on the federation's economic viability. "Torn between defending [what he saw as a frivolous claim] at considerable cost or forfeiting the suit," Cotter lamented that "it is a side of powerlifting that I never dreamed of before I took this job." He was "quite unable to reconcile with my own sense of propriety the sniveling 'strong man,' who, unable to bear the inevitable disappointments in the sport, employs a surrogate in an attempt to probe our weaknesses and bring us to our knees."[84] As of March 1, 1986, legal fees and expenses for the USPF were claimed to be in excess of $55,000, an amount that put significant strain on its budget. In addition, insurance premiums quadrupled to the rate of four dollars per individual participant per year with $9,880 due by February 23, 1986. As a result, the federation had difficulty in funding American teams for the 1986 World Championships in the Netherlands, the Masters' World Championships in Norway, and the Junior World Championships in India. Cotter announced that "it is with [a] heavy heart that I announce that our tradition of fully funding our teams is in jeopardy. We will probably be [only] sending teams consisting of individuals who can provide their own

sponsorship. . . . [This] works against those of limited means who have neither time nor inclination to rustle up sponsors."[85]

Cotter thereafter instituted a program aimed at reducing the risk of
future legal action that had the unintended effect of decreasing his assets for
program development. He announced in an October 1987 issue of *Powerlifting USA* that "it is well said that an ounce of prevention is worth a pound
of cure. On the national level the USPF has engaged lawyers to revise our
bylaws in order to eliminate provisions which might encourage conduct vio-
lative of the law."[86] While it was impossible "to cost the benefits of this exercise," he felt that if "it results in preventing even a single lawsuit, the savings
will be considerable."[87] He proceeded to explain that "the policy of the USPF
has been, and continues to be, strict adherence to the law . . . [with instru-
ments] designed to discourage lawsuits, and where claims have been filed,
an indeflectable determination to defend the case with every resource at the
USPF's command."[88]

During the years that *Frantz v. United States Powerlifting* made its way
through the courts, Brother Bennett's ADFPA—uninvolved in the lawsuit—
continued holding drug-tested contests and attracting new members. Although
the ADFPA cosponsored a few meets with the USPF in its first two years of
operation, that the USPF's Executive Committee refused to implement drug
testing for men until 1986 (following the public humiliation of multiple
doping positives at the Men's, Women's, and Junior World Championships
in 1985), made Brother Bennett and his disciples realize that unbridgeable
differences on the drug question made any sort of alliance between the federations untenable. Instead, Bennett began lobbying for the ADFPA to be
recognized as the official American representative to the IPF—a campaign
that took nearly a decade to see fruition. By 1996, when a renamed ADFPA
officially joined the IPF as USA Powerlifting, the USPF federation it replaced
had less than a third of the members it had possessed in 1985.[89]

Although *Frantz v. United States Powerlifting* was not the only reason
for the fragmentation of powerlifting into several dozen associations, the
case certainly played a role, and a significant one, in the changes seen in
powerlifting over the past two decades. While no antitrust violations were
expressed in the courts' decisions, the sport's leaders imposed their own
interpretations, which focused on the necessity of separate federations. Even
when the law does not in itself require change, it can—as in *Frantz*—do so
indirectly by altering public perceptions; the vast bulk of citizens, after all,
have no legal training. The lawsuit, therefore, helped confirm the notion
among members of the powerlifting community that they could best pursue
their interests by forming their own governing bodies through which they

could implement their own policy preferences. As Frantz himself put it, "It would be nice if we could all be together, but we've all taken separate paths. . . . [The] choice of organization is a personal one."[90] Members of any given federation would, moreover, not be prohibited from participating in other organizations. After having been approached on merging the American Drug Free Powerlifting Association with the USPF, for example, ADFPA president Michael Overdeer responded that "legal advice precludes this as there are issues of financial liability."[91] He continued, "I will advise this body that under U.S. law, the ADFPA cannot arbitrarily deny membership to anyone. . . . You may not ask us to keep any individual or group with a previous or current affiliation from joining the ADFPA without asking the ADFPA to violate United States National Law."[92]

Thus, in a set of outcomes that Frantz and Sternberg clearly did not anticipate, the suit promoted the disintegration of their sport and consequently destroyed any hope for integration into the Olympic movement. When asked for his "opinion of all the alphabet soup of federations in the current day," Frantz responded with the observation that "with so many federations today it can be very confusing to a person."[93] However, he felt that if "our needs were being met I would not hesitate to combine with the USPF. But this would necessitate backing the lifters, not the power hungry leadership overseas."[94] Sternberg felt that "many of the 'alphabets' have been formed out of ego problems. It is pretty confusing. Some have real legitimacy. Others mean nothing."[95] Regarding the possibility of powerlifting becoming an Olympic sport, Frantz stated that "I'm sure it will make the Olympics someday, but not if it is split up in 20 different directions."[96] Steinberg also believed that "powerlifting will not be an Olympic sport any time soon. It's way too splintered."[97] In addition, the lack of a coherent policy toward performance-enhancing drugs led to the further proliferation of anabolic steroids in powerlifting. A 1995 study, for example, found that two-thirds of the powerlifters who responded had used anabolic/androgenic steroids at some point in their lives and concluded that "It is clear that current doping control procedures are not as effective as they need to be."[98]

Once the *Frantz* lawsuit entrenched the idea of parallel federations into the collective consciousness of the powerlifting community, there was no end to the creation of new governing bodies. Powerlifting administrator Judy Gedney, who has been involved in the sport since the mid-1980s, said in a 2005 interview, "The Frantz lawsuit marked a real watershed time for powerlifting. Before the suit, the USPF had contracts with CBS and NBC to cover their national championships, *Sports Illustrated* had run feature stories on a couple of top lifters, and everyone felt like the sport was growing and had real promise."[99] After the suit, Gedney continued, "lifters realized how little authority federations really had if there was always an alternate federation willing to accept them as a lifter. Suddenly there was no need for lifters to obey rules they didn't like. They could just start their own federation and write new rules that suited how they wanted to lift. We lost our TV contracts and record keeping became a joke."[100]

What Gedney and other administrators confirm is that the major impact of the *Frantz* lawsuit was to create a collective consciousness within the powerlifting community that no lifter could be sanctioned for competing in more than one federation. By the late 1990s, powerlifting was no longer recognizable as one coherent sport. Associations varied on drug-testing policies, how long an athlete must abstain from drug use to be considered a "clean" lifter, and whether testing was to be done by urinalysis, polygraph, or voice-stress analysis. Furthermore, some federations began changing the rules for the performance of the actual lifts themselves, allowing types of supportive squat suits and bench press shirts not allowed in other federations, and also changing such matters as how low one had to go in the squat, or whether a bench press had to pause when it touched the chest. These changes to the constitutive rules of powerlifting were fueled by the sport's obsession with records, and by the fact that the proliferation of federations made it possible for a man or a woman to hold American and/or world records in many different federations.[101]

For sports that are not officially part of the Olympic movement (where the hierarchical lines of authority are clearly drawn) the model of multiple federations—resultant to the *Frantz v. United States Powerlifting* decisions—is cause for concern. Although this article focuses on events in powerlifting where the Frantz case originated, at least one other sport—bodybuilding—has also moved to multiple federations with at least nine national and ten international federations existing as of summer 2012. It will not be surprising, given our obsession with records and winning, if other sports follow suit in the coming years.

The tragedy here lies in the fact that powerlifting, a once budding field of athletic endeavor, was destroyed in part by drug use and in part by an ignorance of legal consequences by its leaders and by their personal enmity toward one another. As sociologist John MacAloon noted, "Incompetence can always be rooted out, official co-conspirators can be found, embarrassed, and exiled (if rarely convicted), and ways can at least be sought to raise the voices of true authority above the legalists, public relations specialists and marketing managers. But if there no longer are any such voices and convictions in these organizations, if the public and the rest of the international sport community come to believe that their leaderships and their organizational culture have thrown in the towel in defeat over drugging in sport, then the effect on the overall legitimacy, prestige and deference afforded these bodies will surely be devastating."[102] In powerlifting, it already has been.

Powerlifting remains today a fragmented sport, yet surprisingly popular sport, with little potential for placement on the Olympic program. The many national, regional, and international federations in existence feature widely different regulations on an assortment of subjects—including drug testing. Rather than fostering a shared sense of competition and fandom, this system of conflicting rules and governance structures also dissipates the attention of powerlifters and spectators alike, and seems increasingly driven by what has been described as the Frank Sinatra School of Ethics—the desire to do it "My Way."[103]

SECTION III

THE IMPACT OF SPORT ON LAW AND LAW ON SPORT

"Sport is a microcosm of society" is repeated often enough to be cliché; law, however, is understood to be more of a mirror of society. So what is the significance when a microcosm is mirrored as occurs when sport enters the realm of law? Perhaps the result is a magnification of an issue of some potentially significant aspect of society. Such is the case of the three essays in this section, each of which is rooted in the present day with profound implications for the future—even if the court case itself was years ago.

In 1977 Renée Richards sued the United States Tennis Association for the right to participate in the US Open as a woman.[1] Richards was the first transsexual[2] athlete to fight so publicly to compete professionally with others of their new gender. Although the lawsuit occurred over thirty-five years ago, the issues of transsexual and transgender athletes have become only more resonant. Richards filed her lawsuit in the 1970s during the women's liberation movement and the beginnings of the gay rights movement, but considerably more time would pass before American society more generally and the sporting community particularly would take transgender issues very seriously. In the 1970s, activists for women were lobbying to eliminate laws prohibiting women from serving on juries (*Taylor v. Louisiana* in 1975[3]) and prohibiting single women from obtaining contraceptives (*Eisenstadt v. Baird* in 1972[4]). In the 1970s, gay rights activists fought to convince the American Psychiatric Association to remove homosexuality from the list of psychiatric disorders (which occurred in 1973) and to decriminalize homosexuality in America on a state-by-state basis. Transsexual and transgender rights were even further behind: most support organizations were on the east and west coasts and lobbying was limited. By 2013, women and gays played a more prominent role in American society: US senator Tammy Baldwin (WI) elected in 2012 was the first out gay senator. The 113th Congress opened session in 2013 with six out gay or bisexual members. In 2014 out gay men played in the National Basketball Association (Jason Collins) and were drafted by a team in the National Football League (Michael Sam). Transgender issues are so mainstream that the NCAA and the International Olympic Committee as well as most professional sports leagues in North America now have policies addressing transsexual athletes. An increasing number of high school and youth sports programs are also creating policies to address not just transsexual but also transgendered athletes.

O'Bannon v. NCAA (retitled after consolidation in 2010 as *In re: NCAA Student-Athlete Name & Likeness Licensing Litigation*) is, in 2014, a pending lawsuit. The verdict is anxiously awaited by the past, present, and future athletes wondering whether or not the NCAA and their own schools can continue to profit from the players' image when NCAA rules prohibit the players from profiting from their own image. This lawsuit arises during an era when televised college sport is at an all-time high, when the NCAA signed a $10.8 billion deal with CBS television networks to air the men's basketball tournament from 2011 to 2014. As of 2011, EA Sports, which created and sold video games using past and present NCAA football players, had a life-to-date revenue production of over $868 million on the football video game alone.[5] None of this money goes to the athletes, even after they leave college. Given that star athletes are celebrities in the twenty-first century, and the celebrities can make a large proportion of their income from their image, this lawsuit merges current concerns about money, marketing, celebrity, amateurism, and technology in one complicated antitrust lawsuit.

Major League Baseball (MLB) has for a century, and even more so after Jackie Robinson broke the color line, mined Latin America for its best players. By the 1970s a number of MLB teams had founded baseball academies in Latin America, and often in the Dominican Republic, to teach the game, English, and US culture to the best prospects. Education, though, was not terribly high on the academies' list of important skills, and MLB teams benefited because Latin players were excluded from the draft and could be signed as free agents with much lower salaries and bonuses. Although some exceptional players, like All-Star Pedro Martinez, were obviously very successful and transitioned from the academies to great careers, others were simply used by the academies until it became clear that they were not MLB material—for whatever reason. The situation, ripe for exploitation, is complicated by the fact that US law does not apply to foreign countries. Thus, MLB is limited only by international law, which is notoriously difficult to enforce, and has its own moral compass. A following chapter explores MLB's periodic attempts to create its own rule of law in Latin America and the challenges and failures of past attempts. Given that over 25 percent of MLB players are of Latin descent, and a large number of them come directly from Latin American countries, this issue addresses critical concerns of migration, law, justice, and sport in a global community.

CHAPTER EIGHT

Thirty-Five Years after *Richards v. USTA*

THE CONTINUED SIGNIFICANCE OF TRANSGENDER ATHLETES' PARTICIPATION IN SPORT

Anne L. DeMartini

Introduction

After Caster Semenya crushed her rivals in the 800-meter world championships in 2009, the masculine build and surprising performance of this South African sprinter fueled rumors that she was not "completely female."[1] The resulting international controversy over her eligibility included gender verification testing, a six-month suspension from her sport, and the International Association of Athletics Federation creating new guidelines for female athlete eligibility.[2] Though Caster Semenya is not transgender, her experience illustrates that sport still grapples with questions such as who is "truly" female? who gets to participate in sport and how may they participate? and who should decide?

Examples

There are few examples of openly transgender athletes at elite levels of sport. In 2004, Danish-born, Australian-based golfer Mianne Bagger became the first transsexual woman to compete in a professional golf tournament, having surgically transitioned from male to female in 1995.[3] The most high-profile example of a transgender athlete in soccer was in June 2005 when Martine Delaney, formerly Martin Delaney, was allowed to compete in Soccer Tasmania's women's league.[4] In 2008, Lana Lawless won the RE/MAX World

Long Drive Championship at Mesquite Regional Park by driving the golf ball 254 yards.[5] The media has covered other transgender athletes, including Michelle Dumaresq, a top Canadian mountain biker,[6] Keelin Godsey, a successful Division III NCAA track and field athlete,[7] and amateur triathletes Chris Mosier and Loren Cannon.[8] During the 2010–2011 season, Kye Allums, a transgender male, competed on George Washington University's women's basketball team.[9]

Controversy has surrounded each of these athletes' participation. The press made derogatory comments including claims that the events were not all female[10] and that the transgender athlete's participation on the women's team was unhealthy and may have been the reason for the team's poor performance.[11] Opponents also objected: one second-place finisher used the medal podium to protest by donning a t-shirt that read "100% Pure Woman Champ."[12]

BACKGROUND

The term transgender. is an umbrella that may be used to describe people whose gender expression—an individual's characteristics and behaviors such as appearance, dress, and speech patterns that are perceived as masculine or feminine—is nonconforming to societal norms. Transgender may also refer to individuals whose gender identity—a person's internal, deeply felt sense of being male, female, something other or something in between—is different from their birth-assigned gender.[13] According to Shannon Minter, legal director of the National Center of Lesbian Rights, "the underlying concept is that 'transgender' includes anyone whose behavior, appearance, or identity falls outside of gender stereotypes or outside of stereotypical assumptions about how men and women are supposed to be."[14]

Because of the breadth of gender constructs and the stigma associated with outwardly identifying as a member of the trans-community, the exact number of transgender-identified individuals is difficult to estimate.[15] According to the Human Rights Campaign, there are no concrete statistics on the number of transgender people in the United States. Estimates range anywhere from 0.25 to 1 percent of the US population,[16] to 8 percent of an international sample,[17] to exceeding 20 million worldwide.[18]

Estimates of the number of transgender athletes are even more difficult to obtain. No statistics are kept on the number of transgender student-athletes competing in the NCAA.[19] An accurate count may even be harder to find in sport than in the general population because athletes may be less likely to identify as transgender for fear of discrimination.

DISCRIMINATION

Education and dialogue about transgender people's inclusion in all aspects of society, including sport, is particularly important in light of the discrimination and even violence transgender people encounter. Though disputed, some experts state that a transgendered person's lifetime risk of being murdered is estimated to be more than ten times that of the general population.[20] A California study found students who are transgender or gender nonconforming often face persistent and severe harassment that can involve name-calling, threats of violence, sexual innuendos or sexual harassment, and even physical assault,[21] and 90 percent of transgender youth in a nationwide survey reported feeling unsafe at school because of their gender expression.[22] A recent report from the National Gay and Lesbian Task Force and the National Center for Transgender Equality stated that transgender and gender nonconforming people faced widespread injustices including evidence of discrimination in housing, education, employment, health care, family life, public accommodations, and interactions with law enforcement.[23]

RELATION TO SPORT

Sport pervades United States society, and athletics interweave the fabric of families, friendships, and business connections.[24] Since commentators argue that sport both shapes and reflects the broader culture,[25] examples of transgender people in sport may illustrate the potential for greater inclusion of transgender people in other aspects of society. The issue of transgender participation in sport also has ramifications for sport organizations and sport managers. According to Pat Griffin, director of It Takes A Team! Education Campaign for Lesbian, Gay, Bisexual, Transgender Issues in Sport, "the inclusion of transgender athletes is one of the latest equality challenges for sport governing organizations worldwide."[26]

One of the most notable examples of a transgender person in sport is Renée Richards, who sued the United States Tennis Association for eligibility to compete in the 1977 US Open.[27] Even over thirty years later, the *Richards* case remains relevant to current debate in sport. This chapter attempts to outline the legal and cultural significance of the Renée Richards case. This chapter also identifies how the climate for transgender athletes has changed and how it has remained the same since *Richards*.

SOCIAL AND HISTORICAL CONTEXT

Had Richards brought her case at another point in time, the outcome may have been different. The intersection of the civil rights movements including women's and gay rights and the increasing visibility of women in sport likely contributed to her success in the 1970s.

1960s and 1970s Civil Rights Movements

Frustrated by the delays in enforcing civil rights won in the 1950s, segments of American culture advocated for social change throughout the 1960s, resulting in domestic reforms.[28] The political and cultural trends of the 1960s, including themes of big government, black activism, social protest, and grassroots politics, continued to prosper and dominate life in the United States until the mid-1970s.[29] Through the 1960s and 1970s, multiple protest movements gained traction, focusing on individual rights.[30] The civil rights movement made significant gains for equality for African Americans, especially in the South.[31] Feminists began a campaign seeking to alter women's unequal political, social, and economic status.[32] By the latter part of the decade, the student-led antiwar movement staged passionate protests against the Vietnam War, the gay rights movement built an ever-larger following, and the youth movement rejected the values of the older generation and embraced a back-to-basics peace-and-love lifestyle.[33]

Grassroots activists and national leaders joined forces to obtain for African Americans the basic rights guaranteed to American citizens in the Constitution, including the rights to due process, equal protection of the laws, and the right to vote.[34] This activism culminated in legislation including the federal Civil Rights Act of 1964, prohibiting racial discrimination in employment and public facilities, and the Voting Rights Act of 1965, barring states from obstructing African Americans from voting and ensuring federal oversight of registration and voting.[35]

By the late 1960s, the gay rights movement evolved from its early modest goals and conservative approach to become more radical.[36] Gay rights activists' primary goals were gay liberation, creating a new society that would allow gays and lesbians to freely express and celebrate their love, and obtaining basic civil rights for gays and lesbians, including the repeal of laws in numerous states that make gay sexual activity a crime.[37] By the mid-1970s, almost half of the states had decriminalized private sexual activity among gay men and lesbians, and many communities enacted antidiscrimination laws to protect gay rights in areas such as employment and housing.[38]

The modern women's rights movement, the feminist movement, or the women's liberation movement reemerged in the late 1960s, advocating belief in the full economic, political, and social equality of males and females.[39] These feminists insisted that the "personal is political," asserting that women's individual problems were legitimate, important political issues. The 1963

Equal Pay Act, the 1964 Civil Rights Act, laws prohibiting discrimination in educational and credit opportunities, and Supreme Court decisions expanding the civil liberties of women illustrate the success of the movement.[40]

Women in Sport

Women's increasing participation in sport, traditionally considered a male activity, also reflects the success of the women's movement. The 1970s saw the growing interest of young women in sport, feminism, and improved health, and a demand for greater American success in international sport.[41] In 1971, the Association of Intercollegiate Athletics for Women (AIAW) was established to organize national college championships for women's sports. Then, in 1972, Title IX of the Educational Amendments Act barred sexual discrimination by schools and colleges that received federal assistance, entitling women to parity in the classroom and on the athletic field.[42]

HISTORY OF THE WOMEN'S TENNIS ASSOCIATION

Women's professional tennis began in 1968, with the arrival of the Open era, where male and female pros were awarded prize money at the Grand Slams and other events sanctioned by the International Lawn Tennis Federation (ILTF).[43] However, female pros were still accorded second-class status with significant disparity in paychecks. In 1970, the top women pros organized their first formal protest complaining of discrimination on the part of tournament directors. Nine elite players signed $1 contracts with World Tennis publications publisher Gladys Heldman to compete in a newly created Virginia Slims Tournament Series, which would offer more prize money to the female pros. The Virginia Slims Series debuted with nineteen tournaments in 1971, with a total purse of over $300,000, and Billie Jean King became the first female athlete to cross the six-figure mark in season earnings. A year later, the United States Lawn Tennis Association formed a separate women's tour, signing up Chris Evert and Evonne Goolagong as its headliners. This tour failed to take off, and in mid-1973, the two circuits merged into the Women's Tennis Association (WTA), with King as its first president. That year the US Open, for the first time, offered equal prize money to the men and women and the twenty-nine-year-old King defeated fifty-five-year-old Bobby Riggs 6–4, 6–3, 6–3 in the hugely hyped "Battle of the Sexes" in front of a crowd of 30,472 at the Houston Astrodome, furthering the cause of the women's movement.[44]

Sport Studies scholar Lindsay Pieper notes that Richards's legal challenge to play as a female in the US Open occurred during this time of incredible female advancement, both on and off the court. With women's tennis making progress both publicly and financially, some members of the women's liberation movement and a contingent of professional female tennis players viewed Richards's campaign for inclusion with skepticism.[45]

Renée Richards

BACKGROUND

In the late twentieth and early twenty-first centuries, nonnormative sexuality remains controversial, though the media presents some images of transgender people, including Oscar-nominated films like *Boys Don't Cry*[46] and *Transamerica*.[47] In contrast, in the 1970s the very idea of gender reassignment shocked people. The sex-change operation of Christine Jorgensen had made international headlines two decades before. In an interview, Richards herself cautioned, "You have to put it in perspective," she says. "Nobody had ever heard of doing anything like this."[48]

Renée Richards was born biologically male, named Richard Raskind, in 1934. In her autobiographies, Richards wrote of growing up as a boy in a "house full of women" with a "headstrong" mother and tomboyish sister.[49] Though Richards's parents were well educated and the family wealthy, Richards recounted that her father was rarely home, the family argued vociferously, and by age six she engaged in fantasies that included dressing in women's clothing.[50]

Throughout her autobiographies, Richards spoke of feeling "two different genders struggling for pre-eminence" within him, one male side—Richard—and one female side—Renée.[51] As a young man, Raskind obtained an "upper crust" education at Horace Mann college preparatory school in Riverdale, New York, and attended Yale University in the 1950s.[52] Raskind also found success on the tennis court, winning tennis championships throughout adolescence and participating on the Yale varsity team.[53]

While living outwardly as Richard, Raskind maintained academic and athletic success, even developing strong lifelong male friendships and intimate romantic relationships with girlfriends. During this time, Raskind furtively expressed Renée by traveling into New York City to secretly dress as a woman and attend nightclub revues.[54] After Yale, Raskind attended medical school and during internship decided on a specialty in ophthalmology. After residency, Raskind joined the US Navy, working at the naval hospital and competing in All Navy tennis tournaments.[55]

Raskind engaged in years of psychotherapy and began receiving female hormones, continuing to lead a double life as both Richard and Renée, which proved emotionally draining.[56] After living abroad as a woman for a year,

Raskind returned to the United States, finding exceptional professional success as a surgeon, marrying and fathering a child.[57] After struggling with thoughts of suicide, finally Raskind concluded that the only way he could live a fulfilling life would be to "allow Renée to emerge" permanently.[58] Dr. Roberto Granato at Physicians Hospital in Queens, New York, performed Richards's gender reassignment surgery in 1975.

Following the surgery, now living as Renée, Richards moved to California, joining the eye department at the University of California Medical Center at Irvine and hoping to live "just a quiet" anonymous, new life.[59] Richards established a thriving professional life and played club-level tennis, attempting to stay out of the spotlight by avoiding tournaments. However, the temptation of competition eventually won out and Richards participated in a tournament in La Jolla, where a television journalist "unmasked" her previous identity.[60] Richards held a press conference summing up her life story. In the following publicity, Richards discovered statements from tennis governing bodies denying her eligibility to participate in major championships. Though up to that point, Richards had not considered competing in major tournaments, the refusal "got [her] dander up."[61] This, coupled with thousands of supportive letters pleading with her to stand up for the rights of minorities and an invitation to participate in a major tournament from an old friend, culminated in a semifinal loss in a media-soaked tournament in New Jersey and a decision to pursue professional tennis.[62]

RICHARDS V. USTA

After the sex reassignment operation in 1975, Richards entered nine women's tennis tournaments, winning two tournaments and finishing as runner-up in three. In 1976, Richards attempted to enter the US Open in the women's division. The USTA advised her that in order to qualify she must first pass a sex verification test—the Barr body test.[63] Richards requested that the test be waived on the basis that it was discriminatory, but the USTA denied the request. Richards ultimately failed to appear at a qualifying site, essentially withdrawing her application from consideration.[64]

The following year, Richards, at forty-three years of age, reached the finals of the women's singles at the Mutual Benefit Life Open in August in New Jersey.[65] In order to comply with the USTA's requirements, later that year Richards went to the Institute of Sports Medicine and Athletic Trauma at Lenox Hill Hospital, which had been selected by the USTA and USOC to conduct the sex determination tests for the 1977 United States Open. Doctors at the institute administered the Barr test but due to institute's failure to follow the "standardized procedure" in order to accommodate Richards's herpes condition, "the results were ambiguous." The USTA requested Richards return for a Barr body retest or for the more definitive or elaborate Karyotype test. However, Richards never returned for further testing, and therefore the USTA did not qualify her to play in the United States Open.[66]

In 1977, Richards filed against the United States Tennis Association, United States Open Committee (USOC), and the Women's Tennis Association. Richards claimed a violation of the New York State Human Rights Law, which declares that the state has the responsibility to act to assure that every individual within the state is afforded an equal opportunity to enjoy a full and productive life and prohibits employment discrimination based on age, race, creed, color, national origin, sex, or disability.[67] Richards also claimed a violation of the Fourteenth Amendment to the United States Constitution.[68] Richards sought preliminary injunction prohibiting the USTA from subjecting her to a sex verification test so she would be allowed to compete as a woman, in the women's division, in the 1977 United States Open, the USTA's national championships.[69]

Richards argued that the USTA's requirement that she take the Barr body test, a sex-chromatin test that determines the presence of a second "x" chromosome, to determine whether she was female was "insufficient, grossly unfair, inaccurate, faulty, and inequitable." She stated that the medical community found the use of the Barr body test to exclude athletes from participating in sports events arbitrary, capricious, and without a rational basis. Richards claimed that the USTA's decision to institute the test was specifically designed to exclude her from competition.[70]

Richards presented many affidavits of support. Eugene Scott, tournament chairman of the Mutual Benefit Life Open held in South Orange, New Jersey, in which Dr. Richards played and reached the finals, averred that he invited Richards to play in his tournament as a woman because he recognized her as a woman. He rejected reliance solely on the Barr body test and instead chose to rely on the Phenotype test, which includes the observation of primary and secondary sexual characteristics, which he felt Richards passed.[71]

The defendants argued that the requirement that athletes pass the Barr body test did have the rational basis of ensuring competitive fairness and preventing "female impersonators or imposters."[72] They claimed a male who has undergone "sex change" surgery obtained a competitive advantage as a result of physical training and development as a male. The USTA argued that the Barr body test was a reasonable way to assure fairness and equality of competition when dealing with numerous competitors from around the world and that the use of the test "transcend[ed] the factual background or medical history of one applicant."[73]

The defendants submitted an affidavit of a medical doctor in support of the applicability of the Barr body test for the determination of sexual identity that explained the process and purpose of the test and interpreted how chromosomes may impact competitive athletic ability. Defendants also submitted affidavits in opposition from women's professional tennis players, each stating that based on her experience, "the taller a player is the greater advantage the player has and similarly, the stronger a player is, the greater advantage the player has, assuming like ability." Also, the director of women's tennis for the USTA asserted that she had been unable to find a record of any woman player over age forty who had such a successful competitive record as Richards, a record unparalleled in the history of women's professional tennis.[74]

The court's decision explored the definition of a transsexual[75] and relied on Richards's surgeon, Dr. Roberto Granato, who explained the sex reassignment surgical process and Richards's prior and subsequent endocrinological testing and administration of female hormones.[76] Dr. Granato believed Richards did not possess an unfair advantage "when competing against other women. Her muscle development, weight, height and physique fit within the female norm" and concluded that except for reproduction, Richards should be considered a woman, classified as a female and allowed to compete as such. Richards presented several other medical views that supported that Richards should be considered female, that the Barr body test is inadequate to determine one's sex for purposes of athletic competition, and that she would not have an unfair advantage when competing against other women.[77]

Richards also submitted an affidavit from women's tennis professional star Billie Jean King in support of the plaintiff's application. Billie Jean King stated that she and Dr. Richards were doubles teammates in one tournament and that she participated in two tournaments in which Dr. Richards played and she judged that Richards "does not enjoy physical superiority or strength so as to have an advantage over women competitors in the sport of tennis."[78]

The New York Supreme Court granted the preliminary injunction Richards requested and found that the defendants violated Richards's rights under the New York Human Rights Law.[79] The court's reasoning stated the requirement that Richards pass the Barr body test in order to be eligible to participate in the women's singles of the United States Open was grossly unfair, discriminatory, and inequitable.

The court indicated that it believed the defendants knowingly instituted the test for the sole purpose of preventing the plaintiff from participating in the tournament since the USTA's decision to require a sex determination test for the 1976 US Open was a direct result of Richard's attempt to compete. Until August 1976, there had been no sex determination test in the ninety-five-year history of the USTA national championships, other than a simple Phenotytpe test (observation of primary and secondary sexual characteristics) and the USTA had not required the sex-chromatin test for sanctioned tournaments other than the US Open. The USTA permitted each tournament committee to make its own determination as to whether to use the chromatin test.[80] The court stated that the only justification for using a sex determination test in athletic competition is to prevent fraud and the court rejected any suggestion that Richards was attempting to engage in fraud by desiring to play professional tennis as a woman. The court opined, "When an individual such as plaintiff, a successful physician, a husband and father, finds it necessary for his own mental sanity to undergo a sex reassignment, the unfounded fears and misconceptions of defendants must give way to the overwhelming medical evidence that this person is now female."[81]

The court, however, did not go as far as to strike completely down the Barr body test, since it appeared to be recognized as an acceptable tool for determining sex. The court did order that the Barr body test was not and should not be the sole criterion for determining an individual's sex when the circumstances warrant consideration of other factors.[82]

AFTER THE COURT DECISION

The court decision was not a broad sweeping victory for transgender athletes' access to athletic participation. In a 2009 interview, Richards commented that the judge indicated his decision was an individual decision for her situation and noted that the judge's decision did not indicate that all transgender athletes should be allowed to play professional sports, only that "this woman at 44 at her current persona, condition, physicality and so on, [. . .] she is entitled to play in the US Open."[83] Since the judge did not make a blanket decision on transgender participation, he essentially ruled that future judgments would be made on a case-by-case basis where an authoritative institution, like a court, would determine if the athlete was female enough to be allowed to compete.[84] Therefore, Richards's legal victory alone did not force dramatic change in sport or society.[85]

After the court decision, Richards pursued a professional tennis career. She played in the 1977 US Open, losing in the doubles finals. She won the US Open thirty-five-and-over singles championship in 1979, but was ousted in the first round of the 1981 tournament. Soon after, she ended her own competitive tennis career and briefly coached Martina Navratilova.[86] By 1982, Richards had returned to medicine full time to live a private life. She later explained that she was tired of the public scrutiny she endured and felt that her notoriety exacted an emotional and financial price.[87] Her decisions led to a lengthy estrangement from her sister[88] and a tumultuous relationship with her son.[89] In interviews since the court decision, Richards is often quoted as being an unwilling role model and refuses to acknowledge her role as an activist for transgender issues.[90]

The court decision divided female professional tennis players. Some women opposed Richards, recognizing that while she had legally earned the right from the New York Supreme Court to participate, she still possessed an unfair biological advantage. Other female competitors, who demanded complete equality to men, interpreted the backlash against Richards as detrimental to both the quest for gender equality and the plight of women's tennis. They believed that denying her inclusion was hypocritical, rejecting supposed biological restraints and holding more nonnormative views of gender.[91] Billie Jean King, both a leader in the women's liberation movement and one of the most prominent figures in women's tennis, served as one of the first professional female tennis players to support Richards, and also as the most important. Over time, as Richards produced only mediocre competitive results, opponents' fears were assuaged and advocacy for Richards grew. Following King's lead, other female professional tennis players eventually understood that to dispute Richards's acceptance "would signify adherence to the cultural ideology of male superiority in athletics, and thus counter their claims that female competitors deserved equality."[92]

CONTINUED SIGNIFICANCE AFTER *RICHARDS V. USTA*

Renée Richards's experience remains relevant today. The current questions surrounding transgender athletes' participation are not new. Transgender athletes today confront many of the same arguments Richards did thirty-five years ago. Questions arose that were complex, profound, and practical: What constitutes gender? What makes one a "man" or a "woman?" Are transgender people fair competition in women's sports? Would hormonal therapy to "correct" an individual's birth gender violate doping policies that prohibit testosterone? Which locker room should transgender athletes use?[93]

RECENT CASES

Few transgender athletes have used the court system to gain access to athletics participation since *Richards*. The news media reported in October 2010 that Lana Lawless sued the Ladies Professional Golf Association alleging that the LPGA's "female at birth" policy discriminates in violation of California's state civil rights law.[94] Lawless dropped the case in May 2011 after the LPGA voted to change its policy.[95] As of June 2013, no other cases of transgender athletes suing for access to athletic participation had been published.

Other Legal Avenues

Renée Richards won her case against the USTA under specific New York State laws. Currently, a transgender athlete may have some further legal protections from discrimination, though the protections are still limited. A transgender athlete who is attempting to compete as a professional may find some protection from employment antidiscrimination statutes while an intercollegiate or interscholastic athlete who wants to participate may find protection under educational statutes. Constitutional provisions and state and local laws may provide some protection in both situations.

Title VII

Title VII of the Civil Rights Act of 1964 prohibits employment discrimination based on an individual's race, color, religion, sex, or national origin.[96] For a number of decades, whether or not legal protection existed for transgender employees was somewhat unclear. In the 1970s, some federal courts held that Title VII did not protect transgender employees from discrimination.[97] Recently, the Supreme Court's increasingly expansive interpretation of Title VII in other contexts undercuts the rationales in these past decisions, allowing a few federal circuits to issue favorable decisions holding that transgender, or more broadly, gender nonconforming persons, are protected from discrimination under Title VII and other sex discrimination statutes.[98] Until the Supreme Court resolves the issue, circuits will remain split on whether Title VII's protection against discrimination "because of sex" applies also to sexual orientation and transgender discrimination.[99]

Constitutional Provisions

If an athletic organization receives government funding or is highly entangled with the government, courts consider the organization a state actor and it must adhere to both the US Constitution and appropriate state constitutions.[100] The Equal Protection Clause of the Constitution requires that all people similarly situated be treated similarly.[101] Where laws or government practices treat people differently based on sex, the state must meet the higher standard of intermediate scrutiny, showing at least that the classification serves important governmental objectives, and that the discriminatory means employed are substantially related to those objectives.[102]

If courts applied intermediate scrutiny to policies that exclude transgender athletes from participation in accordance with gender identity, the policies would likely fail.[103] However, courts generally have not applied heightened scrutiny in cases involving discrimination on the basis of gender identity.[104] Some courts construed sex discrimination to include gender-non-conformity discrimination for purposes of the Equal Protection Clause,[105] and a federal district court did so for the benefit of a transgender plaintiff,[106] but existing precedent extending the Constitution's protection to transgender athletes is still limited.[107]

Title IX

Transgender student-athletes may find additional protection from discrimination under Title IX or state student rights laws. Title IX of the Education Amendment Acts of 1972 prohibits discrimination based on sex in education programs and activities receiving federal financial assistance.[108] No case law currently exists regarding the direct applicability of Title IX to transgender student-athlete eligibility. However, some courts have found that Title IX protects students from peer harassment based on their gender nonconformity since that harassment is considered "on the basis of sex."[109] Since courts interpret the provisions of Title IX through relevant case law respecting Title VII, the current split among courts over the scope of Title VII will have a significant impact on the claims of transgender students.[110] Therefore, jurisdictions that interpret Title VII's definition of "sex" more broadly may also interpret Title IX's "on the basis of sex" to include protection against discrimination based on gender nonconformity, which could include transgender student-athletes. Additionally, California, Illinois, Iowa, Maine, Maryland, Minnesota, New Jersey, Oregon, Vermont, and the District of Columbia have enacted Student Rights Laws that explicitly prohibit discrimination or harassment based on gender identity or expression in schools.[111]

State and Local Antidiscrimination Laws

Due to the exclusion of explicit sexual orientation and gender identity protections under current federal antidiscrimination laws and Congress's failure to pass supplemental legislation to create such protections, most plaintiffs must seek relief under state and local laws.[112] State or local statutes that explicitly prohibit sexual orientation or gender identity discrimination create the most potential for successful claims.[113]

As of May 2014, eighteen states and the District of Columbia have statewide laws that include gender identity and/or expression as a category of antidiscrimination,[114] and at least 156 counties and cities have such laws.[115] The National Gay and Lesbian Task Force estimated in 2012 that 44 percent of people in the United States lived in a jurisdiction that has such laws.[116] Since 2012 Delaware and Maryland have enacted laws prohibiting discrimination based on gender identity and/or expression. Additionally, fifteen states and the District of Columbia have hate crimes laws that include gender identity and/or expression.[117] Students may have more protection, as some states prohibit educational institutions specifically from discriminating on the basis of gender identity and many educational institutions have campus nondiscrimination policies that include gender expression.[118]

Courts, commissions, and attorneys general and executive orders in fifteen states have interpreted existing state law to include some protection against discrimination for transgender individuals.[119] Over the past decade, courts and administrative agencies have found that transgender plaintiffs, who had been discriminated against because of their gender identity, had a right of action under existing state and/or local antidiscrimination laws.[120]

In other cases, transsexual plaintiffs have been able to find relief through state disability statutes, as long as the statutes do not follow the Americans with Disabilities Act (ADA), which explicitly excludes gender identity disorders.[121] However, many states still do not allow claims under disability statutes, usually focusing on a rationale that a transgender condition does not affect the major life activity of working.[122]

ATHLETIC ORGANIZATIONS' POLICIES

The landscape for transgender athletes has changed since *Richards,* even if not solely due to the outcome of the case. Though many athletic governing organizations still have yet to address transgender eligibility, some have created policies.[123] These other organizations followed in the footsteps of the International Olympic Committee's (IOC) 2003 adoption of a policy establishing criteria for transgender athletes to participate in the Olympics. This IOC policy, known as the Stockholm Consensus, focuses primarily on male-to-female transitions and completion of a surgical transition as a criterion for participation.[124] The policy allows that individuals undergoing sex reassignment after puberty may be eligible for participation under particular conditions including that "surgical anatomical changes have been completed, including external genitalia changes and gonadectomy, legal recognition of their assigned sex has been conferred by the appropriate official authorities, and hormonal therapy appropriate for the assigned sex has been administered in a verifiable manner and for a sufficient length of time to minimize gender-related advantages in sport competitions."[125] The policy also requires that "eligibility should begin no sooner than two years after gonadectomy," and allows a confidential case-by-case evaluation.[126]

In 2005, both the United States Golf Association and USA Track & Field adopted the IOC policy.[127] Since the IOC policy went into effect, the Ladies Golf Union (Great Britain), the Ladies European Golf Tour, and Women's

Golf Australia created policies governing transgender athlete participation using the IOC policy as a guideline.[128] Other sport organizations using the IOC's policy as a template include USA Rugby, USA Hockey, USA Track and Field,[129] and the Football Association (Britain's soccer governing body).[130] The Gay Games Federation and the Gay and Lesbian International Sport Association also adopted policies enabling transgender and transitioned athletes to compete in the Gay Games and the OutGames.[131]

In contrast, the National Collegiate Athletic Association (NCAA) does not follow the IOC. Until 2011, the NCAA had no formal policy governing participation by transgender athletes in competition, but provided a non-binding position statement to its member institutions.[132] The former NCAA position statement did not prohibit transgender student-athletes from competition, but required that athletes compete in the gender designated on their official state government documents: a driver's license, birth certificate, or passport.[133] In September 2011, the NCAA approved a new policy based on a report from the National Center for Lesbian Rights and the Women's Sports Foundation that allows transgender student-athletes to participate in sex-separated sports activities in their reassigned gender if the athlete's use of hormone therapy is consistent with the NCAA policies and current medical standards. A trans male (female to male) student-athlete who has received a medical exception for treatment with testosterone for gender transition may compete on a men's team but is no longer eligible to compete on a women's team. A trans female (male to female) student-athlete being treated with testosterone suppression medication for gender transition may continue to compete on a men's team until completing one calendar year of documented testosterone-suppression treatment, at which time the student-athlete becomes eligible to compete on the women's team.[134]

In 2008, the Washington Interscholastic Activities Association (WIAA) became the first state association to enact a policy on transgender participation in high school athletics.[135] The first draft of the WIAA policy followed the IOC policy, which requires surgery, but commentators resoundingly condemned the validity of the policy as applied to high school students since gender reassignment surgeons require patients to be at least eighteen.[136] After collaboration with groups including the National Center for Lesbian Rights, the Washington State Human Rights Commission, the American Civil Liberties Union of Washington, Advocates for Informed Choice, and the Colorado High School Activities Association, the 2008–2009 WIAA policy allows student-athletes "to participate in WIAA activities in a manner that is consistent with their gender identity, irrespective of the gender listed on a student's records."[137] Not all high school athletic associations have followed the WIAA's lead. Both the Connecticut Interscholastic Athletic Conference and the Colorado High School Activities Association created policies that required student athletes to have completed a surgical transition and hormone therapies before they would be eligible to compete in their reassigned sex.[138]

Future Views

ADVOCACY

Though there has been progress toward more transgender athletes' participation in sport since Renée Richards, transgender athletes still have a long journey to reach full inclusion. Most of the largest and most popular sport organizations in the United States still have not created policies regarding transgender athletes' eligibility.[139] Additionally, commentators and human rights groups have criticized many of the organizations that do have policies, including the IOC, as unnecessarily restrictive.[140] The IOC guidelines set complicated barriers to entry for athletes that have no connection to athletic performance. Many countries do not allow for legal recognition of transsexual people in their transitioned sex. Athletes may not desire surgery for privacy or personal reasons or may not be able to afford it. The amount of time it takes to undergo surgery and legal recognition is often far greater than the amount of time it takes to lose an athletic advantage via hormone treatment. Elite competition requires an athlete to be at the top of his or her sport, which allows for a very short window of opportunity to compete.[141]

Transgender plaintiffs continue to have varying results in legal cases. While the Supreme Court has ruled that transgender employees cannot be explicitly denied protection from discrimination,[142] few courts have held that federal law explicitly protects them.[143] While a growing number of states and municipalities have enacted some legal protections for transgender people, the majority still have not.[144] Transgender people still endure discrimination and violence.[145]

Dean Spade, assistant professor at Seattle University Law School and founder of the Sylvia Rivera Law Project, a nonprofit law collective that provides free legal services to transgender, intersex, and gender nonconforming people who are low income and/or people of color calls for the addition of laws prohibiting discrimination on the basis of gender identity and expression and significant changes in the law regarding the regulation and administration of gender categories in order to reduce the legal and policy barriers to transgender survival.[146]

Many gay, lesbian, and transgender advocacy organizations are now focusing their efforts on securing congressional passage of the Employment

Non-Discrimination Act (ENDA) for federal-level legal reform.[147] The proposed bill would prohibit discrimination against employees on the basis of sexual orientation and gender identity.[148] Another potential federal law would help protect transgender public school students. The Student Non-Discrimination Act prohibits discrimination and harassment on the basis of the students' actual or perceived sexual orientation or gender identity.

APPLICATION TO ATHLETICS

Athletic organizations can work to ensure transgender athlete equality and access to participation opportunities. In the think tank report, On the Team: Equal Opportunity for Transgender Student-Athletes, Pat Griffin and Helen Carroll demand school policies focus on maximizing inclusiveness and "enable all student athletes, regardless of their gender identity or expression, to compete in a safe, competitive, and respectful environment free of discrimination."[149] They note that specific policy requirements may differ depending on the level of athletics. They recommend that high school student-athletes be allowed to participate in athletics consistent with their gender identities, regardless of whether a transgender student has undergone any medical treatment.[150] For collegiate student-athletes, they recommend institutions allow participation in any sports activity so long as that athlete's use of hormone therapy, if any, is consistent with the national governing body's existing policies on banned medications.[151]

Commentator Erin Buzuvis argues that in addition to empirical research about the sex-based competitive advantages, policymakers must also consider the purported educational benefits of sport and the benefits of diverse and inclusive teams.[152] Buzuvis argues that policies governing participation by transgender athletes should allow transgender athletes to compete in a manner consistent with their gender identity as the default rule and should carve exceptions from this default rule only when doing so is consistent with educational, scientific, and legal considerations.[153]

The Women's Sports Foundation (WSF) position paper on the participation of transgender athletes in women's sports recommends physical accommodations to ensure the fair and appropriate inclusion of transgender athletes.[154] Both WSF and Griffin as well as Carroll elaborate that physical accommodations include ensuring access to locker rooms, showers, and toilet facilities appropriate for an athlete's gender identity and providing athletes who desire increased privacy with accommodations that best meet their needs and privacy concerns. Additionally, transgender athletes should be permitted to dress consistently with and wear the team uniform of their preferred gender identities. Teammates, coaches, and all others in the school should refer to transgender student-athletes by a student's preferred name and the pronoun references to transgender student athletes should reflect the student's gender and pronoun preferences.[155]

Conclusion

In conclusion, Renée Richards's groundbreaking case against the USTA remains relevant today. *Richards v. USTA* endures as the primary example of a transgender athlete using the legal system to gain access to sporting competition. Today, more sport organizations have policies governing transgender athletes' participation and transgender people have growing legal protections. However, sport continues to struggle with issues of fairness and inclusion of transgender athletes. While the cultural and legal landscape has progressed, transgender athletes still face discrimination in both sport and broader society. The sport industry should move toward a more inclusive model, so future transgender athletes will not have to follow in Richards's footsteps.[156]

CHAPTER NINE

"Clean Up the Abuses"

BUILDING A RULE-OF-LAW CULTURE FOR MAJOR LEAGUE
BASEBALL'S OPERATIONS IN LATIN AMERICA

Arturo J. Marcano and David P. Fidler

Here We Go Again?

In July 2012, a documentary called *Ballplayer: Pelotero*[1] caused controversy in professional baseball. The film focused on events in 2009 concerning two 16-year-old prospects in the Dominican Republic and depicted problems with how Major League Baseball (MLB) operates in that country. MLB commissioner Bud Selig criticized the documentary by asserting that it was inaccurate, contained misrepresentations, and did not reflect changes MLB had made in the Dominican Republic since 2009.[2]

For us, as lawyers who have worked for over a decade to identify, analyze, and remedy problems connected with MLB's behavior in Latin American countries,[3] Selig's response to *Ballplayer: Pelotero* was, to quote Yogi Berra, "déjà vu all over again."[4] We have repeatedly encountered arguments from MLB and its defenders that critiques were not accurate and did not take account of steps MLB had made to improve its operations in Latin American countries. Often these arguments admitted problems existed (just not the ones critics emphasized) that MLB had already addressed.

However, the reality has been that MLB has been forced to make changes many times because of multiplying problems identified and publicized by reporters and critics of MLB. Contrary to intentions, problems multiplied as MLB added more rules to regulate its activities in Latin American countries, primarily the two biggest sources of foreign talent—the Dominican Republic and Venezuela. This conundrum pointed to not only emergence of new problems that existing rules did not address but also a culture of persistent rule bending and breaking. The history of MLB's development of a system of rules and institutions to govern its Latin American operations involves the failure of a "rule-of-law culture" to take root and grow.

Talking in terms of the "rule of law" concerning MLB's operations in Latin American countries might seem odd because the concept typically applies to the behavior of governments. In this traditional sense, the rule of law is a political philosophy under which governments exercise power according to established rules.[5] This objective requires not only rules but also institutions that promulgate, implement, interpret, and enforce rules. Experts also emphasize the need for societies to have a culture in which people respect rules and institutions and their functions: "The rule of law is as much a culture as a set of institutions, as much a matter of the habits, commitments, and beliefs of ordinary people as of legal codes. Institutions and codes are important, but without the cultural and political commitment to back them up, they are rarely more than window dressing."[6]

However, MLB plays such a powerful role in the process through which amateur players in Latin America are recruited, signed, and trained by MLB teams that using rule-of-law thinking produces insights worth exploring. Other chapters in this volume analyze how sports and legal rules and institutions intersect, as, for example, happened with decisions by the US Supreme Court.[7] The history of MLB's involvement in Latin America is, however, one in which MLB rather than governments and formal legal systems has been the major rule-making and rule-implementing actor. Given this reality in the globalization of baseball, a rule-of-law lens requires from MLB and its stakeholders appropriate and effective rules, institutions to apply them fairly, and a shared culture of commitment to the values the rules and institutions embody.

With the help of *Ballplayer: Pelotero,* this chapter explores the failure of a rule-of-law culture to develop with MLB's adoption of more rules and institutional capacity for its activities in Latin America. We reflect on how the evolution of MLB's rules and institutional capabilities for its Latin American endeavors reached the point MLB realized it had to engage in deeper, more systemic reforms in order to transform the entire enterprise. Our analysis moves from the initial context of no rules through the stage of rule multiplication to, finally, MLB's most recent efforts to change how it accesses talent in Latin America. We do not claim that reforms have created the missing rule-of-law culture. Rather, we explore whether these reforms have potential to be the foundation for building such a culture for MLB's future operations in Latin America.

A Tale of Two *Peloteros*

Ballplayer: Pelotero tells the stories of two Dominican teenagers, Miguel Angel Sanó and Jean Carlos Batista, who come from impoverished backgrounds they are desperate to escape through baseball.[8] Although alike in these respects, Sanó and Batista had different personalities and worked for their goals in different circumstances. Nicknamed *Bocatón* or "Big Mouth," Sanó is a confident extrovert surrounded by an extended family, his *buscon* (or independent trainer), a lawyer, and a professional agent. Sanó was pegged as one of the very best Dominican sixteen-year-old prospects in 2009, with the potential to pull a record-breaking bonus of $5,000,000 or more.

By contrast, Batista had no entourage other than his *buscon* and mother. His father died when he was young, and he missed his mother while training for tryouts and still felt his father's absence. Compared to *Bocaton*, Batista was quiet and introspective but still intense about baseball. He asserted that only Sanó was a better prospect, although Batista and his *buscon* aimed for a smaller bonus of around $1,500,000. The film depicted Batista's first try-out as a bit of a disaster, with Batista wildly missing first base after fielding a ground ball and badly striking out in his first at bat. Sanó did nothing but impress at his tryouts, with one MLB scout marveling how easy playing baseball seemed to Sanó. Of the two, Batista was the underdog, and, when his determination produced better tryouts, both players seemed on the cusp of achieving their dreams as the July 2 signing day for international amateur prospects approached.

However, things fell apart for both players. At an April tryout involving Rene Gayo, director of Latin American scouting for the Pittsburgh Pirates, Gayo remarked to Sanó's *buscon,* Vasilio "Moreno" Tejeda, that Sanó's "size, the way he talks to you, his maturity—he doesn't seem like a kid. So that's a real concern." Two weeks later, allegations emerged in the media that Sanó was lying about his identity and age, which intensified the required investigation MLB was conducting on his eligibility. Based on these investigations, MLB suspends players who commit age or identity fraud for one year. The investigation turned into an agonizing process that left Sanó and his family feeling victimized and helpless. Sanó cooperated with the investigation, including undergoing DNA tests and bone-density scans that supported his claimed identity and age. And, yet, the investigation continued. Rob Plummer, Sanó's agent, asserted that, under MLB's system, Sanó was guilty until proven innocent.

With this cloud hanging over his head, Sanó and his support team sought assistance on July 1 from Porfirio Veras, head of the Dominican

Baseball Commission, a Dominican government agency. Instead of helping, Veras told them how the system really works:

> I want to be very clear about this. There is only one MLB. It's a monopoly. And it's their monopoly. They're the ones who govern the business, and make the rules of the game. We're limited to merely advising you. People take advantage of poverty here. I am totally clear. This is happening because he's poor.

With the MLB investigation ongoing, no MLB team made Sanó an offer. Only one team, the Pittsburgh Pirates, appeared interested in Sanó after July 2, but this interest is a source of controversy in the film. Sanó, his family, and agent believed that Rene Gayo circulated the allegations about Sanó's age and identity and then colluded with investigators in MLB's Dominican office to be in a position to sign Sanó for a reduced bonus. After a meeting at the MLB office at which, for some reason, Gayo was present, Sanó's lawyer stated that the MLB investigator and Gayo told Sanó that his problems would go away if he signed with the Pirates. In anger and frustration, the lawyer stated: "Why would an [MLB] investigator care which team you're going to sign with? This is a mafia, understand? A mafia, that's what it is."

After MLB concluded its investigation on July 24 by confirming Sanó's identity but stating it could not verify his age, Sanó's family conducted its own investigation, which included secretly taping a meeting with Gayo. At this meeting, Gayo told the family:

> We can sign right now. All you have to do is say OK, and we can sign. The only real offer he has is mine for $2 million. . . . Unfortunately, this is a country of lies. And even though you are telling the truth, you have to pay for that. . . . According to MLB, he was going to be suspended for a year, but now he's not. What I did is get him amnesty. I have influence. All you have to do is cooperate.

Rob Plummer tried to use the tape to demonstrate to other teams what was happening to Sanó, but he encountered no interest. Plummer concluded that teams did not want to hear that Sanó was sixteen because, with the cloud hanging over his age, he commanded less signing bonus money. "Smells like collusion to me," Plummer observed, "Major League Baseball might have an interest in trying to keep the bonuses down."

In the end, Sanó signed in September with the Minnesota Twins for $3.15 million and, thus, avoided the need to ink with the Pirates. In the film, Sanó's story ends with him cruising the streets in a new SUV, enjoying the new home he bought his family, and being designated as one of the Twins' rising minor league stars.[9]

As part of due diligence on every Dominican prospect that might sign, MLB began its investigation of Jean Carlos Batista in June. Batista's *buscon*, Astín Jacobo, stated that he had no worries because he had seen no hints that Batista or his mother had lied about his age or identity. Batista got an offer to sign on July 2 with the Houston Astros for $450,000—the highest bonus the Astros had ever offered a Dominican prospect. Although Jacobo wanted Batista to accept, Batista rejected the offer after the Astros refused to increase the bonus to $600,000. Houston signed another player for less money, and Batista had no other offers. In the meantime, MLB's investigation of Batista—delayed because of a backlog of cases—came back inconclusive in September, meaning that investigators had identified problems. This development prevented Batista from accepting an offer made that month by the Arizona Diamondbacks.

In October, the film depicted Jacobo revealing that Batista was not sixteen but was seventeen. "They lied," Jacobo sadly said. For committing age fraud, MLB suspended Batista for one year. After the suspension, the Houston Astros signed Batista for $200,000. Jacobo sued Batista and won damages related to the age fraud. This outcome brings to mind a scene early in the film when Batista is hanging out with other players at Jacobo's training facility, and one of the players said, "A lot of us have pulled off tricks so we can sign. People change their ages and all that. But that's what you have to do." Batista looked straight at the camera after this statement.[10]

Reactions to *Ballplayer: Pelotero*—A Culture of Abuse

Ballplayer: Pelotero involved engaging storytelling by the filmmakers, but film critics frequently connected the stories to problems associated with how MLB teams recruit prospects in the Dominican Republic. Reviews repeatedly emphasized the abusive nature of MLB's system:

- The film "depicts a recr uitment process that . . . [is] all about the dehumanizing power of money, and growing kids into superstars at bargain-basement prices."[11]
- It "shows a shady business in which scouts and the teams they represent try to manipulate teenage players, and to some extent the players do some manipulating of their own."[12]
- The documentary is "a damning film" that exposes a "flawed," "shameful" and "potentially exploitative system" that "is being gamed from all sides of the table—the story of the collision of youthful dreams and a cutthroat adult cartel."[13]

- "The potential for chicanery is rife, . . . what starts out as an inspirational tale of two young hopefuls quickly becomes a backstage drama in which both of their potentially budding baseball careers become mired in controversy."[14]
- In the film, "the suits who run MLB are the real bad guys here, treating the aspiring ballplayers as so much sausage."[15]
- Sanó's and Batista's "childhoods have long since disappeared, replaced by the reality that they are the merchandise of the U.S. national pastime."[16]
- MLB appears as "another massively powerful corporation that exploits the needy[.]"[17]
- The film exposes the "bizarre, plantation-style world of Dominican youth baseball" where "young *peloteros* are a lot like sugar cane, the country's other principal cash crop."[18]

These reactions highlighted how the film exposed a system that targets children living in poverty and subjects them to manipulation and exploitation. Critics of MLB's activities in Latin America, including us, have argued for years that these aspects of the system threaten the human rights of children recognized in international law.[19] How the system has long functioned constitutes an enduring failure of MLB to live up to its responsibilities under international human rights law to respect, protect, and fulfill the human rights of children it recruits, signs, and trains to play professional baseball. The human rights aspects of MLB's activities in Latin America connect to the emphasis rule-of-law thinking places on respect for fundamental human rights.[20]

These reactions from film critics also raise many questions, but, for this chapter's purposes, we are interested in how the documentary depicts MLB's operations in the Dominican Republic fostering a culture of abuse even after numerous MLB efforts to address abuses, including adoption of new rules and creation of new institutional capabilities. A decade ago, we chronicled a Venezuelan teenager's tragic journey through MLB's system in Latin America, and a key theme was MLB's failure to adopt rules to govern its activities in Latin America and develop institutional capacities to oversee their implementation.[21] Disciplining the exercise of power requires rules and institutions that support their implementation and enforcement, so the lack of both on MLB's part helped explain the culture of abuse our book analyzed.

The context for *Ballplayer: Pelotero* is different. The film touches on important rules MLB adopted in the past decade, including rules on abuse of performance-enhancing drugs and age and identity fraud. Unlike the time period of the events described in our book, Sanó's and Batista's journeys involve encounters with a MLB office in the Dominican Republic equipped with staff to investigate compliance with MLB rules. And, as reactions to the documentary demonstrate, the film depicted a culture of abuse concerning the process through which MLB recruits young prospects in the Dominican Republic. How, despite rules and institutional capabilities, could *Ballplayer: Pelotero* still depict a culture of abuse concerning MLB's operations in the Dominican Republic?

Ballplayer: Pelotero does not answer this question. In keeping with good storytelling, it presented real-life complexities, opinions, accusations, and innuendo and let the viewer make judgments about what the film depicted. Surprisingly given its response to *Ballplayer: Pelotero* and the harsh judgments rendered in many film reviews, a helpful place to start in understanding the culture of abuse the documentary revealed is critical analysis produced by MLB itself.

The Alderson Report

Ballplayer: Pelotero concentrated on events in the Dominican Republic that took place from March to October 2009. At exactly the same time, MLB undertook a review of its operations in that country. In response to yet more scandals emerging from the Dominican Republic involving age and identity fraud, performance-enhancing drugs, and corruption by MLB team officials, MLB commissioner Selig appointed a committee in May 2009 "to examine Major League Baseball and Club operations in the Dominican Republic."[22] Selig named Sandy Alderson—a Harvard Law School graduate, former marine, experienced MLB team executive, and a highly respected figure in professional baseball—as chair of the committee. The committee "decided to explore the current problems affecting baseball operations in the Dominican Republic first, and then to consider issues with broader, longer term implications."[23] It issued recommendations for existing problems in a September 2009 memorandum known as the "Alderson Report." This document was strategic in outlook because it recognized the depth of the problems, the extent of the short-term reforms required, the need for long-term changes, and MLB's responsibility to engage in deep reform.

This strategic outlook is remarkable when viewed against the typical pattern of MLB responses to problems in its Latin American operations. Time and again, MLB responded defensively, reactively, and inadequately to problems its approach to recruiting and training children and young men living in poverty in developing Latin American countries produced and perpetuated. This ad hoc, piecemeal, and nonstrategic approach—what Rob Ruck described as "aborted and timid efforts . . . to address the exploitation of young baseball talent"[24]—meant MLB ran from problem to problem, usually after embarrassing publicity, rather than proactively and strategically identifying issues and addressing them through comprehensive reform.

This pattern produced rules and new institutional capabilities, but the reactive adoption of additional rules as more problems emerged produced an ineffective patchwork of rules overseen by inadequate institutional personnel and resources. Some examples illustrate this pattern of behavior. In response to teams signing players as young as thirteen and fourteen years old, MLB established sixteen years of age as the minimum signing age in 1984.[25] However, MLB did not create institutional capacities in its two biggest markets for foreign talent, the Dominican Republic and Venezuela, to oversee compliance with the rule. Eventually, MLB established an office in the Dominican Republic in 2000 and assigned it the task of addressing violations of the signing-age rule by MLB teams.[26] Similarly, in response to criticism that teams did not routinely provide Spanish-speaking players with Spanish-language contracts, MLB began in 2001 to require that teams provide Spanish translations of signing documents to players, a requirement also overseen by the Dominican office established in the same year.[27]

This pattern continued as other problems arose. In response to disclosures and outside criticism about poor playing and living conditions in MLB teams' minor league baseball facilities—known as "baseball academies"—in the Dominican Republic and Venezuela, MLB adopted standards for such facilities in 2002 and assigned the MLB office in the Dominican to oversee their implementation.[28] Media disclosures of rampant abuse of performance-enhancing drugs by Dominican prospects and players forced MLB to adopt in 2004 rules about such drugs and establish a drug-testing and education program for minor league activities in the Dominican Republic and Venezuela.[29] Revelations that MLB teams were abusing tryouts by hiding promising prospects in their baseball academies until they were old enough to sign contracts produced, in 2006, a new MLB rule to prevent this behavior from continuing.[30]

But the problems simply kept multiplying. On the heels of scandals involving performance-enhancing drugs came awareness that prospects were increasingly engaging in age and/or identity fraud when signing with MLB teams. So, the MLB office in the Dominican Republic was tasked with investigating the ages and identities of prospects and punishing those who engaged in such fraud. MLB also knew that such fraud—as well as use of performance-enhancing drugs—were encouraged and practiced by many *buscones* in the Dominican Republic, leading to calls for MLB to regulate how teams used *buscones* in the recruitment and signing process. The development of more rules and investigation procedures confronted many prospects in Latin America with processes with little transparency and sense of fairness, as Miguel Sanó discovered. Even MLB teams complained about the investigations, describing them "as perfunctory, riddled with incompetence and subject to the very corruption that they were designed to stop."[31] In 2008 and 2009, MLB fired investigators for inadequate performance and corruption.[32] Finally, scandals emerged in which MLB team officials were involved in corruption by taking kickbacks from *buscones* and skimming money from player signing bonuses.[33]

Viewed against this pattern of MLB's prior responses to problems, the Alderson Report is remarkable. Jonathan Mahler, a contributor to the *New York Times Magazine*, described it as "an ambitious reform blueprint" where MLB "finally seemed poised to end its long history of exploiting Latin Americans[.]"[34] The report jettisons any pretense that MLB had brought short-term problems and long-term challenges in the Dominican Republic under control. It identified problems, recommended actions, acknowledged MLB's responsibility to undertake reform, and warned about difficulties MLB would face with reform.

More specifically, the Alderson Report identified problems with MLB operations in the Dominican Republic, including:

1. Use of performance-enhancing drugs, including insufficient MLB activities to reduce such use;
2. Age and identify fraud, including poor quality MLB age and identity investigations;
3. Behavior of *buscones*;
4. Prevalent corruption among MLB team officials;
5. Problems with signing bonuses;
6. Continued issues with tryouts in MLB baseball academies;
7. Difficulties working with the Dominican government;
8. Inadequate MLB social initiatives, such as player education; and
9. Ineffective structure, staffing, financing, and functioning of MLB's Dominican office.

This litany of issues involves more problems than *Ballplayer: Pelotero* touched upon.[35] The committee communicated that the problems were too many, too serious, too pervasive, and too entrenched for "business as usual" to guide MLB.

Although it focused on short-term problems, the committee noted the potential need for more fundamental changes, such as an international draft.[36] This aspect of the committee's work suggested it was skeptical that fixes to immediate problems would address adequately the pervasiveness and depth of the abuses. Talk of an international draft had been around for years before the Alderson Report,[37] but the talk never materialized into action. The report linked the short-term and long-term problems, which brought prospects for an international draft more into the reform spotlight.

The Alderson Report's examination of short-term problems also revealed the intertwined nature of these issues. For example, the report acknowledged that *buscones* contribute to abuse of performance-enhancing drugs, age and identify fraud, corruption among MLB team officials, problems with signing bonuses, and the adverse impact these problems have on MLB's Dominican office.[38] Fortunately, the two *buscones* featured in *Ballplayer: Pelotero* were not engaged in any such behavior, again illustrating how more comprehensive the Alderson Report's critique of the system was compared to what the documentary depicted.

The cancer the *buscon* system represents has been recognized for years without MLB seriously addressing it.[39] The Alderson Report captured team complicity in *buscon*-related corruption by observing that team officials "were hesitant to confront these [corrupt] buscones out of a concern that the Clubs would be denied access to the buscones' players."[40] This reprehensible behavior reflected a governance vacuum. As the report stated, "[t]here is no system currently in place to regulate the conduct of buscones."[41] As the multi-billion-dollar enterprise[42] that created the opportunities and incentives *buscones* have to sell prospects to MLB clubs, this failure falls on MLB.[43] The Alderson Report constituted the first MLB attempt to address the *buscon* problem more forthrightly.

The scale and substance of the Alderson Report's recommended reforms communicated that MLB bears comprehensive responsibility for the problems in the Dominican Republic and elsewhere in Latin America. With this in mind, Anderson called for stricter protocols and more efficient institutional capabilities. In terms of new rules, the report called for new regulations on age and identity fraud, tryouts at MLB baseball academies, *buscones,* and corruption by MLB team officials . In terms of new rules, the report called for new regulations on age and identity fraud, tryouts at MLB baseball academies, *buscones,* and corruption by MLB team officials. Institutionally, the committee argued that (1) the MLB office in the Dominican Republic "is inadequately organized and insufficient" to achieve MLB's interests, and (2) staff and departments in the commissioner's office in New York "should discharge greater responsibility in their oversight of their areas of authority in the Dominican Republic."[44] Acknowledgment of problems with the Dominican office and its relationship with headquarters demonstrated that the office's establishment in 2000 did not achieve strategic reform. The committee emphasized the need to strengthen MLB's governance and institutional capabilities with respect to its Latin American operations.

MLB efforts to implement the Alderson Report showed signs that MLB officials understood the need to supplement the recommended new rules and institutional capabilities with a significant shift in attitudes about the problems with MLB's operations in Latin America. As chair of the committee, Alderson was MLB's point man on reform, and, during trips to the Dominican Republic in 2010, he was brutally clear about the need for fundamental change in declaring that "the system as it currently exists cannot continue" and emphasizing the urgency of the need to "clean up the abuses."[45] Such messages took aim at the culture of abuse that tainted MLB's operations in the Dominican Republic, and MLB began to make changes, including firing the head of the Dominican office in March 2010. [46] The following summarizes the recommendations and demonstrates that the committee approved an ambitious agenda for "critical short term issues."[47]

Performance-enhancing drugs

- Expand educational programs, including for *buscones* and unsigned young players
- Explore initiatives with the Dominican government on educating younger players
- Investigate allegations that *buscones* facilitate PED use

Age and identity fraud

- Strengthen MLB Department of Investigations in combating age and identity fraud
- Register players at their first point of contact with MLB teams (e.g., at tryouts)
- Perform investigations before an MLB team signs a player
- Prohibit players on the suspended list from attending MLB tryouts
- Require players and *buscones* to attest to a player's age and identity
- Defer payment of signing bonuses

Baseball academy tryout process

- Improve regulation of MLB tryouts at baseball academies by:
  Prohibiting tryouts before formal registration;
  Computerizing records of player entry and exit from baseball academies;
  Randomly inspecting academies; and
  Implementing an annual closed period in which no team can host an unsigned player at an academy

Regulation of buscones

- Lobby Dominican government to enact and enforce legislation regulating *buscones,* including penalties for facilitating PED use and age and identity fraud
- Reach out to the US Embassy for help working with the Dominican government

- Establish voluntary registration system for *buscones* and provide them with information on MLB rules and programs, including PED programs
- Require *buscones* to attest to a player's age and identity

Corruption by MLB team employees

- Subject team employees working in Latin America to background checks
- Require annual statements that employees have not received anything of value from players or their representatives
- Bar any employee who has engaged in corruption from MLB employment for a significant period of time and encourage criminal prosecution

Scouting talent in Latin America

- Develop MLB scouting function to track players from an early age and maintain player database to reduce age and identity fraud and prepare for possible international draft

Social initiatives

- Retain an experienced person in the Dominican office to focus full-time on community initiatives and public relations and partner with organizations interested in helping MLB on social issues (e.g., USAID, NGOs)

MLB office in the Dominican Republic

- Expand and restructure the office
- Establish or augment functional areas, including head of the office, Department of Investigations, Baseball Operations, Community Affairs/ Public Relations, Legal, Security, MLB International, and Labor
- Retain adequate office space to allow the office to perform these functions
- Deploy appropriate technologies to perform functions recommended
- Increase office's budget significantly

Source: Alderson Report

Past MLB's responses tended to blame others—prospects, players, *buscones,* "bad apples" on MLB teams, or the Dominican government—for problems in Latin America. The Alderson Report discussed the need for action by others, such as Dominican government regulation of *buscones,* but it avoided passing the buck for its Dominican operations. MLB officials started to emphasize this responsibility more. Robert Manfred, executive vice president for Labor Relations, admitted, in connection with age and identity fraud, that "we recognize our responsibility . . . and that we have to constantly reevaluate the way we do business to make sure we are not creating perverse incentives to engage in behavior we know is wrong."[48]

But the culture shift attempted in the wake of the Alderson Report had to include participants outside MLB. In trips to the Dominican Republic to pursue reform, Alderson encountered opposition and protests by people, such as *buscones*, with vested interests in how the existing system operated. Alderson responded harshly by criticizing *buscon*-organized protests involving players as "another example of kids being manipulated and victimized."[49] Alderson warned in April 2010 that, if MLB and its stakeholders could not "clean up the abuses, I think there's a very strong likelihood there will be an international draft."[50] This warning echoed the committee's discussion of the potential need for an international draft—the most radical option available and the one most feared by Dominicans, but perhaps the only one capable of ending the culture of abuse and producing sustainable root-and-branch reform.

The New Basic Agreement

The Alderson committee set July 2, 2010, as the deadline for implementation of its recommendations.[51] Although MLB began implementation of some recommendations, such as creating a registration system for Dominican prospects, MLB by no means achieved the ambitious reform agenda the committee recommended. Indeed, doubts emerged about whether MLB was serious about, or capable of achieving, the kind of comprehensive reform laid out in the Alderson Report. Doubts multiplied when Alderson—the central figure of the reform effort—resigned to become the general manager of the New York Mets in October 2010.[52] However, reform of MLB operations in Latin America was not dead, as disclosure at the end of 2011 of the terms of the Basic Agreement 2012–2016 negotiated by MLB and the Major League Baseball Players Association (MLBPA) revealed.[53]

Through collective bargaining, the MLBPA and MLB negotiate agreements to establish the terms of the overall relationship between MLB teams and players represented by the MLBPA. Historically, Basic Agreements have not addressed MLB's operations in Latin America because the MLBPA does not have collective bargaining authority over Latin American amateur prospects. The Basic Agreement for 2003–2006 established a World-Wide Draft Subcommittee tasked to expand the existing amateur draft to include all amateurs regardless of residence.[54] However, it could not reach agreement, and the free agency system in Latin America continued. Thus, in an unprecedented move by the MLB and MLBPA, the Basic Agreement for 2012–2016 included the most radical changes ever made to MLB operations in Latin American countries, and these changes have eclipsed in importance many recommendations made in the Alderson Report. Until the end of 2016, efforts to end the culture of abuse portrayed in *Ballplayer: Pelotero* and analyzed by the Alderson Report will center on the new Basic Agreement's provisions on international amateurs.[55]

In brief, the Basic Agreement (1) establishes a draft-like mechanism—the "Signing Bonus Pool"—that limits signing bonuses for international amateur players, (2) creates an International Talent Committee through which MLB and the MLBPA will negotiate on a formal international draft and address other problems related to MLB's international operations, and (3) tasks an Education/Vocational Committee to assist international players who do not make it to the major leagues to transition into education or work after their baseball careers end.

The Signing Bonus Pool (SBP) mechanism caps what teams can spend on signing bonuses for international amateurs and—after the 2012–2013 signing period during which every MLB team had a fixed amount for signing bonuses—it allocates bonus amounts and signing slots to MLB teams in inverse order based on the prior season's winning percentage. Teams with losing records will be allocated more money, which will give them more opportunities to sign top prospects than they might have under the free agency system. Thus, the SBP mechanism functions like a draft in controlling the costs of signing amateur players and seeking more competitive balance among teams. The SBP mechanism imposes penalties on teams that exceed their signing bonus limits,[56] but it excludes from a team's allocation (1) six signing bonuses of $50,000 for the 2012–2013 seasons; and (2) an unlimited number of signing bonuses of $7,500 or less for the 2012–2013 seasons, and $10,000 or less for the 2014–2016 seasons.

Under the Basic Agreement, the International Talent Committee is "to discuss the development and acquisition of international players, including the potential inclusion of international amateur players in a draft, and to examine the rules and procedures pursuant to which international professional players sign contracts with Clubs."[57] The list below provides all of the matters on which the International Talent Committee shall provide advice to MLB and the MLBPA. This agenda includes some issues identified by the Alderson Report, such as the need to regulate *buscones*, but it goes beyond the report's reforms in, for example, tasking the committee to advise on what age is appropriate for prospects to sign contracts with MLB teams—an indication of potential willingness to raise the eligibility age from sxiteen to, perhaps, eighteen.

The Basic Agreement also establishes a "permanent Education/Vocational Committee consisting of representatives of both parties to assist international players who are not drafted, or are released prior to reaching the

Major Leagues, with their transition to educational/vocational programs or the workforce."[58] This mandate addresses criticism leveled at MLB that its operations in Latin American countries harm educational and vocational prospects of the vast majority of players who will not make it to the major leagues. It also responds to the Alderson Report's emphasis on the need for MLB to improve its social initiatives, including in education:

Commissioner on the following matters:

1. If there is an international draft, whether international players should be part of a single worldwide draft (including players currently covered by the Rule 4 Draft) or a separate draft (or drafts).
2. The appropriate age at which international amateur players should be signed to professional contracts.
3. If there are to be multiple drafts, whether players from Puerto Rico should remain in the Rule 4 Draft or instead be part of an international draft.
4. The development of appropriate country-by-country plans for playing and development opportunities for players prior to draft eligibility, including expansion of the El Torneo Supremo.
5. The development of appropriate plans to provide undrafted or unsigned players (including players age 18 to 21) from Latin America with an opportunity to continue their development, including the creation of a new league or leagues, or the addition of centrally operated Clubs in the Dominican Summer League (DSL).
6. Whether and how regulations should be put in place regarding representation of international amateur players (e.g., "independent trainers" and agents).
7. Improving the education and acculturation programs of Clubs at their international academies.
8. What safeguards should be established in relation to any signing bonus payments made to international amateur players.
9. The laws of the countries from which international players are signed and how those laws should affect the actions of the parties.
10. What actions are necessary in order to achieve the negotiation of a revised agreement between MLB and the Mexican League that allows players greater choice of where to play and promotes a fair and open system of player movement.
11. What actions are necessary in order to achieve the negotiation of revisions to the protocol agreements with the Korean Professional Baseball League, the Japanese Professional Baseball League, and the Taiwan R.O.C. League to accommodate a draft.
12. How Cuban players should be treated under an amateur talent system in light of the legal and political factors that affect their signability.

Source: Basic Agreement, 265–66.

Each element of the Basic Agreement's provisions on international amateur players is more complex than described above, but even these incomplete descriptions communicate adoption of radical changes (e.g., the SBP
mechanism), the potential for more drastic reform (e.g., an international
draft), and efforts to address long-standing problems associated with the
existing system (e.g., signing sixteen-year-old prospects, the need to regulate *buscones*, and problems associated with the system signing thousands of
teenage players MLB knows will never play in the major leagues). Further, no
longer is reform solely in the hands of MLB because the MLBPA is involved in
all aspects of the Basic Agreement relating to international amateur players.

Implementation of the Basic Agreement, 2012–2013

As of May 2014, the Basic Agreement has been in effect for two signing
seasons, providing some evidence to examine how its provisions on international talent have been implemented. In its first two years, the SBP mechanism appears to have achieved its primary objective of controlling costs for
MLB teams in signing players in Latin America. From the 2012 to the 2013
signing seasons, spending on international players decreased from a total of
$96,000,000 to $87,226,600, with the scheduled amount for the upcoming
2014 season set by the SBP mechanism at $79,194,000, meaning that SBP
implementation has decreased the amount MLB teams spend on international players for three straight years. During this period, the amounts MLB
teams spend on drafted players has increased.[59] According to MLB, of the
approximately 400 prospects signed by MLB teams during the 2012 signing
season, 10 players received signing bonuses of at least $1 million, 62 players
signed for bonuses of more than $250,000, and 328 players (or 82 percent)
signed for less than $250,000.[60] Stakeholders in this process acknowledge
that the SBP mechanism has allowed MLB "to systematically lower signing
bonuses," which has produced complaints that Latin American prospects
are being "penalized" under this mechanism.[61] Referring to the SBP mechanism's exclusions for low signing bonuses operable during the 2012 signing
season, one director of international scouting for a MLB team said, "We've
got so many guys we've given less than $50,000 . . . I'm not bragging—every
organization is like that."[62]

For the 2014 season, the SBP mechanism eliminates the six $50,000
signing bonuses each MLB team had, which did not count against the team's
SBP spending allocation. Starting with the 2014 season, the SBP mechanism
permits each MLB team an unlimited number of signing bonuses of up to
$10,000—a change that will contribute to most Latin prospects signing for
small bonuses.

The MLB and the MLBPA failed, however, to reach agreement on implementing an international draft.[63] According to MLB, "agreement was not reached on some of the mechanics and procedures related to such a draft."[64] The MLBPA gave a different reason, stating that, "[a]t this time, the players are not prepared to accept an international draft."[65] A group of over 150 Latin American players on MLB teams signed a petition opposing a draft,[66] but information about the views of other MLB players has not been made available by MLBPA.

The differences in the MLB's and MLBPA's explanations of the unsuccessful negotiations raise more questions than answers, but neither party has provided information on what happened, leaving those interested in this issue confronting a lack of transparency. However, the negotiations themselves apparently lacked transparency because even MLB "teams are in the dark about what MLB has in the works with its international draft talks."[67] Further, the negotiating process itself came in for criticism because "team officials and player representatives have expressed concerns that decisions about a draft are being made by people without experience in international scouting or international amateur player development, and argue that the amateur players being affected don't have anyone looking out for their interests."[68] Given what is known, MLB and the MLBPA will not, in all likelihood, reach agreement on an international draft before the current Basic Agreement ends in 2016, and whether they agree to try again in the next agreement remains to be seen.

The Basic Agreement also established an International Talent Committee, with an ambitious agenda extending beyond questions of an international draft, and an Educational/Vocational Committee to address problems Latin American players confront after being released by MLB teams before reaching the major leagues. However, as of this writing, neither MLB nor the MLBPA has released sufficient information about what these committees have done, if anything, over the course of their existence.[69] Although the Basic Agreement is producing cost control for MLB teams, the lack of information about the International Talent Committee and Educational/Vocational Committee on long-standing problems connected to MLB practices in Latin America perhaps suggests little, if any, progress on objectives unrelated to reducing MLB team expenses in signing Latin American players.[70]

Toward a Rule-of-Law Culture in MLB's Activities in Latin America?

The Basic Agreement's provisions on international amateurs ensured that, to paraphrase Alderson, the prior system will not continue, at least until the end of 2016 when the agreement terminates. The Basic Agreement provides that, if MLB and the MLBPA "fail to reach a new Basic Agreement by the end of the 2016–2017 signing period, the status quo will revert to the system governing international signings prior to the execution of the new Basic Agreement."[71] As of May 2014, we did not have enough information to determine whether the Basic Agreement has ended the culture of abuse depicted in *Ballplayer: Pelotero* and analyzed in the Alderson Report by fostering better rules, more robust institutions, and a new culture of habits, commitments, incentives, and beliefs that support rule-based behavior and protect children and young men living in poverty from exploitation and manipulation. Without more transparency from MLB and the MLBPA, especially about the International Talent Committee and the Educational/Vocational Committee, the Basic Agreement's impact on key problems with MLB operations, and their consequences, in Latin America is uncertain.

From available information, the Basic Agreement's main achievement appears to be cost control for MLB teams signing Latin American prospects. Part of that achievement—excluding small signing bonuses from counting under the signing bonus caps—means that the vast majority of Latin American prospects signed will receive small bonuses. This outcome is reminiscent of when almost all signing bonuses for Latin American prospects were under $10,000—the heyday of what Samuel Regalado called "Latin players on the cheap."[72]

In conversations with people involved in recruiting Latin prospects, we have noted another disturbing impact of the Basic Agreement and the SBP mechanism—MLB teams are attempting to recruit, develop, and establish strong relationships with fourteen-year-old children. This trend results from the convergence of two things. First, for many years, MLB teams have worked to reach informal agreements with fifteen-year-old prospects before the official July 2 signing date, which undercuts the letter and spirit of the seventeen-year-old rule. This widely known and MLB-tolerated practice takes many top fifteen-year-old prospects off the market before they are old enough to sign contracts. This practice means MLB teams are recruiting younger prospects to develop relationships that might help the teams reach these informal agreements when the prospects are fifteen years old. Second, limited signing bonus money under the SBP mechanism reinforces the incentive to establish connections with fourteen-year-old prospects. MLB teams want to identify as early as possible prospects the teams believe should be allocated portions of their signing bonus pools. The limits on signing bonuses increase the competitive pressure MLB team scouts face in finding top prospects, which fuels the desire to recruit younger prospects. This trend constitutes the latest manifestation of one of the most disturbing aspects of MLB behavior in Latin American countries—the deliberate targeting of children.

A major theme of our 2002 book was the need for "people who care about the future of the game of baseball to begin restructuring governance for Major League Baseball's activities with respect to Latin children and young men."[73] In our years of working on these issues, the Basic Agreement contains the most far-reaching governance changes to MLB's Latin American operations ever made, with more reforms potentially emerging from the International Talent Committee and the Education/Vocational Committee. However, if all the Basic Agreement achieves in Latin America is cost control for MLB teams, then MLB and—this time—the MLBPA will have squandered an opportunity and failed their responsibilities to "clean up the abuses" that characterize how MLB brings Latin American children and young men into its system.

CHAPTER TEN

"A Matter of Basic Fairness"

Ed O'Bannon Takes the NCAA to Court

Daniel A. Nathan

Ed O'Bannon Jr., tall, lithe, and blessed with "superb athleticism," was an All-American basketball player and a history major at University of California, Los Angeles (UCLA).[1] As a senior, he led the Bruins to the 1995 National Collegiate Athletic Association (NCAA) national championship and was named the Most Outstanding Player of the tournament.[2] Soon thereafter, O'Bannon won the John R. Wooden Award, which honors the nation's best college basketball player, and was selected by the New Jersey Nets as the ninth pick in the National Basketball Association (NBA) draft.[3]

Unfortunately for O'Bannon and the Nets, he had a lackluster and brief NBA career, partly due to injuries, partly because he "was sick of the NBA."[4] He played for the Nets only for a season and a half before being traded to the Dallas Mavericks; and he averaged a mere 5.0 points per game during his two-year NBA career.[5] O'Bannon subsequently became a pro basketball vagabond: over eight years, he played in Italy, Spain, Greece, Argentina, and Poland.[6] In 2009, O'Bannon became the assistant promotions manager at a Toyota dealership in Henderson, Nevada, a Las Vegas suburb. He is an affable, thoughtful, well-spoken, conscientious, financially secure family man (he is married and has three children).[7]

Ed O'Bannon is also the lead plaintiff in an important class-action lawsuit against the NCAA. The original suit also named the College Licensing Company (CLC), which "manages branding and merchandising for the NCAA, as well as many colleges and universities" and, since 2007, is a division of IMG Worldwide, Inc., a global entertainment and marketing company, and Electronic Arts (EA) Sports, the popular, multi-billion-dollar video

game company, which is headquartered in Redwood, California as defendants; the latter two are in the process of settling.[8] O'Bannon's lawsuit was
filed in July 2009, in US District Court, Northern District of California, and
claimed that the NCAA, the CLC, and EA Sports had violated antitrust statutes and misappropriated former college athletes' likenesses in violation of
right of publicity laws. The suit was originally filed as *O'Bannon v. NCAA
and CLC*, but was consolidated with other similar suits in 2010 and became
known as *In re NCAA Student-Athlete Name & Likeness Licensing Litigation*.[9]

Many legal observers and members of the media have noted that the
lawsuit may end up being meaningful and possibly historic. According to
legal scholar Michael McCann,

> The stakes of O'Bannon v. NCAA [*sic*] are enormous. If O'Bannon and
> former student-athletes prevail or receive a favorable settlement, the NCAA,
> along with its member conferences and schools, could be required to pay
> tens of millions, if not hundreds of millions, of dollars in damages—
> particularly since damages are trebled under federal antitrust law. The mar-
> ketplace for goods may change as well, with potentially more competition
> over the identities and likenesses of former college stars.[10]

At the same time, the *O'Bannon* case is not just about money. The *New
York Times* reported, "The significance of this case appears to transcend
financial reward, as it cuts to the core of the N.C.A.A.'s amateurism ideals."[11]
Sports commentator Frank Deford took it a step further and declared that
the case "may conceivably lead to the end of amateurism in big-time college
football and basketball."[12]

That would be a desirable outcome, in my view, because the NCAA's
version of amateurism is exploitative, hypocritical, and ethically dubious.
However, it seems unlikely that the case will be as revolutionary as Deford
imagines (and hopes). First, the suit may turn on very specific legal grounds
and its implications may be narrow. In addition, despite its inconsistencies,
the NCAA's version of amateurism is deeply entrenched and has weathered
many assaults.[13] Further, the *O'Bannon* lawsuit did not originally argue that
current student-athletes should be compensated for the use of their likenesses; rather, it contends that "the NCAA has unreasonably and illegally
restrained trade in order to commercially exploit *former* student-athletes
previously subject to its control, with such exploitation affecting those individuals well into their post-collegiate competition lives" (emphasis added).[14]
"When you're in school you're obligated to live up to your scholarship,"
O'Bannon makes clear. "But once you're done, you physically, as well as your
likeness, should leave the university and the NCAA."[15] Later, however, after

obtaining more evidence during the pretrial discovery stage, the plaintiffs amended the suit and "now seek to change the way current athletes are compensated for the use of their images."[16]

This chapter examines the *In re NCAA Student-Athlete Name & Likeness Licensing Litigation* lawsuit: its history, some of the contexts in which it is best understood, and some of the issues at stake. I am not qualified to provide a purely legal commentary on the *O'Bannon* matter. Many of those have been published in law review journals and many more will be once the lawsuit is resolved, which will take several years; the case is scheduled for trial in 2014. Likewise, since it is unwise to predict a case's significance before it is adjudicated, I do not propose to do that, either. Instead, this chapter will use the *O'Bannon* lawsuit as an opportunity to reflect on some of the ways in which thousands of student-athletes who play revenue-generating sports (that is, Division I basketball and football players) have been exploited by a disingenuous intercollegiate athletic system that is rife with hypocrisy.[17]

II.

Before turning to the lawsuit itself—its chronology, arguments, evidence, precedents, and contexts—it is worthwhile to consider who is most responsible for it. According to Dan Fitzgerald, an attorney and sports law blogger:

> After his professional basketball career ended, O'Bannon grew frustrated that various entities continued to profit from his and his teammates' collegiate success at UCLA while they received nothing. O'Bannon was connected with Sonny Vaccaro, who is credited with introducing commercialism to college basketball through his marketing efforts on behalf of sneaker companies. Vaccaro, now an outspoken advocate for the rights of student-athletes, connected O'Bannon with an international law firm experienced in dealing with high-profile class action suits. A lawsuit ensued.[18]

This assessment of the events leading up to the lawsuit is a good start and needs to be developed further.

To begin, O'Bannon's level of frustration at having his likeness used without his permission and without being compensated for it is difficult to gauge. On more than one occasion, O'Bannon has shared a revealing, useful anecdote about seeing his likeness in an EA Sports video game. In a March 2011 episode of *Frontline*, entitled "Money and March Madness," correspondent Lowell Bergman interviewed the former UCLA star:

> Bergman: [*voice-over*] O'Bannon first discovered that he was included in this video game when he was visiting a friend.

     O'Bannon: He asked me if I had ever seen this game and that I was in it.

     Bergman: Was it the UCLA team?

     O'Bannon: UCLA team, yeah. Immediately, seeing yourself on the video game—I'm thinking to myself, "Wow, they got me on a video game." And while this kid was playing, he almost whispers it in my ear. It was like, "You know, the crazy thing about this is you didn't get paid." They didn't ask me for my image. They didn't ask me, you know, for my left hand, for my sweet jump shot.

     Bergman: And you don't get a piece of the action, basically.

     O'Bannon: [None] whatsoever. No.[19]

If he is frustrated or upset, and we can assume he is, O'Bannon is also reasonable and principled. "Things need to change in how the NCAA does business," O'Bannon explains. "And what better time than now? What better person than me?"[20]

Second, O'Bannon's connection to Sonny Vaccaro, the successful former basketball "shoe-company guru" who "invented the practice of paying college basketball coaches to outfit their players in his company's gear," is stronger and longer than Fitzgerald suggests.[21] It extends back to when O'Bannon was a teenager and "attended Vaccaro's Nike basketball camp."[22] Like many current and former athletes, O'Bannon respects and trusts Vaccaro. To some observers, journalist Sam Laird writes, Vaccaro is seen "as an advocate for young athletes, many of them poor and black, in search of a better life through sports." Others consider "him as the personification of a system that uses young basketball players to generate millions of dollars for the shoe companies and the N.C.A.A. but subordinates education to dreams of endorsement deals and N.B.A. careers."[23] Both perspectives have merit.

Nonetheless, Vaccaro is an outspoken and persistent critic of the NCAA and the intercollegiate athletic system he helped create. In fact, one could argue that *In re NCAA Student-Athlete Name & Likeness Licensing Litigation* is largely a Vaccaro initiative. He was the one who brought this matter to the attention of civil litigator Michael D. Hausfeld, whose firm, Hausfeld, LLP, "has recovered billions in worldwide class action suits ranging from reparations from price fixing cartels to benefactors of slave labor."[24] In addition, Vaccaro worked with Hausfeld to find "the perfect lead plaintiff," that is, O'Bannon, who says he was "honored" to serve in that capacity.[25] Staying involved, Vaccaro is an unpaid consultant for the plaintiffs in *In re NCAA Student-Athlete Name & Likeness Licensing Litigation*.

One might ask, what is Vaccaro's interest in this issue? What motivates him? In *Varsity Green: A Behind the Scenes Look at Culture and Corruption in*

College Athletics (2010), business reporter Mark Yost notes that Vaccaro experienced an acute guilty conscience. Yost writes that Vaccaro "was ashamed of himself. He was ashamed of the business he'd created. He was ashamed of how he and the schools and the sneaker companies had made money off these kids all these years."[26] And he wanted to do something about it. With his usual enthusiasm and penchant for self-promotion, Vaccaro says that initiating and participating in the *O'Bannon* case is "the greatest thing I've ever done. This might be the first time I didn't do it for myself or a company I work for. I don't hate the NCAA. I can't overthrow the NCAA. All I've ever asked for is fairness for the kids. Just do the right thing."[27] Precisely what "the right thing" is is debatable.

Of course, it is Michael Hausfeld, his former co-lead counsel, Jon T. King, and their many associated attorneys (including lawyers from Boies, Schiller & Flexner, LLP, and several other antitrust law firms) who have done the complex legal work necessary to prosecute the lawsuit.[28] When the original class-action complaint was filed in July 2009, Hausfeld explained: "No one has a right to own or control another persons' image or likeness for eternity without providing fair compensation. Former student athletes should have a voice in how their own images or likenesses—once they are no longer students—are used throughout their lifetime."[29]

The defendants, who are represented by Miller, Canfield, Paddock and Stone PLC, among others, assert that individuals who consent to participate in NCAA-sponsored competition, via completing and signing Form 08-3a, an eligibility and release form that all NCAA athletes must sign, have effectively relinquished "the right of publicity of their names and images in perpetuity."[30] More specifically, Form 08-3a reads: "You authorize the NCAA [or a third party acting on behalf of the NCAA (e.g., host institution, conference, local organizing committee)] to use your name or picture in accordance with Bylaw 12.5, including to promote NCAA championships or other NCAA events, activities or programs."[31] It is worth pointing out that the form does not use the phrase "in perpetuity." The previously mentioned bylaw 12.5, which is in the NCAA's over 400-page manual, is almost five pages long, with numerous subsections and exceptions. Interestingly, bylaw 12.5.1.1.1, "Promotions Involving NCAA Championships, Events, Activities or Programs," which was adopted in 2003, states: "The NCAA [or a third party acting on behalf of the NCAA (e.g., host institution, conference, local organizing committee)] may use the name or picture of an *enrolled student-athlete* to generally promote NCAA championships or other NCAA events, activities or programs" (emphasis added).[32] It makes no mention of *former* student-athletes, like O'Bannon and those in his class.

Form 08-3a is an important component of *In re NCAA Student-Athlete Name & Likeness Licensing Litigation*. The plaintiffs contend, "Form 08-3a is purposefully misleading, incomplete and ambiguous on its face, and student-athletes, including minors, must sign it under duress and without informed consent."[33] The complaint further asserts:

> Form 08-3a is evidence of the NCAA's repeated attempts to obfuscate issues about sales of merchandise by referring to the vague and ambiguous concept of "promot[ion] of NCAA championships or other NCAA events, activities or programs of college athletics." The ambiguous word "support" also appears in the "Institutional, Charitable, Education or Nonprofit Promotions Release" mandated by Article 12.5.1.1 of the Bylaws. No reasonable person, upon reading Form 08-3a, and the "Institutional, Charitable, Education or Nonprofit Promotions Release" described below, would interpret phrases such as "support educational activities," or "generally promote NCAA championships or other NCAA events, activities or programs" to specifically grant a license in perpetuity for former players' images to be used for profit, over many years, in DVDs, on-demand video, video games, photographs for sale, "stock footage" sold to corporate advertisers, "classic games" for re-broadcast on television, jersey and apparel sales, and other items.[34]

Many legal scholars and other observers agree with the plaintiffs on this point, but we will learn what other "reasonable" people think about this argument if and when the case is tried. For its part, the NCAA, according to its general counsel Donald Remy, says it "doesn't restrict athletes from profiting from their college accomplishments through post-college commercial endorsements and other ventures."[35]

When it was part of the suit, EA Sports defended itself by asserting that "the constitutional right to free speech under the First Amendment means it doesn't need permission to use the players' likenesses because the videos have enough creative elements that, as a whole, they are more than a depiction of any one athlete."[36] The video game company correctly noted that there is unresolved tension between the right of publicity and the First Amendment right to free speech and expression. At the same time, attorney Scott R. Chandler explains "that the First Amendment does not automatically trump the right of publicity in the video game context."[37] The *O'Bannon* case exemplifies this point, for the court ruled that EA's "depiction of collegiate athletes in its video games not only did not satisfy the transformative use test [which is derived from copyright law's fair use doctrine and requires that a work contain 'significant transformative elements' in order to trump the right of publicity] but also that the use of the athletes' identities and likenesses was not of public interest and should not be granted First Amendment protection in this context."[38] The court has a point; it is difficult to see how a video game is in the public interest, other than the pleasure it gives gamers and the tax revenue it generates.

In December 2009, the O'Bannon complaint survived several motions to dismiss.[39] A month later, at the court's request, *O'Bannon* was consolidated with a previously filed class-action lawsuit, *Keller v. EA, NCAA, and CLC,* in which former Arizona State University and University of Nebraska quarterback Sam Keller alleged that the defendants deprived him and his class members of their publicity rights.[40] Those are rights that prevent the commercial use of someone's likeness without that person's consent.[41] As a result of the consolidation, the renamed *In re NCAA Student-Athlete Name & Likeness Licensing Litigation* has two distinct claims for relief: antitrust violations and right of publicity demands.

Wasting little time, the defendants again tried to have the case dismissed in February 2010. Once again, US District Court judge Claudia Wilken denied the request, although she did dismiss the "common law accounting claims against the NCAA and Collegiate Licensing."[42] Both sides claimed victory. Jon King of Hausfeld argued that the denial of the motion to dismiss was significant because it "opens the door to the discovery process, and we soon can begin collecting evidence from the NCAA, taking depositions, and uncovering everything that it wanted to hide and keep from the public's and athletes' view."[43] Meanwhile, NCAA spokesperson Erik Christianson declared unconvincingly, "We're pleased that the court recognized defects in some of the claims made by plaintiffs and dismissed those. The court's other rulings at this preliminary stage of the cases do not diminish the NCAA's confidence that we will ultimately prevail on all of the claims."[44]

The resubmitted consolidated and amended complaint, dated March 10, 2010, is a long, interesting, and in many ways persuasive document. These are some of its arguments and evidence. In the introduction to the antitrust claims section, the plaintiffs allege: "The NCAA's conduct is blatantly anticompetitive and exclusionary, as it wipes out in total the future ownership interests of former student-athletes in their own images—rights that all other members of society enjoy—even long after student-athletes have ceased attending a university."[45] On the face of it, the NCAA's actions seem remarkably unfair. Yet one thing the court will have to decide (if the case is tried) is whether this alleged "anticompetitive and exclusionary" activity is an *unreasonable* "restraint of trade," as per Section 1 of the Sherman Antitrust Act.[46]

Thereafter, the amended complaint lists all the antitrust plaintiffs individually, cataloging their athletic accomplishments, and the ways in which the defendants profit from the "sale of his image, likeness and/or name." Later, it does the same for the right of publicity plaintiffs. Of the NCAA, the complaint contends that, despite its lofty ideals and rhetoric, the association's "true interest is in maximizing revenue for itself and its members, often at the expense of its student-athletes. While extolling the virtues of 'amateurism' for student-athletes, the NCAA itself runs a highly professionalized and commercialized licensing operation that generates hundreds of millions in royalties, broadcast rights and other licensing fees each year."[47] It is undeniably true that the NCAA generates a great deal of money due to the labor/play of athletes, who compete for its member institutions, all of which have made significant investments in maximizing athletic performance. In 2010–11, the NCAA reported that its "revenue was $845.9 million, most of which came from the [television] rights agreement with Turner/CBS Sports" to broadcast the annual Division I men's basketball tournament.[48]

The document also describes and critiques the previously mentioned Form 08-3a, which it claims "is an adhesion contract due to the unequal bargaining power of the parties and the take it or leave it nature of the contract."[49] Later, the plaintiffs assert that the form does not in fact "convey, transfer, or grant any rights of the student-athlete to the NCAA, its member institutions, or its licensees" and that "the NCAA has created an anti-competitive and unconscionable perpetual release relating to image rights."[50] It also reasserts that the NCAA's form constitutes "an unconscionable contract and is the product of anticompetitive conduct and agreement."[51] Because "there are no acceptable substitutes for major college football or major college basketball," the lawsuit contends, athletes in those sports have no real recourse but to accept the NCAA's rules, which are nonnegotiable.[52]

The plaintiffs go to great lengths to demonstrate that EA Sports attempts to create images of college athletes as realistically as possible, and that it does so with great success, visually and financially. After presenting numerous examples, the complaint alleges: "Defendants deliberately and systematically misappropriate players' likenesses to increase revenues and royalties at the expense of student-athletes."[53] Again, the revenues are substantial. In 2011, EA Sports reported more than $3.5 billion in revenue, none of which was shared with the current or former college athletes depicted in EA's video games.[54] Yet EA pays the National Football League Players' Association (NFLPA) nearly $35 million annually for similar usage of pro players' likenesses and names in its video games.[55] (In perhaps a bit of foreshadowing, more than 2,000 *former* NFL players won a class-action lawsuit against the NFLPA and its licensing subsidiary for excluding them from licensing agreements with EA for its Madden NFL video games. The retired NFL players' case was tried in the US District Court, Northern District of California; they won their suit and were awarded $28.1 million.)[56]

One of the most noteworthy features of the complaint is the "Description of Revenue Streams Relating to the Commercial Exploitation of Images of Former Student-Athletes" section.[57] The NCAA, a not-for-profit organization, and the CLC make money by selling media rights for televising games, from DVD and On-Demand sales and rentals, video clip sales to corporate advertisers and others, by providing website content, and licensing photos, action figures, trading cards, posters, video games, rebroadcasts of "classic" games, jerseys, T-shirts, and other apparel (e.g., some schools sell "game worn" uniforms).[58] A conservative estimate of the annual revenue generated from these sources is in the hundreds of millions.[59] This is not in dispute. What is contested is whether the NCAA, the CLC, and EA Sports have ever legitimately received the "class members' consent, written or otherwise, to use their likenesses, images, names, or other distinctive appearances."[60] The plaintiffs obviously think not, and as result argue that the class members are entitled to damages.[61]

EA Sports, undeterred by the court's refusal to dismiss it from the lawsuit in February 2010, tried again. In May 2011, Judge Wilken assented to the request and dismissed the antitrust claims against the video game company, although it still faced the publicity rights claims.[62] It was a short-lived victory, however. For in late July, Wilken reinstated the antitrust claims against EA Sports, as a result of "'significant' new allegations that EA agreed to not [sic] offer payment to athletes once they left their college sports careers, in addition to [the] NCAA's rule prohibiting compensation of current student athletes."[63] Wilken added that the new allegations and evidence proffered by the plaintiffs "suggests that EA was actively participating to ensure that former student-athletes would not receive any compensation for the use of their images, likenesses and names."[64]

Slowly but surely, the case appears to be moving to trial, as it seems unlikely that O'Bannon and his fellow plaintiffs (whose ranks now include basketball Hall-of-Famers Oscar Robertson and Bill Russell) will settle this matter out of court. Not only is there a great deal of money at stake, but many of the former athletes are fighting for a principle in which they believe.

III.

In re NCAA Student-Athlete Name & Likeness Licensing Litigation is best understood in several contexts. This litigation is far from an isolated event. Lawyer and legal scholar Christian Dennie notes that the NCAA "has been involved in a plethora of lawsuits relating to nearly every conceivable area of the law, including antitrust, United States constitutional challenges, state constitutional challenges, tortious interference with a contract, and complaints that NCAA bylaws are applied arbitrarily and capriciously."[65]

More specifically, *In re NCAA Student-Athlete Name & Likeness Licensing Litigation* is not the first time that the NCAA has faced a serious antitrust challenge. In the early 1980s, the University of Oklahoma and the University of Georgia teamed up to challenge the NCAA's limit on the number of football games that could be televised, claiming that the association's TV monopoly violated the Sherman Antitrust Act. A federal district court agreed; the NCAA appealed the ruling. "When the case finally reached the U.S. Supreme Court in 1984, a 7–2 decision resulted, the first time the Supreme Court had ruled amateur sport to be in violation of antitrust laws," writes historian Ronald A. Smith. "The justices ruled that the NCAA TV plan was a purely commercial venture in which the universities participated solely for the pursuit of profits."[66] In the 1990s, the NCAA tried to restrict assistant basketball coach salaries. A class-action suit against the NCAA resulted, and, "after five years of often tortuous legal wrangling," the courts found that the NCAA's policy had an anticompetitive effect and was in violation of antitrust law.[67] After mediation, the "1,900 assistant college coaches whose salaries were found to have been illegally restricted" received a $55.4 million settlement.[68] And there have been other matters, including the National Invitation Tournament antitrust case against the NCAA's Division I men's basketball tournament, and a suit concerning the NCAA's prohibition against "the use of lawyers by players to discuss professional contracts."[69]

Obviously the NCAA has a history of imposing anticompetitive policies that challenge or violate antitrust law.[70] Why? This can be partly explained in a word: control. Beyond trying to manage its 400,000 athletes and more than 1,000 member institutions, the NCAA controls a vast, profitable commercial endeavor, despite its 501(c)(3) status.[71] It does so with great difficulty: logically, legally, and ethically.

Some of these difficulties can be traced to the NCAA's Division I Manual, which includes the organization's constitution and bylaws. The fundamental problem is the unresolved (and probably unresolvable) tension between the organization's stated ideals and the way it conducts business. According to the NCAA, its "basic purpose" is "to maintain intercollegiate athletics as an integral part of the educational program and the athlete as an integral part of the student body and, by so doing, retain a clear line of demarcation between intercollegiate athletics and professional sports."[72] Yet when it comes to big-time college sports, that "clear line of demarcation" is tissue thin, if it exists at all. Everything about, say, Southeastern Conference or Big

Ten basketball and football is professionalized, from the coaches' and staff members' salaries, to the facilities in which the players practice and play, to the time, energy, and expertise devoted to the endeavor to the media's coverage of it.[73] Although many observers have noted that the only people in intercollegiate athletics who do not make money are the athletes, in reality they *are* compensated to play their sports, in the form of "grants-in-aid," otherwise known as athletic scholarships.[74] A full ride, however, is not a free ride (nor is it always "full," as some athletic scholarships do not cover all the costs of a college education). Nor do all athletes receive any scholarship money let alone a full scholarship.[75] Most athletes who compete in Division I sports work long hours and extremely hard (in and out of season), so much so, argue law professors Robert A. McCormick and Amy Christian McCormick, that their "daily burdens and obligations not only meet the legal standard of [an] employee, but far exceed the burdens and obligations of most university employees."[76] This situation contributes to a significant disconnect between rhetoric and reality that makes it challenging to take the NCAA's "basic purpose" seriously.

The hypocrisy begins with the NCAA's assertion that its athletes "shall be amateurs" (that is, unpaid) and "their participation [in athletics] should be motivated primarily by education and by the physical, mental and social benefits to be derived. Student participation in intercollegiate athletics is an avocation, and *student-athletes should be protected from exploitation by professional and commercial enterprises*" (emphasis added).[77] Clearly most Division I coaches demand time, physical, and emotional commitments of their athletes that are well beyond what can be considered avocational. (The same is true of some Division II and III programs.) Worse, the very organization that is supposed to be protecting athletes "from exploitation by professional and commercial enterprises" is, as the plaintiffs *In re NCAA Student-Athlete Name & Likeness Licensing Litigation* argue, perpetrating that exploitation. Some NCAA administrators are aware of the problems of "crass commercialism," to borrow a phrase from Wallace Renfro's 2009 "State of the Association" speech. Renfro was the NCAA's vice president at the time and declared: "Generation of much needed revenue does not justify the exploitation of student-athletes. We can—and we should—debate the nature of proper commercial conduct. However, one principle is not subject to debate: commercial exploitation of student-athletes is not permissible. Period."[78] It is reasonable to assume that this exhortation should also apply to *former* student-athletes, like O'Bannon and his class members.

In re NCAA Student-Athlete Name & Likeness Licensing Litigation also needs to be understood in legal contexts. Fortunately, many legal scholars have written about it. Predictably, no consensus emerges from the scholarship on the *O'Bannon* matter. Yet for different reasons, most legal scholars and lawyers who have studied *In re NCAA Student-Athlete Name & Likeness Licensing Litigation* at some point indicate that the plaintiffs have made strong arguments and that the status quo is troubling—financially, legally, and ethically—and needs to be reformed. Not everyone agrees, however. Writing in the *Journal of Intellectual Property Law*, Mary Catherine Moore argues that "college athletes should not be compensated for the use of their likenesses in video games because video games are expressive works protected by the right to free speech, because college athletes have contractually agreed to give up their right of publicity to play NCAA sports, and because any potential compensation structure would be too costly and convoluted to implement effectively."[79] These are all debatable points. The latter, though, seems especially unsatisfactory. Yes, equitably compensating former athletes for the use of their likenesses is complicated and would be expensive, but those are not compelling reasons to continue an exploitative and perhaps illegal practice. Conversely, Julia Brighton contends that the "NCAA has unfairly profited at the expense of college athletes, and the court should fashion relief for the class of plaintiffs to address the unjust enrichment. The NCAA should remedy the situation by creating a system of trusts into which profit-sharing payments could be deposited for college athletes while they are still subject to the rules of amateurism."[80] The court may compel the NCAA to do just that, which strikes me as reasonable.

Many of the law review notes, comments, and articles about this case stress that it is unfair for the NCAA to profit at its athletes' expense when the athletes themselves, while in school, are not allowed to do so. It is possible, write Kristal S. Stippich and Kadence A. Otto in the *Journal of Legal Aspects of Sport*, that the court "could conclude that if the system of amateurism is indeed essential to intercollegiate athletics, then the schools and the NCAA, not just the student-athletes, should be required to abide by amateurism principles."[81] For those who value consistency, such a ruling would be satisfying.

Several scholars have concluded that the plaintiffs are correct. Attorney Andrew B. Carrabis, for example, asserts:

> The NCAA and its exclusive license agreements should not be permitted to use a student athlete's identity, image, or likeness without the student athlete's consent when the likeness is used for commercial gain in the marketplace. Federal courts should apply a rule of reason analysis to alleged Sherman Act violations by the NCAA particularly as it relates to the exclusive licensing agreement with EA Sports. The NCAA bylaws are inequitable

to student athletes by unfairly allowing the NCAA and private companies such as EA Sports to exploit student athletes for monetary gain. It is time the NCAA realizes this and creates trust funds for future collegiate athletes once they leave the cell-like parameters of the NCAA's constitution.[82]

In "Involuntary Servants: The NCAA's Abridgement of Student-Athletes' Economic Rights in Perpetuity Violates the Thirteenth Amendment," John K. Tokarz makes a more aggressive argument. Critical of "the NCAA's romanticized amateurism ideal and its outward promises of student-athlete protection," Tokarz declares:

> the NCAA has created a multi-billion dollar industry on the backs of essentially unpaid workers. Worse yet, the NCAA has broken its promise that academic pursuit would not be compromised in the pursuit of success on the playing field. The trade-off between amateurism and commercialism—that student-athletes would remain unpaid because they were in school primarily for academic pursuit—was palatable when the pursuit of academic excellence was not just a front and the dollars at stake were still "amateur." However, the system has devolved into a commercial free-for-all marked by athletic departments that cash checks from professional marketing agencies while the university leaders turn their heads as student-athletes are exploited.[83]

Tokarz takes his argument further: "Unforgivingly," he writes, "the NCAA has extended this exploitive relationship in perpetuity by forcing student-athletes to sign away their image rights for their entire lives." One could argue that the "NCAA's rules preventing a student-athlete from earning money from the use of his image make sense while he is still enrolled in college," but not after he is no longer a student-athlete. "This draconian restriction begins to resemble 'the inseparable incidents of the institution' of slavery, such as 'compulsory service of the slave for the benefit of the master' and, thus, constitutes a violation of the Thirteenth Amendment."[84] Since the plaintiffs have not evoked the Thirteenth Amendment, it is unlikely that the court will consider it in its deliberations. Obviously Tokarz is one of many people troubled by the NCAA, which he describes as "a hypocritical institution that has largely lived above the law by touting an agenda that is clearly at odds with reality," and thinks that "drastic change" is necessary.[85]

Many people see that change coming, thanks partly to O'Bannon and his class members. "The NCAA is at a crossroads," observes Jeffrey J. R. Sundram in the *Tulane Law Review.*

> As the organization becomes more and more commercialized, the likelihood that its actions will face antitrust scrutiny continues to increase.

> The current lawsuit brought by O'Bannon represents the potential end of judicial acceptance of amateurism as a pro-competitive benefit. O'Bannon has already taken a giant first step in surviving a motion to dismiss and gaining access to NCAA financials through discovery. The availability of that information increases the possibility that, if not O'Bannon, the right plaintiff could come along and financially destroy the NCAA. The question is whether the NCAA will resist the allure of commercialism and make the changes necessary to preserve amateurism and keep its protection.[86]

Historically, the NCAA has not demonstrated that it can "resist the allure of commercialism" or effectively reform intercollegiate athletics.[87]

In re NCAA Student-Athlete Name & Likeness Licensing Litigation is also embedded in larger cultural and historical contexts. From one perspective, the NCAA's policies and practices regarding the marketing and selling of its athletes' likenesses are unexceptional and unsurprising. Like most corporations and many not-for-profit organizations, the NCAA's leadership and members apparently feel pressure to grow, to generate new revenue streams, to maximize their resources and (tax-exempt) profits. This is basically standard operating procedure in the United States. After all, this is widely acknowledged to be a country and historical moment in which just about everything, seemingly, is commercialized, privatized, and/or monetized, from health care to education to garbage collection and recycling. According to sociologist John Brueggemann, "The logic of the market—that everything is for sale and we should strive to get as much as we can—has pushed beyond the economic sphere into other parts of our lives."[88] This is much to our detriment, he argues, in terms of the quality of our interpersonal relationships, moral lives, and civil society.

Higher education, of course, has not been impervious to this phenomenon, as Derek Bok makes clear in *Universities in the Marketplace: The Commercialization of Higher Education* (2003). The former president of Harvard University, Bok acknowledges that commercialization has multiple causes, yet worries that it "may be changing the nature of academic institutions in ways we will come to regret. By trying so hard to acquire more money for their work, universities may compromise values that are essential to the continued confidence and loyalty of faculty, alumni, and even the general public."[89] One might say the same of the NCAA and its member institutions. Yet because Bok is historically minded, he recognizes that intercollegiate athletics, "as practiced by most major universities, are the oldest form of commercialization in American higher education."[90] It is not a compliment.

Indeed, intercollegiate sport has been commercialized from the beginning. "From the first contest," an 1852 rowing contest between Harvard and

Yale university men on Lake Winnipesaukee in New Hampshire, sponsored by a train company, explained Ronald A. Smith, "intercollegiate sport has been a commercial enterprise, and professionalism followed closely on its heels."[91] More than 150 years later, the scale of that commercialization has changed exponentially, to the point that big-time intercollegiate athletics "leads a schizophrenic existence, encompassing both amateur and professional elements," economist Andrew Zimbalist observed. "The courts, IRS, and sometimes the universities themselves cannot seem to decide whether to treat intercollegiate athletics as part of the educational process or as a business. The NCAA claims that it manages college sports in a way that promotes both the goals of higher education and the financial condition of the university. Critics say it does neither."[92] The Pulitzer Prize–winning writer Taylor Branch is one of those critics. He is direct and correct: "Big-time college sports are fully commercialized. Billions of dollars flow through them each year. The NCAA makes money, and enables universities and corporations to make money, from the unpaid labor of young athletes."[93] It clearly profits from the likenesses of its former athletes, too.

The point to be stressed here is that, broadly speaking, the business practices being contested in *In re NCAA Student-Athlete Name & Likeness Licensing Litigation* are part of a long tradition of commercialization, exploitation, and hypocrisy. Yet the plaintiffs' assertion of their rights and demand for their fair share of the NCAA's profits are relatively new. But they have precedents, which several of the chapters in this book illustrate. Influenced by the civil rights movement and an empowering spirit of change in the 1960s and early 1970s, athletes such as prizefighter Muhammad Ali, basketball player Spencer Haywood, and baseball player Curt Flood also took their grievances to court, with mixed results. A few observers have called O'Bannon the "Curt Flood of college sports."[94] The analogy is not precise and the historical conditions are much different. Yet like *Flood v. Kuhn* (1972), which Flood lost but nevertheless helped introduce free agency to professional sports, the O'Bannon case has the potential to be a dramatic game changer: for the NCAA, its member schools, thousands of current and former athletes, as well as how we think about amateurism in the United States. It could and should force us to rethink entrenched (i.e., largely antiquated and bankrupt) notions of "student-athletes" and the proper role of intercollegiate athletics in higher education and American culture.

IV.

By the time this book is published, the O'Bannon lawsuit may be resolved; or not, as it is the kind of case that could go on for many years. There is, after all, a great deal at stake. Not just money, although there is a lot of that, but fundamental principles and values, such as respect, fairness, honesty, and responsibility, things that the NCAA claims to promote.[95] "College sports has become a multi-billion dollar business due to thousands of former student-athletes like myself," Ed O'Bannon explains. "I'm participating in this case to stand up on behalf of all former players who have been treated unfairly. It is not about personal gain for me, but a matter of basic fairness."[96] Even a cynic can admire that sentiment.

It will be interesting to see what happens. "If there is any case that should be won it's O'Bannon," says business professor Allen Sack, the author of *Counterfeit Amateurs: An Athlete's Journey Through the Sixties to the Age of Academic Capitalism* (2008). "This one I truly believe that the athletes should win on the basis of the law, but there are never guarantees in these cases."[97] Sack is right, certainly about there being no guarantees. Court cases, like athletic contests, are open-ended rather than scripted events. Anything can happen.

What is certain, though, is the NCAA's commitment to its version of amateurism (no matter how irrational and hypocritical) and its financial interests, neither of which should be underestimated. One of our finest sports critics, Frank Deford, sees the matter clearly: "The NCAA is influenced by all the money at stake. It mouths crazy, old-fashioned moral pretense, keeping its players as serfs, yet is primarily just looking after the economic welfare of its so-called educational constituents."[98] To their credit, the NCAA and some of its members have tried for generations to reform intercollegiate athletics, to promote equality of conditions and to stamp out corruption in its many forms. In general, they have not been successful.[99]

There are many reasons for this, but chief among them is that the NCAA has long tried to hold together competing, essentially incompatible ideas: most notably, that athletes in revenue-producing sports should play for all manner of reasons (to build character, to honor one's school and community, for the love of the game), *except* for financial gain, while everyone else involved in the endeavor profits handsomely. After all these years, this situation is hard for many to accept. "Human nature," Deford suggests, "tells us that it is impossible to expect that the performers wouldn't also want to share in some of the bounty."[100] At the very least, Ed O'Bannon and his fellow plaintiffs do. Yet they also want much more than that. O'Bannon and many of his class members want to be respected and they want a more equitable dispersal of the NCAA's massive revenues; in a word, they want justice, which rarely comes without a struggle.

Coda

That struggle continues, for the foreseeable future, and probably beyond.

Slowly and dramatically, the *O'Bannon* case is wending its way through the courts. In late August 2012, after collecting more evidence during the pretrial discovery stage, the plaintiffs significantly modified their lawsuit. They claimed that to make it more inclusive, they intended to expand the class action to include *current* Division I football and men's basketball players, not just former athletes.[101] Predictably, the NCAA and its co-defendants (who later decided to settle) responded almost immediately, filing a motion asking the court "to end the class-certification process, in part because they contended the plaintiffs had changed their legal strategy in a way that was unfair."[102] Donald Remy, the NCAA executive vice president and general counsel, added:

> Unable to prove their original claims regarding former student-athletes, plaintiffs have now abandoned those claims and are attempting to assert new claims on behalf of current student-athletes. Unfortunately, this about face runs them smack into a very old argument, and one that the NCAA has defeated in court many times. Plaintiffs now claim that the NCAA's financial aid rules restrain "trade" by preventing schools from "paying" for "labor" of certain current student-athletes by offering to share media royalties with those student-athletes. They want to be cut in on TV revenues, but every court that has examined this type of issue has said that plaintiffs have no right to such a claim. Many courts, including the United States Supreme Court, have repeatedly rejected the notion that the NCAA's financial aid rules violate the Sherman Act by preventing these sorts of commercial transactions between schools and current student-athletes. Plaintiffs want the court to believe that student athletes are the same as professional athletes and unionized employees—which is pure fiction.[103]

Actually, the plaintiffs did not abandon their initial claims; they added to them. Remy is correct, though, that student-athletes are not "the same as professional athletes and unionized employees," who are usually well represented by legal counsel, have collective bargaining agreements, and are often well compensated for their labor.

In January 2013, Judge Claudia Wilken denied the defendants' motion, asserting that they could make their "arguments supporting denial of the motion for class certification on its merits" at the class-certification hearing, which took place on June 20.[104] At that hearing, Judge Wilken informed the plaintiffs that in order for the class to include current Division I football and men's basketball players they needed a current athlete to be part of the injunctive class and that they had until July 19 to find one.[105] At the time, the National College Players Association executive director Ramogi Huma (a former UCLA linebacker) said several current players might join the lawsuit. "The players have a lot of interest in this, a lot at stake in this," Huma asserted. "There's no aura of fear or insurgency. It's all support for what Ed O'Bannon is doing."[106] Huma's claim may have been hyperbolic, but it was not just posturing.

A month later, six current college athletes, at least one from each of the biggest and most significant athletic conferences (the Atlantic Coast Conference, the Big Ten, the Pacific-12, and the Southeastern Conference), joined the plaintiffs.[107] One of them, University of Arizona linebacker Jake Fischer, a Pac-12 All-Academic honoree, explained: "I stepped forward for the future well-being, safety and health of student-athletes. We [a reference to his teammate, placekicker Jake Smith] have both met a ton of people since we've been here who have lingering effects from injuries, not getting a great education, not having all the capabilities or the opportunities that a regular student would have, and honestly, we would just like to try to fix that."[108] Fischer and Smith joined the lawsuit after meeting with their coach, Rich Rodriguez, who understood and backed their position. "They're two conscientious guys," Rodriguez said, "and they're both really appreciative of playing college ball. It's not like they're disenchanted with the system. They love being student-athletes. But with the likeness issue, they wanted to see if they could have a voice for college athletes, and I said I support that."[109] What NCAA administrators and attorneys thought of Rodriguez's statement was not reported.

The day before, by the way, and seemingly not coincidentally, the *Wall Street Journal* noted that the NCAA had announced "that it won't renew its contract with videogame maker EA Sports—the most tangible effect so far of an antitrust lawsuit filed against the association."[110] ESPN's legal analyst Lester Munson called it "a surprise move." According to Munson, "They'll never admit it at NCAA headquarters in Indianapolis, but there is little doubt that the O'Bannon litigation and the possibility of a settlement prompted the EA decision."[111] Nonetheless, despite the NCAA's decision to sever its relationship with the multi-billion-dollar video game company, the lure of all that money did not disappear. Thus two days later *USA Today* reported: "More than 150 colleges, conferences and bowl games have approved a three-year contract extension with EA Sports that will continue production of the company's college football video game despite the ongoing legal controversy surrounding it."[112] The deal allows EA Sports "to use schools' logos, trademarks, stadiums, mascots, and other school-specific indicia in a college football video game that EA produces and sells."[113] So, even without the

NCAA's imprimatur, acronym, and logo, this revenue stream will continue to flow.

Not having a crystal ball, I don't know how this case and story ends. Obviously no one does. That is part of its appeal—that, and the fact that the stakes are so high and that justice may eventually be served. A persistent (and convincing) critic of the NCAA, columnist Joe Nocera argues, "if O'Bannon wins, and players have to be compensated for use of their likeness, it will be the first small step toward giving the players a share, at long last, of the riches their work produces."[114] If that happens, and I suspect that it will, eventually, it will not be a "small step" but a huge leap forward. Nocera understands, however, that the struggle is not over: "Whether through O'Bannon or some other means, the day is coming when the players will be paid. The only question is when."[115] Perhaps.

At this date, May 29, 2014, less than two weeks before the case is set to go to trial, the fight is far from over. The NCAA has a long tradition of winning legal battles, in part because it has amazing resources and stamina.[116] So it is possible that the NCAA will out argue and/or outlast the plaintiffs. Then again, O'Bannon and his lawyers are similarly skillful and committed to seeing this case all the way through. His sense of competition seemingly provoked, O'Bannon told the *New York Times* in June 2013: "You can't just throw some dollars in my face and watch me go away. I want systemic change. That's what we're here for."[117] If that is true, and I am convinced that we should take O'Bannon at his word, this potentially landmark case could go all the way to the US Supreme Court.

CHAPTER ELEVEN

Epilogue

With increased attention given to sport since 1945, it should not be too surprising that sixty years later US Supreme Court nominee John Roberts, when asked by US senators how he might approach his job should he become chief justice, responded with a baseball analogy. "Judges are like umpires," said the nominee. "Umpires don't make the rules; they apply them. The role of an umpire and a judge is critical. They make sure everybody plays by the rules. But it is a limited role. Nobody ever went to a ball game to see the umpire . . . I will remember that it's my job to call balls and strikes and not to pitch or bat."[1] This relationship to sport, of course, was not the first time a person of Roberts's distinction had incorporated America's national pastime as part of an argument. In 1972, for instance, Justice Harry Blackmun, who read the majority position in *Flood vs Kuhn*, delivered what historian Allen Guttman described as an "unpersuasive opinion . . . [with a] lengthy rolecall [*sic*] of the heroes of baseball and his evocation of the glories of the game."[2] Others simply and cynically referred to it as Blackmun's "Ode to Baseball."[3] Indeed, Court observers recognized that, in this case, baseball references in official capacities were quite common. "Nothing in the law of sport matches the frequency of baseball's interaction with the institutions of the law or the tendency of lawmakers who speak of sports to talk in baseball terms," claimed Ross E. Davies, a law professor at George Mason University.[4]

While the two justices' remarks could be written off as simply exaggerated hyperbole, the comments, nonetheless, illustrated the continued marriage between sport, American culture, and the practice of law in everyday life. Sport, as demonstrated in each of the essays in this volume, not only played a vital role in helping to shape our culture in the postwar era, but also did the same in the arena of jurisprudence. And the decisions rendered in many of these cases, and others like them, continue to resonate today. On many counts, challenges to collective bargaining rights, use of imagery, constitutional precedent, and free agency, among other issues, were models for change that impacted the larger world beyond the athletic sphere. As the story of Jackie Robinson's pioneering actions that cracked baseball's color barrier in 1947 is without question the Olympus of athletic accomplishments in the realm of social justice, other individuals, through the courts, also took on injustice and either broke legal ground or set the wheels in motion for changes that raised the level of consciousness on issues that impacted Americans all.

Historian Peter Levine was correct in his description that sport, as seen by some, was an "incubator of American individualism and an example of the opportunity, equality, and mobility that Americans enjoy," while to others it mirrored "the worst tendencies in American society."[5] This could not be truer when it came to the conundrum that connected sport and the law. Muhammud Ali, Spencer Haywood, and Curt Flood, for instance, were all celebrated figures and champions in their respective sport. But, many also despised them. Still, their athletic legacy grew and was cemented as a result of their pursuit of justice through the court system.

To be sure, even had they not pursued litigation, all three were major figures. But, as sports fans discovered, their principles were such that, even at the risk of public and legal retribution, they willingly put their careers on the line in the quest of their rights and social justice. Ali's case set, what some consider, a new precedent for the Supreme Court in determining conscientious objector cases. Dating back to 1917 and the implementation of the Selective Service Act, the High Court struggled with identifying clear legal parameters on how one might be classified as a "conscientious objector." In the passing years, such cases were effectively a "work in progress." But the attention given to Ali's case was something of an anomaly that the 1971 Court's predecessors had not experienced. Ali's boxing celebrity, along with his very public persona and convictions, all which came at a time when there then appeared to be little evidence that the Vietnam War was in decline, increased the need for the Burger Court to establish a clear protocol for what constituted a "conscientious objector." And they did so in this case.

Basketball and baseball also held the spotlight in 1971 and 1972, respectively. Spencer Haywood, who for two years was already a professional in the American Basketball Association with the Denver Rockets when he triggered legal action, employed the Sherman Antitrust Act against the National Basketball Association, who, he argued, "restrained" players like himself to sign contracts prior to four years beyond high school. Driven in part by a sense of moral conviction, Haywood successfully forced the NBA to relax its four-year rule and thus open the door for players to sign contracts once they reached the minimum age of adulthood. And Curt Flood, while he lost a seemingly insurmountable antitrust exemption case against the major leagues, nonetheless, lit the fuse that led to the demise of baseball's reserve clause. Flood, of course, was not the first to mount such a challenge to baseball, but he was the first high-profile player to do so. He gave frequent interviews on the matter and attempted to galvanize the players to join in his crusade. And in the backdrop of an era that is best defined by the large-scale push back to social convention, the *Flood* case was no small matter. Ali, Haywood, and Flood, also, were not alone.

Not all of the pioneers were themselves household figures. Danny Gardella, a lesser-known utility major league player in the 1940s was, in reality, the first player to draw blood from baseball's iron-clad reserve clause almost thirty years before the world heard of Curt Flood. In a 1946 class-action lawsuit, Gardella effectively forced Commissioner Happy Chandler to capitulate and lift his penalty that had blackballed Gardella for having played in Jorge Pasquel's "outlaw" Mexican League. Gardella and his lawyer demonstrated the vulnerability of baseball over its antitrust exemption, bringing the future of the exemption into question. The case therefore set the tone for future arguments against the reserve system. If Gardella had not been in severe economic difficulty he might well have carried his suit to conclusion, rather than settle out of court, and could then have ended baseball's antitrust exemption.

As it developed the two subsequent cases relevant to the reserve clause, the *Toolson* case and the *Flood* case, produced victories for MLB and its defense of the reserve system and its antitrust exemption. However, the *Flood* case set the stage for the arbitration ruling by Peter Sietz that struck down the reserve clause and led to a form of free agency. The precise form of free agency was hammered out over the years in the collective bargaining process.

Sports and the law also brought into focus the struggles of Renée Richards, who fought both public stigma over her transformation from being a male to battling in the legal arena for her right to compete as a tennis professional. Unwilling to be banned from competing in the US Open and be mute on the issue of her rights, Richards, on legal grounds, brought down the conventional standards then seen in professional tennis that discriminated on the basis of gender. More important, like many of the lawsuits described in this anthology, the *Richards* case was about freedom, power, and control. Renée Richards wanted the freedom to identify with the gender she believed she really wanted and the freedom to live fully as that gender. Given that sports have long relied on a fundamental dichotomy between men and women, her boundary-crossing was not well received; her mere existence as a tennis player demanded that sport learn to define sex and begin to defend its justification for the rigid separation of most men's and women's athletics. This process continues to this day: in the 2012 London Olympics, Caster Semenya won a silver medal in the 800-meter race after sitting out almost eleven months while undergoing gender testing. Her success at the

Olympics, however, brought the issue of what defines gender back into the public discussion and her failure to win gold-triggered allegations that she deliberately tanked the race to avoid additional controversy.[6] Left largely un-discussed in the mainstream media is why men and women compete separately. Eventually the reasons for segregation might help define sex and gender for the purposes of sport. Richards opened a door that will remain open as long as sport divides men from women without science, sport, or society being able to clearly define either.

Powerlifting was the centerpiece of *Frantz v. United States Powerlifting*, which also addressed antitrust issues but in a different context. Rather than free agency, what was at stake in this case was the degree of control athletic federations can exert over its member athletes, and how much power an international federation can exercise on national organizations and/or its members. Complicating the case were conflicting views on drug use within the lifting community.

More than anything the course and outcome of this case illustrated the dangers of unintended consequences that can flow from a legal dispute. The proliferation of organizations of lifters and the inability of any one group to control the sport resulted in a lack of clear and uniform rules and regulations. This made it unlikely that powerlifting would gain the necessary international approval that could lead to participation of any of the sanctioning bodies in international competition including the Olympic Games. Indeed, the court decision led to something resembling anarchy.

The powerlifters who sued to be allowed to compete in multiple federations unwittingly contributed to the decline of the powerlifting their federations in the public eye. But eventually, these same powerlifters successfully seized control for themselves. If the lifter did not like the rules of one federation, he or she could compete in a different federation. While the multitude of federations may have hindered the growth of the sport, ironically, these various organizations arguably empowered the individual athletes in the short term.

Injustice was a theme consistent in most, if not all, of the aforementioned cases, and the quest to eradicate it also was seen in the transnational arena where reformers exposed the practices of major league operatives who exploited Latino youths in the Caribbean. Looking to sidestep the recommendations even from its own watchdog commission, which produced "The Alderson Report," Major League Baseball, international lawyers contended, had ignored or abandoned "rule of law" protocols in its effort to tap into the wealth of talent found in that region, irrespective of the consequences to its under-aged prospects. The exploitation of athletes was also not exclusively one that took place in the Caribbean.

Similarly, MLB does the same thing with young Latin baseball players. Using the American Dream image of achieving wealth and success playing a game that they love, MLB teams have been able to use and discard young players without much limitation on their behavior and then to sign the best to contracts and signing bonuses below market value. Although the Alderson Report offered suggestions for reform, MLB has not adopted all of those suggestions and one component of the agreements is still capping signing bonuses for Latin players. Given that the number of MLB players from Latin America has consistently increased over the last twenty years and shows no signs of abating, the capped signing bonus saves MLB money and limits the opportunities of the Latin players. MLB hopes to avoid an international draft, and ordinarily drafts restrict player freedom, but one wonders if an international draft in these circumstances, without a clear rule of law, might actually benefit the players.

Ed O'Bannon believed that justice had eluded him and other college athletes as well. A former star basketball player for the UCLA Bruins who, in 1995, helped lead them to a national title, he bristled at NCAA position that upon graduation athletes had no say in the use of their own images while universities effectively bilked them for millions of dollars. To O'Bannon, the NCAA platitudes from which it painted itself as an institution, which promoted players who competed for "the love of sport," was a smokescreen for what was, in fact, the exploitation of athletes. Taking action in the form of a 2009 lawsuit, O'Bannon opened up a Pandora's box that the NCAA had for so long sought to avoid: the clouded line between amateurism and commercialization. To the former player, it was matter of "basic fairness."

Similarly the *O'Bannon* case is also about control and power. The athletes who want a piece of the profits from their images simply want the right to control and profit from that image. The National Collegiate Athletic Association policy of having amateur college athletes renounce the rights to their image, apparently in perpetuity in the context of college sport, gives all power to the NCAA and its member institutions and nothing to the athlete as an individual. College athletes are given a large stack of forms at the beginning of their career, which usually starts when they are as young as eighteen years of age, and told by authoritative adults to sign them. While theoretically the athletes know that they do not have to sign away their rights, as a practical matter, they often believe that if they fail to sign everything, they will not be allowed to play the sport they love and may lose any scholarship or benefits that they have from being an athlete. The NCAA and their member schools, *O'Bannon* has made clear, take advantage of the youth and inexperience of these athletes and have since discovered an additional way to profit from their lack of freedom, power, and control. This case seeks to wrest some of that power from the NCAA.

To be sure, as amplified in the essays in *Sport and Law: Historical and Cultural Intersections* the legal relationship with sport and culture was, and continues to be, a vital component found in the "new social history" method of examining American culture from "the bottom up." With such fodder as the Cold War, advancements in communicative technologies, civil rights, gender, human rights, and transnationalism, that served as a backdrop for action, individuals and groups from an array of ethnicities, classes, and cultures actively sought to either change or protect their constitutional rights. And sport figures and their institutions, who opted to use the law books in lieu of athletic equipment, were vital players in the construction of a newer American profile and the continuing quest for social justice and a level playing field.

Thoughts Regarding
Scholarly Methods

Sport and law have been inexorably intertwined in the United States for more than a century, and arguably they are two of the most powerful and dominant institutions in American society. The structures of the law and sport are similar. In each case, separate bodies that do not directly participate in either the practice or enforcement create the rules. Both sport and law have arbitrators who enforce those rules. As well, they profess great concern about fairness and level playing fields, and yet neither achieves complete fairness or level playing fields. Wealth, for example, is an advantage in both fields. Law and sport are credited with building character and building better citizens, and although neither is an American creation, in the United States we like to maintain that we put our unique stamp on both. The two are also pragmatically entangled. Lawyers are involved in sport: after the Black Sox scandal of 1919, Judge Kenesaw Mountain Landis was named the first commissioner of baseball, and in 2013, NBA commissioner David Stern and NHL commissioner Gary Bettman were attorneys. Athletes sometimes follow up their sporting careers with careers in law: Supreme Court justice Byron White was runner up for the Heisman Trophy as the best college football player in 1937 and former Minnesota Viking lineman Alan Page through 2013 was a justice on the Minnesota Supreme Court. Frequently law and sport become overtly meshed together when judges are asked to make legal decisions about sport as in the periodic labor dispute or to interpret sports' adherence to laws like Title IX.

Not surprisingly, the study of law and sport has also been intertwined. Legal scholars have long written law review articles about the law and sport. For example, Gilbert H. Montague published "Antitrust Laws and the Federal Trade Commission, 1914–1927" in 1927, which included a discussion of baseball's exemption.[1] In 1939, Fredric A. Johnson published "Baseball Law."[2] Johnson's is among the first scholarly discussions to focus primarily on the connection between law and sport. Lawyers' interest in sport is so extensive that a number of law reviews such as the *Marquette Sports Law Journal* and the *Sports and Entertainment Law Journal* along with more than a dozen others focus specifically on the intersection from a lawyer's perspective.[3] Many, like Deborah Brake, who authored a detailed work on Title IX, have authored scholarly books on law and sport.[4] Legal scholars have also ventured into more popular approaches like Roger I. Abrams's *Sports Justice: The Law and Business of Sport*.[5] Abrams wrote a very accessible description of a number of legal issues in sport, some of which went to trial, and explored their implication on the game and society. Additionally lawyers have collaborated with nonlawyers to provide interdisciplinary examinations of sports law. andre douglas pond cummings and Anne Marie Lofaso edited an anthology, *Reversing Field: Examining Commercialization, Labor, Gender, and Race in 21st Century Sports Law*, which contained work by sociologists as well as practitioners in the field of sport business.[6]

Early sport history analysis of law in North America appeared in the 1970s; Canadian scholars were just as involved as US historians. At the inaugural North American Society for Sport History conference in 1973, Lorne W. Sawula of the University of Alberta presented a paper examining the role of the Canadian government in sport and the legislative attempts to solidify that involvement.[7] That same year, Al-Tony Gilmore historicized the Jack Johnson criminal prosecution for violations of the Mann Act in "Jack Johnson and White Women: The National Impact."[8] The first volume of the *Journal of Sport History* included Thomas Jable's historical look at the seventeenth-century blue laws in Pennsylvania.[9] Subsequent works studied topics as varied as John Marshall Carter's evaluation of crime and sport in thirteenth-century England (a surprising number of violent attacks after chess games appear in the records) published in the *Canadian Journal of Sport History*,[10] and, in the same journal, R. C. Watson and John C. MacLellan examined the history of criminal charges stemming from ice hockey games in Canada, beginning with a manslaughter case in 1905.[11] In 1998, in the *Sport History Review*, Kevin Wamsley explored how Canadian laws against gambling and their subsequent enforcement in the early twentieth century reflected institutionalized racism and classism.[12]

The twenty-first century has continued to see historians examine the nexus between law and sport. Some are focused on law in its historical context, like Sarah K. Fields's *Female Gladiators: Gender, Law, and Contact Sport in America*, which explored how school-aged girls in the United States used the law to gain access to contact sport and the social backlash that hindered that access.[13] Thomas M. Hunt's book *Drug Games: The International Olympic Committee and the Politics of Doping, 1960–2008* examined the historical response of the IOC to doping, using legal sources and a subtle administrative law analysis.[14] Other books acknowledge the significance of law and lawsuits in broader sport history, as Ying Wushanley did in *Playing Nice and*

Losing: The Struggle for Control of Women's Intercollegiate Athletics, 1960–2000[15] when he analyzed the effect of *Kellmeyer v. NEA*,[16] a lawsuit challenging rules prohibiting female athletes from receiving athletic scholarships. Similarly, Ronald A. Smith placed Title IX in a historical context in *Pay for Play: A History of Big-Time College Athletic Reform*.[17] Many scholars have addressed issues of law and sport history a bit more tangentially in articles, presentations and books.

Historians are not the only scholars without law degrees to have also studied sport and law. A number of different disciplines have examined the intersection of sport and law and published their findings in articles, books, and in dedicated journals. For example, sport sociologist Wilbert Leonard discussed the role of sport and law in society generally in *Sociological Perspective of Sport*,[18] and Jay Johnson and Margery Holman explored the role of law in preventing hazing in *Making the Team*.[19] Sport philosophers publish on the topic generally in *Fair Play: Journal of Sport, Philosophy, Ethics and Law*. Others have examined doping, law, and sport extensively—focusing largely on the role of law more broadly as in the concept of the rules established by sporting organizations rather than laws of a nation. Ross Comber, for instance, looked primarily at the North American experience in *Drugs and Drug Use in Society*,[20] whereas Verner Møller provided a more international perspective in *The Ethics of Doping and Anti-Doping: Redeeming the Soul of Sport?*[21] Like historians, other sport scholars have considered legal issues in a myriad of other books and articles.

Sport management scholars have analyzed the practical application of law in sport settings and have a dedicated journal for the topic: *Journal of Legal Aspects of Sports*. It is worth noting, however, that several prominent sport management legal scholars have law degrees. Reflecting the involvement of lawyers and the fact that the field so values a rudimentary legal understanding, most graduate programs and many undergrad programs in sport management require a course in Sports Law—which in turn has spawned dozens of textbooks on the topic as well as the hornbook *The Essentials of Sports Law* by Glenn M. Wong.[22]

Thus, while the scholarly examination of the intersection between law and sport has been extensive, it also begs the question: how might a multidisciplinary examination of sport and law be thoroughly approached? Obviously each scholar approaches this query with his or her own specialties and strengths, but there are some general approaches that are worth discussing.

For most of the essays in this anthology, the scholars begin with the published legal decision, and any appeals, that might have followed. This is, however, a matter of entering the story in the middle. The published legal decision comes after a number of other events and often after a number of intervening years. Like all histories, when the story begins is rarely clearly defined; the beginning is a nebulous moment when one or both parties is so unhappy with a situation that they turn to the law to protect their interests. That moment, though, comes after a series of other moments that have helped lead to the untenable situation in which the courts are asked to intervene. The published decision usually tells some of the story of what led to the lawsuit and the decision usually explains the legal justifications for the court's decision. The published decision reaches into the past, but it does so only through the eyes of the judge writing the decision. The published decision tells part of a history and it tells it largely through the court's perspective, but that published decision is a beginning, or at least an entry point, for the sports law historian.

So the scholar begins in the middle with the published decision and must work both backward and forward and on multiple disciplinary fronts. On the legal front, the scholar must determine where in the legal history the published decision lies. Relatively few lawsuits that are filed with the courts actually go to trial. The vast majority are dropped by the parties, dismissed by the courts, or otherwise settled out of court. Those lawsuits that proceed to trial do not necessarily result in a published decision as the first level of court is the trial court for states and the district court for the federal level. Trial court judges never publish their decisions, in part because usually the court does not make the decision: a jury does. The jury keeps no record of their deliberations and unless the jurors choose to speak to the press, no one knows why they reached their decision. Even when a judge makes a decision without a jury, whether by dismissing the case, granting summary judgment for one party, or reaching a conclusion based on the merits of the case, the trial court judge publishes no decision. At most the judge will make comments from the bench, which might be recorded and published by reporters present in the courtroom. Thus no trial court level decision has a published decision. Only if the case is appealed to a state court of appeals or eventually a state supreme court will the decision be published. Federal district court judges publish decisions at their discretion, and these opinions are often at the beginning of a series of legal appeals. Thus the published decision with which a scholar starts is never the beginning; it is usually smack in the middle of a larger legal story and always in the middle of a larger historical and cultural story. For the scholar, though, the research often begins with the published decision. The published decision can be found in the physical books with the decisions available in law libraries both private and public as well as in online databases. Lexis-Nexis and Westlaw are two of the more popular and thorough online legal databases available through many university and college libraries. Many decisions, however, are available through other online databases like the Legal Information Institute of Cornell University Law School[23] and Justia.com, which can be found through simple and free online searches.

The scholar, after reading the initial publication, must then look to see if there are any preceding published opinions. For example, Richard Crepeau focused on the US Supreme Court's decision in *Flood v. Kuhn*. The Supreme Court, however, was hearing an appeal and there were a number of prior published legal decisions from lower-court judges. One scholarly approach to contextualize legal history is to look at any prior published opinions as well as any published court memos or documents. Sometimes these decisions and documents provide additional factual information about the people involved or more details about the story behind the law. These documents often contain different legal arguments and conclusions. The prior decisions and court documents are earlier chapters in the story. Similarly, sometimes the published decisions are appealed. Daniel A. Nathan, for example, explores the Ed O'Bannon case, which at the time of publication had not yet been fully litigated. Future studies will consider all the published decisions that have followed the publication of his essay.

One storyline for the sport historian interested in law is the evolution of law itself and to understand these, one must go to the work of legal scholars. Most of these scholars publish in law reviews, which are available in online databases like Westlaw and Lexis-Nexis as well as other databases found online. Law review articles themselves are amazing resources that are heavily footnoted. Finding a case note (which focuses on a single decision) or an article involving a specific topic (like antitrust law) provides a wealth of information both in the text and the footnotes—most case notes have a two-to-one page ratio of footnotes to text. Law review articles can range in length from twenty pages to hundreds of pages; some of the best legal scholars publish few books and many law review articles.

In addition to tracing the legal history of a case, most sport historians interested in law focus on contextualizing the historical and cultural backgrounds of the participants and the situation. In many ways this is much like doing "regular" history. Primary sources are of value for the sport law historian. Most scholars rely on contemporary accounts of events from newspaper and magazine articles for perspectives and reactions to the lawsuits as they occurred and the decisions as they were published. Contemporary sources also help to contextualize the era surrounding the controversy. In addition to news reports, many of the essays in this anthology refer to autobiographies written, or cowritten, by the participants involved in the cases. These historians have used the words of the individuals themselves, as suspect and self-serving as those words may at times be, to try to extrapolate a version of what occurred and what motivated the participants. Primary sources like letters, memos, journals, and other unpublished documents kept by the participants can be useful.

Further, secondary sources can help immensely. All historians build on the work of other historians and the work of a sport historian examining the law is no different. The essays in this anthology rely on secondary sources about the parties themselves, including biographies of the plaintiffs, the defendants, and sometimes the judicial figures. Many of the secondary sources cited in the notes refer to scholarly examinations of the role of a sport in American history as well as other non-sport-specific histories. Consider Samuel O. Regalado's essay on Muhammad Ali. Not only does Regalado place his work in the context of sport historians but also within the work of historians examining the history of the Vietnam War. The lawsuit Ali filed was set against a political and cultural backdrop that Regalado described in great detail to contexualize the choices that Ali made and the price that he paid, even though he won the lawsuit in the end.

The challenge and reward of the type of research that sport historians looking at law have is to take a mosaic of images of a moment in time from several different disciplines, specifically law and history, and kaleidoscope those pieces into a different interpretation of the history. Some of these essays examine legal cases that have been scrutinized by lawyers and historians alike. Others focus on more obscure moments. All attempt to provide a unique vision by combing through a variety of documents from both historical and legal sources. The end result is a broader interpretation and understanding of specific legal cases as contextualized within the larger social, political, and cultural history of the time.

Notes

Chapter One: Introduction

1. Thurgood Marshall, "The Bicentennial Speech," given at the Annual Seminar of the San Francisco Patent and Trademark Law Association in Maui, Hawaii, May 6, 1987. Available at http://www.thurgoodmarshall.com/speeches/constitutional_speech.htm (accessed February 14, 2010).

Section I: The Burger Supreme Court and Sports

1. Frank Litsky and Richard Sandomir, "Jim McKay, Who Told of the Triumph and Tragedy in Sports, Is Dead at 86," *New York Times*, June 8, 2008, 32.

Chapter Two: Clay, aka Ali v. U.S.

1. David Remnick, *King of the World: Muhammad Ali and the Rise of an American Hero* (New York: Random House, 1998), 290.

2. Ibid.

3. Ibid., 291.

4. While race and sport was not at issue in the petitioner's claim, those two components did, of course, factor into the thinking of some, if not all, of the justices in the 1971 Burger Court. For the greater social and cultural implications of *Clay, aka Ali v. U.S.* (1971), historian Jeffrey T. Sammons, as noted in several citations within this essay, has contributed the topic's most insightful work.

5. David Remnick, *King of the World*, 291.

6. Ibid., 287.

7. Ibid., 288.

8. Ibid., 289.

9. Benjamin G. Rader, *American Sports: From the Age of Folk Games to the Age of Spectators* (Englewood Cliffs, NJ: Prentice-Hall, 1983), 331.

10. Muhammad Ali with Richard Durham, *The Greatest: My Own Story* (New York: Alfred A. Knopf, 1975), 175.

11. Benjamin Rader, *American Sports*, 291.

12. Muhammad Ali, *The Greatest*, 175.

13. Ibid., 156.

14. Ibid., 157.

15. Jeffery T. Sammons, *Beyond the Ring: The Role of Boxing in American Society* (Urbana: University of Illinois Press, 1988), 203.

16. "Clay Guilty in Draft Case; Gets Five Years in Prison," June 20, 1967, http://www.nytimes.com/learning/general/onthisday/big/0620.html (accessed May 1, 2006).

17. John R. Vile, *Great American Lawyers: An Encyclopedia, Volume 2* (New York: ABC-CLIO, 2001), 138.

18. *United States v. Seeger*, 380 U.S. 163 (1965).

19. Lawrence M. Baskir and William A. Strauss, *Chance and Circumstance: The Draft, the War, and the Vietnam Generation* (New York: Alfred A. Knopf, 1978), 77.

20. John Whiteclay Chambers II, *Draftees or Volunteers: A Documentary History of the Debate over Military Conscription in the United States, 1787–1973* (New York: Garland Publishers, 1975), 77. Further numbers on the number of inductees during World War One is found in the United States Selective Service Webpage. See http://www.sss.gov/induct.htm (accessed February 22, 2010).

21. Chambers, *Draftees or Volunteers*, 297; *Arver v. U.S.*, 245 U.S. 366 (1918).

22. *U.S. v. MacIntosh*, 283 U.S. 605 (1931).

23. Mulford Q. Sibley and Philip E. Jacob, *Conscription of Conscience: The American State and the Conscientious Objector, 1940–1947* (Ithaca, NY: Cornell University Press, 1952), 50.

24. Chambers, *Draftees or Volunteers*, 418–19; Selective Service System, http://www.sss.gov/induct.htm (accessed November 24, 2006).

25. *Sicurella v. United States*, 348, U.S. 385 (1955).

26. Ibid.

27. *United States v. Seeger,* 380 U.S. 163 (1965).

28. Selective Service System, http://www.sss.gov/induct.htm (accessed November 24, 2006).

29. Baskir and Strauss, *Chance and Circumstance*, 70.

30. Ibid.

31. Ibid.

32. Ibid., 74.

33. Ibid.

34. Jeffrey T. Sammons, *Beyond the Ring: The Role of Boxing in American Society* (Urbana: University of Illinois Press, 1988), 204.

35. Ibid.

36. Michael E. Lomax, "Revisiting *The Revolt of the Black Athlete*: Harry Edwards and the Making of the African-American Sport Studies," *Journal of Sport History* 29, no. 3 (2002): 469–79.

37. Ibid.

38. Jeffrey Sammons, "Rebel with a Cause: Muhammad Ali as Sixties Protest Symbol," in *Muhammad Ali: The People's Champ,* ed. Elliott J. Gorn (Urbana: University of Illinois Press, 1995), 170.

39. Ibid.

40. Baskir and Strauss, *Chance and Circumstance,* 77.

41. Bob Woodward and Scott Armstrong, *The Brethren: Inside the Supreme Court* (New York: Simon and Schuster, 1979), 12.

42. Kermit L. Hall, *The Oxford Companion to the Supreme Court of the United States* (New York: Oxford University Press, 1992), 104.

43. Alpheus Thomas Mason, *The Supreme Court from Taft to Burger* (Baton Rouge: Louisiana State University Press, 1980), 316.

44. Michael Oriard, "Muhammad Ali: The Hero in the Age of Mass Media," in Gorn, ed., *Muhammad Ali: The People's Champ,* 16.

45. *United States v. Seeger*, 380 U.S. 163 (1965).

46. Bruce Allen Murphy, *Wild Bill: The Legend and Life of William O. Douglas* (New York: Random House, 2003), 415–16.

47. Roger K. Newman, *Hugo Black: A Biography* (New York: Pantheon Books, 1994), 580.

48. Ibid., 591.

49. Jeffrey Moore, "Opposition to the Iraq War Reaches New Level," Gallup, April 24, 2008, http://www.gallup.com/poll/106783/opposition-iraq-war-reaches-new-high.aspx. (accessed July 21, 2013).

50. Juan Williams, *Thurgood Marshall: American Revolutionary* (New York: Random House, 1998), 275–76.

51. Ibid., 278.

52. *Gillette v. United States*, 401 U.S. 437 (1971).

53. Sammons, *Beyond the Ring*, 216.

54. Ibid., 217.

55. Ibid.

56. Woodward and Armstrong, *The Brethren*, 138.

57. *Clay, aka Ali v. United States*, 403 U.S. 698 (1971).

58. Sammons, *Beyond the Ring*, 215; *Welsh v. United States*, 398 U.S. 333 (1970).

59. Woodward and Armstrong, *The Brethren*, 138.

60. Ibid., 138–39.

61. Baskir and Strauss, *Chance and Circumstance*, 79.

62. Othello Harris, "The Revolt of the Black Athlete," in Gorn, ed., *Muhammad Ali: The People's Champ*, 66.

63. Roy Strom, "As Muhammad Ali Turns 70, Lawyers Look Back on High Court Case," *Chicago Daily Bulletin*, January 17, 2012, http://www.chicagolaw bulletin.com/News-Extra/Muhammad-Ali-Turns-70.aspx (accessed August 19, 2012).

64. Gwen Knapp, "World Cheers Ali and Atlanta III Boxing Legend Lights Olympic Flame," *SF Gate*, July 20, 1996, http://www.sfgate.com/sports/article/World-cheers-Ali-and-Atlanta-Ill-boxing-legend-3134398.php (accessed August 19, 2012).

65. Stan Wilson, "Muhammad Ali Returns to the Olympic Stage, Once Again, in London," *CNN News Report*, July 2012, http://articles.cnn.com/2012-07-27/worldsport/sport_olympics-muhammad-ali_1_jeanie-kahnke-ali-center-spokeswoman-muhammad-ali/3 (accessed August 19, 2012).

CHAPTER THREE: ODD BEDFELLOWS

1. *Haywood v. National Basketball Assn.*, 401 U.S. 1204 (1971) [Haywood I]. Neither the district court nor the court of appeals published their decisions in granting and then staying the injunction; the first published opinion is Douglas's.

2. Spencer Haywood with Scott Ostler, *Spencer Haywood: The Rise, the Fall, the Recovery* (New York: Amistad Books, 1992), 11–12.

3. Ibid., 18–20.

4. Ibid., 72–81.

5. Ibid., 92–103.

6. Ibid., 104.

7. "'Spencer Haywood,' NBA History," http://www.nba.com/history/players/haywood_summary.html (accessed May 5, 2006).

8. Haywood, *Spencer Haywood*, 130.

9. Terry Pluto, *Loose Balls: The Short, Wild Life of the American Basketball Association as Told by the Players, Coaches, Movers, and Shakers Who Made It Happen* (New York: Fireside Press, 1990), 181–82.

10. "'Spencer Haywood,' NBA History."

11. Haywood, *Spencer Haywood*, 134, 142–45.

12. *Denver Rockets, etc. v. All-Pro Management Inc.*, 325 F. Supp. 1049 (CD Cal. 1971) [Haywood II]. At the same time that Haywood filed the suit against the NBA, he also filed a suit to have his contract with the Denver Rockets voided. Sam Schulman settled that case out of court; Haywood, *Spencer Haywood*, 153.

13. For a complete explanation of injunctive relief, see Lisa Pike Masteralexis, "Judicial Review, Standing, and Injunctions," in *Law for Recreation and Sport Managers*, 3rd ed., ed. Doyice J. Cotten and John T. Wolohan (Dubuque, IA: Kendall/Hunt Publishing, 2003), 426–33.

14. Haywood I at 1205.

15. Haywood I at 1206.

16. Douglas authored three autobiographies: *Of Men and Mountains* (New York: Harper and Brothers, 1950); *Go East, Young Man* (New York: Random House, 1974); and *The Court Years, 1939–1975: The Autobiography of William O. Douglas* (New York: Random House, 1980) (published posthumously). Multiple scholars have written biographies on Douglas, including, in order of publication, James C. Duram, *Justice William O. Douglas* (Boston: Twayne Publishing, 1979); Edwin P. Hoyt, *William O. Douglas* (Middlebury, VT: Paul S. Eriksson Publishing, 1979); James F. Simon, *Independent Journey: The Life of William O. Douglas* (New York: Penguin Books, 1980); and Bruce Allen Murphy, *Wild Bill: The Legend and Life of William O. Douglas* (New York: Random House, 2003).

17. Simon, *Independent Journey*, 21.

18. Murphy, *Wild Bill*, 24.

19. Douglas, *Go East, Young Man*, 13.

20. Simon, *Independent Journey*, 39.

21. Howard Ball, "Loyalty, Treason and the State: An Examination of Justice William O. Douglas's Style, Substance, and Anguish," in *"He Shall Not Pass this Way Again": The Legacy of Justice William O. Douglas*, ed. Stephen L. Wasby (Pittsburgh: University of Pittsburgh Press, 1990), 7.

22. Donald W. Jackson, "Commentary: On the Correct Handling of Contradictions within the Court," in Wasby, *"He Shall Not Pass this Way Again,"* 59; L. A. Powe Jr., "Justice Douglas, the First Amendment, and the Protection of Rights," in Wasby, *"He Shall Not Pass this Way Again,"* 76; Melvin I. Urofsky, "William O. Douglas as Common Law Judge," in *The Warren Court in Historical and Political Perspective*, ed. Mark Tushnet (Charlottesville: University of Virginia Press, 1993), 79.

23. G. Edward White, "The Anti-Judge: William O. Douglas and the Ambiguities of Individuality," *Virginia Law Review* 74 (1988): 46.

24. *Griswold v. Connecticut*, 381 U.S. 479 (1965).

25. Murphy, *Wild Bill*, 366–67.

26. Ibid., 429–38.

27. Haywood I at 1204–7.

28. *Flood v. Kuhn*, 407 U.S. 258 (1972) (Douglas, J., dissenting).

29. Haywood I at 1206–7.

30. No evidence exists to suggest that anyone requested that Douglas recuse himself given that he had grown up in Washington State and that the SuperSonics were based in the same state.

31. Urofsky, "William O. Douglas as Common Law Judge," 71.

32. *Haywood v. Merrill*, 401 U.S. 952 (1971).

33. Haywood II at 1061.

34. Ibid. at 1062.

35. Ibid. at 1066.

36. Haywood, *Spencer Haywood,* 152.

37. Ibid., 148–53.

38. "'Spencer Haywood,' NBA History."

39. Haywood, *Spencer Haywood,* 168–84.

40. Ibid., 185–209.

41. Ibid., 240–60. Haywood's section on his drug usage and his early attempts at recovery in his biography is, not surprisingly, a bit hazy. After leaving the Bullets in 1983, he notes very few dates until his divorce in 1987. Sometime after 1985 he entered rehab.

42. Interview with Michael Tillery, "The Spoken Word," The Black Sports Network, http://blacksportsnetwork.com/articles/qa/The%20Wood_060806.asp (accessed January 17, 2007); Irv Moss, "Hardwood Success, Controversy Followed Star," *Denver Post*, December 31, 2006, http://www.denverpost.com/nuggets/ci_4930559 (accessed January 17, 2007).

43. Tim Povtak, "After 40 Years, Spencer Haywood Finally Gets His Thanks." February 2, 2010, http://www.aolnews.com/2010/02/02/after-40-years-spencer-haywood-finally-gets-his-thanks/ (accessed December 16, 2011).

44. Murphy, *Wild Bill*, 492–507. Ironically, Ford replaced Douglas with John Paul Stevens, a man who would join Douglas as one of the Court's most consistently liberal justices.

45. Moss, "Hardwood Success."

46. Johnette Howard, "Spencer Haywood is Still Waiting," April 11, 2013, http://espn.go.com/nba/story/_/id/9160941/spencer-haywood-waiting-hall-fame-call (accessed April 15, 2013). Howard argued that Haywood's induction was long overdue. Sam Amick, "Spencer Haywood Misses Cut for Naismith Hall of Fame," April 2, 2014, http://www.usatoday.com/story/sports/nba/2014/04/02/spencer-haywood-naismith-memorial-basketball-hall-of-fame-nba/7231089/(accessed May 13, 2014).

47. Murphy, *Wild Bill*, 105.

48. See Daniel A. Applegate, "The NBA Gets a College Education: An Antitrust and Labor Analysis of the NBA's Minimum Age Limit," *Case Western Reserve Law Review* 56 (2006): 825–56 (arguing that the NBA's eligibility requirements are protected from antitrust law as nonstatutory labor exemptions); Kevin J. Cimino,

"Student Work: The Rebirth of the NBA—Well, Almost: An Analysis of the Maurice Clarett Decision and Its Impact on the National Basketball Association," *West Virginia Law Review* 108 (2006): 831–71 (arguing that the NBA's eligibility rule requiring players be one year beyond their high school graduation would not survive a court review because eligibility is a mandatory subject for collective bargaining). *Clarett v. National Football League*, 369 F.3d 124 (2nd Cir. 2004) concluded that football's age limitation was legal because it was part of the collective bargaining agreement.

49. "NBA Board of Governors Ratify 10-year CBA," December 8, 2011, http://www.nba.com/2011/news/12/08/labor-deal-reached/index.html (accessed December 16, 2011).

Chapter Four: The *Flood* Case, 1972

1. Curt Flood with Richard Carter, *The Way It Is* (New York: Trident Press, 1971), 194–95.

2. Robert F. Burk, *Much More Than a Game: Players, Owners, and American Baseball since 1921* (Chapel Hill: University of North Carolina Press, 2001), 177–78.

3. Roger I. Abrams, *Legal Bases: Baseball and the Law* (Philadelphia: Temple University Press, 1998), 56–57.

4. Ibid., 59.

5. Andrew Zimbalist, *May the Best Team Win: Baseball Economics and Public Policy* (Washington, DC: Brookings Institute Press, 2003), 18.

6. *Toolson v. New York Yankees, Inc.*, 346 U.S. 356 (1953), 357.

7. Brad Snyder, *A Well-Paid Slave: Curt Flood's Fight for Free Agency in Professional Sports* (New York: Viking Press, 2006), 21–23.

8. Zimbalist, *May the Best Team Win*, 18.

9. Snyder, *A Well-Paid Slave*, 130.

10. *Flood v. Kuhn*, 407 U.S. 258 (1972).

11. Snyder, *A Well-Paid Slave*, 133.

12. Ibid., 159–89, offers an excellent summary of the testimony on both sides of the case. Among those questioning Goldberg's strategy are Snyder, *A Well-Paid Slave*, and Neil F. Flynn, *Baseball's Reserve System: The Case and Trial of Curt Flood v. Major League Baseball*, (Springfield, IL: Walnut Park Group, 2006).

13. Ibid., 191–92.

14. Ibid., 257–60.

15. Ibid., 264–74, offers a summary of Goldberg's presentation.

16. Ibid., 283–91.

17. Bob Woodward and Scott Armstrong, *The Brethren: Inside the Supreme Court* (New York: Simon and Schuster, 1979), 186–92.

18. Ibid., 188.

19. Snyder, *A Well-Paid Slave*, 305.

20. Alex Belth, *Stepping Up: The Story of Curt Flood and His Fight for Baseball Players' Rights* (New York: Persea Books, 2006), 183.

21. Woodward and Armstrong, *The Brethren*, 190–91.

22. Snyder, *A Well-Paid Slave*, 300–306 and 310–11; Flynn, *Baseball's Reserve System*, 290–91.

23. Benjamin Rader, *Baseball: A History of America's Game* (Urbana: University of Illinois Press, 1994), 192; David Voigt, *American Baseball: From Postwar Expansion to the Electronic Age,* vol. 3 (University Park: Pennsylvania State University Press, 1983), 211–12.

24. Charles Alexander, *Our Game: An American Baseball History* (New York: MJF Books, 1991), 281–82; Burk, *Much More Than a Game,* 302; John Thorn, "Our Game," *Total Baseball,* 6th ed. (New York: Total Sports, 1999), 10; G. Edward White, *Creating the National Pastime: Baseball Transforms Itself, 1903–1953* (Princeton, NJ: Princeton University Press, 1996), 326.

25. Lee Lowenfish, *The Imperfect Diamond: A History of Baseball's Labor Wars,* rev. ed. (New York: DeCapo Paperback, 1991), 213–14; Marvin Miller, *A Whole Different Ballgame: The Sport and Business of Baseball* (New York: Birch Lane Press, 1991), 194–96.

26. Charles P. Korr, *The End of Baseball as We Know It: The Player's Union, 1960–1981* (Urbana: University of Illinois Press, 2002), 100–101; Leonard Koppett, *Koppett's Concise History of Major League Baseball* (Philadelphia: Temple University Press, 1998), 338–41; and Belth, *Stepping Up,* 187.

27. Korr, *The End of Baseball as We Know It,* 122; Jules Tygiel, "Revisiting Curt Flood," Paper delivered at Frostburg State University, Frostburg, Maryland, November 2006, 33 (copy of paper generously supplied to me by Jules Tygiel).

28. Bowie Kuhn, *Hardball: The Education of a Baseball Commissioner* (New York: Times Books, 1987), 89–90.

29. Miller, *A Whole Different Ball Game,* 197–98.

30. Belth, *Stepping Up,* 172.

31. Snyder, *A Well-Paid Slave,* 349–52, direct quotation on 349; Michael Lomax, "'Curt Flood Stood Up for Us': The Quest to Break Down Racial Barriers and Structural Inequality in Major League Baseball," in *Ethnicity, Sport, Identity: Struggles for Status,* ed. J. A. Mangan and Andrew Ritchie (London: Frank Cass, 2004), 44–70.

32. Abrams, *Legal Bases,* 126–27; Flynn, *Baseball's Reserve System,* 310.

33. Zimbalist, *May the Best Team Win,* 22–23.

34. Belth, *Stepping Up,* 200.

35. Flynn, *Baseball's Reserve System,* 318.

36. Zimbalist, *May the Best Team Win,* 24–33.

CHAPTER FIVE: HOW THE BURGER COURT CAME TO BE

1. William L. O'Neill, *Coming Apart: An Informal History of America in the 1960's* (New York: Quadrangle Books, 1971), 360.

2. James T. Patterson, *Grand Expectations: The United States, 1945–1971* (New York: Oxford University Press, 1996), 678.

3. Theodore H. White, *The Making of the President—1968* (New York: Atheneum, 1969), x.

4. Ed Cray, *Chief Justice: A Biography of Earl Warren* (New York: Simon and Schuster, 1997), 496.

5. Cray, *Chief Justice,* 250; Dwight D. Eisenhower, *The White House Years,* vol. 1, *Mandate for Change, 1953–1956* (Garden City, NY: Doubleday, 1963), 226–29.

6. G. Edward White, *Earl Warren: A Public Life* (New York: Oxford University Press, 1982), 143.

7. Eisenhower, *Mandate for Change*, 228.

8. Ibid.

9. Earl Warren, *The Memoirs of Earl Warren* (Garden City, NY: Doubleday, 1977), 261.

10. Ibid.

11. Stephen E. Ambrose, *Eisenhower*, vol. 2, *The President* (New York: Simon and Schuster, 1984), 128.

12. Cray, *Chief Justice*, 250.

13. Ibid., 253.

14. For measured accounts of the events described in this paragraph, see Warren, *Memoirs*, 260–61, 269–71; White, *Earl Warren*, 144–53; Bernard Schwartz, *Super Chief: Earl Warren and His Supreme Court* (New York: New York University Press, 1983), 1–7; and Jim Newton, *Eisenhower: The White House Years* (New York: Doubleday, 2011), 112–15.

15. Bruce Allen Murphy, *Fortas: The Rise and Ruin of a Supreme Court Justice* (New York: William Morrow, 1988), 272.

16. Murphy, *Fortas*, 286.

17. Cray, *Chief Justice*, 497.

18. Murphy, *Fortas*, 287.

19. Cray, *Chief Justice*, 497.

20. Ibid.

21. Ibid., 498.

22. Laura Kalman, *Abe Fortas: A Biography* (New Haven, CT: Yale University Press, 1990), 328.

23. Robert Dallek, *Flawed Giant: Lyndon Johnson and His Times, 1961–1973* (New York: Oxford University Press, 1998), 233.

24. Murphy, *Fortas*, 285.

25. Dallek, *Flawed Giant*, 559. More generally, see Kalman, *Abe Fortas*, 327–28, and Murphy, *Fortas*, 272–300.

26. Kalman, *Abe Fortas*, 329.

27. Ibid.

28. Ibid.

29. Kalman, *Abe Fortas*, 328–29. See also Cray, *Chief Justice*, 497–501; Kalman, *Fortas*, 335–51; Dallek, *Flawed Giant*, 557–63; and Murphy, *Fortas*, 441–62.

30. Kalman, *Abe Fortas*, 326–27, 351–56.

31. Dallek, *Flawed Giant*, 563–64; Murphy, *Fortas*, 477–526.

32. Kalman, *Abe Fortas*, 364.

33. Ibid., 374.

34. Cray, *Chief Justice*, 508–10; Schwartz, *Super Chief*, 760–62; Jim Newton, *Justice for All: Earl Warren and the Nation He Made* (New York: Riverhead Books, 2006), 502–3; Kalman, *Abe Fortas*, 322–27, 359–74.

35. Cray, *Chief Justice*, 511–13.

36. Ibid., 513.

37. Ibid.

38. Ibid.

39. Ibid., 513–14.

40. "Introduction," *Significant Supreme Court Opinions of the Honorable Warren E. Burger, Chief Justice of the United States* (Manila: Philippine Bar Association, 1984), n.p.

41. Donald E. Boles, *Mr. Justice Rehnquist, Judicial Activist: The Early Years* (Ames: Iowa State University Press, 1987), 3–9; Sue Davis, *Justice Rehnquist and the Constitution* (Princeton, NJ: Princeton University Press, 1989), 3–7.

42. Boles, *Mr. Justice Rehnquist*, 4.

43. Davis, *Justice Rehnquist*, 3.

44. Boles, *Mr. Justice Rehnquist,* 9.

45. George V. Higgins, *The Friends of Richard Nixon* (Boston: Little, Brown, 1974), 159; Kermit L. Hall and Kevin T. McGuire, eds., *The Judicial Branch* (New York: Oxford University Press, 2005), 169.

Section II: Antitrust Law and Sports

1. 15 U.S.C. 1 §§1–2.

2. Lawrence M. Friedman, *A History of American Law*, 3rd ed. (New York: Simon and Schuster, 2005), 346–49.

3. *Chicago Board of Trade v. United States*, 246 U.S. 231, 238 (1918).

4. Glenn M. Wong, *Essentials of Sports Law*, 3rd ed. (Westport, CT: Praeger, 2002), 441.

5. *Molinas v. Podoloff*, 190 F. Supp. 241 (S.D.N.Y. 1961).

6. See *Clarett v. National Football League*, 369 F.3d 124 (2nd Cir. 2004).

7. *Standard Oil Co. of New Jersey v. United States*, 221 U.S. 1 (1911). For a general introduction to antitrust law and its history, see also Ernest Gellhorn, William E. Kovacic, and Stephen Calkins, *Antitrust Law and Economics in a Nutshell*, 5th ed. (Minneapolis, MN: West Publishing Co., 2004).

8. 172 F.2d 402 (1949).

9. *Frantz v. United States Powerlifting Federation,* 1986 U.S. Dist. LEXIS 18174 (N.D. Ill. 1986); *rev'd in part and remanded,* 836 F.2d 1063 (7th Cir. Ill. 1987); *rev'd and remanded by* 1988 U.S. Dist. LEXIS 5694 (N.D. Ill. 1988).

Chapter Six: Danny Gardella and Baseball's Reserve Clause

1. *Gardella v. Chandler,* 79 F. Supp. 260 (SDNY, 1948), *rev'd and remanded,* 172 F.2d 402 (2nd Cir. 1949), *aff'd* 174 F.2d 919 (2nd Cir. 1949).

2. "Rickey's Charge That Reserve Clause Foes Lean to Communism Brings Sharp Denial," *New York Times*, April 14, 1949, 33.

3. "Gardella Counsel Query Chandler on World Series, All-Star Moneys," *New York Times*, September 20, 1949, 39.

4. Richard Goldstein, "Danny Gardella, 85, Dies; Challenged Reserve Clause," *New York Times*, March 13, 2005, 46.

5. Maury Allen, "Danny Gardella: Baseball's King of Laughter," March 21, 2005, http://www.thecolumnists.com/allen/allen68.html (accessed August 19, 2013).

6. See Jerold J. Duquette, *Regulating the National Pastime: Baseball and Antitrust* (Westport, CT: Praeger, 1999); Albert Theodore Powers, *The Business of Baseball*

(Jefferson, NC: McFarland & Company, 2002); Warren Freedman, *Professional Sports and Antitrust* (New York: Quorum Books, 1987); and Lee Lowenfish and Tony Lupien, *The Imperfect Diamond: The Story of Baseball's Reserve System and the Men Who Fought to Change It* (New York: Stein and Day, 1980).

7. Bryan De Salvatore, *A Clever Base-Ballist: The Life and Times of John Montgomery Ward* (Baltimore: Johns Hopkins University Press, 2001), 160–61.

8. Quoted in Andrew Zimbalist, *Baseball and Billions: A Probing Look into the Big Business of Our National Pastime* (New York: Basic Books, 1992), 3.

9. *Federal Baseball Club of Baltimore v. National League of Professional Baseball Clubs*, 259 U.S. 200 (1922).

10. Robert F. Burk, *Much More Than a Game: Players, Owners, and American Baseball since 1921* (Chapel Hill: University of North Carolina Press, 2001), 9.

11. Duquette, *Regulating the National Pastime*, 15.

12. For a biographical sketch of Danny Gardella, see Lowenfish and Lupien, *Imperfect Diamond*, 155–68.

13. Ibid., 156.

14. Allen, "Danny Gardella: Baseball's King of Laughter."

15. William Marshall, *Baseball's Pivotal Era, 1945–1951* (Lexington: University Press of Kentucky, 1999), 45.

16. "Gardella Reveals Jump from Giants," *New York Times*, February 19, 1946, 29.

17. "A Jolly Good Feller," *Baseball Magazine*, February 1946, 29.

18. "Gardella in Mexico," *New York Times*, February 23, 1946, 22.

19. Quoted in Marshall, *Baseball's Pivotal Era*, 49.

20. Ibid.

21. G. Richard McKelvey, *Mexican Raiders in the Major Leagues: The Pasquel Brothers vs. Organized Baseball, 1946* (Jefferson, NC: McFarland & Company, 2006), 70.

22. George Vecsey, "Ray Dandridge, The Hall of Fame and *Fences*," *New York Times*, May 10, 1987, S3.

23. McKelvey, *Mexican Raiders in the Major Leagues*, 92–93.

24. Lee Lowenfish, *Branch Rickey: Baseball's Ferocious Gentleman* (Lincoln: University of Nebraska Press, 2007), 394.

25. Shirley Povich, "Hard to Quell the Pasquels," *Sporting News*, May 16, 1946, 10 paperofrecord.hypernet.ca (accessed August 19, 2013).

26. Ibid.

27. Mark Winegardner, *The Veracruz Blues* (New York: Penguin, 1996); and Steve Crinti, "Baseball in America: The Game of Imperialism in Winegardner's *The Veracruz Blues*," *Studies in Contemporary Fiction* 47, no. 4 (2006): 389–406.

28. Quoted in Duquette, *Regulating the National Pastime*, 45.

29. Harry Grayson, "Lawyer's Trip to Dentist Office Led to Filing of Gardella Suit," *Sporting News*, March 2, 1949, 2, paperofrecord.hypernet.ca (accessed August 19, 2013).

30. Lowenfish and Lupien, *Imperfect Diamond*, 159–60.

31. Ibid., 162–64.

32. Ibid.

33. Ibid.

34. Quoted in Duquette, *Regulating the National Pastime*, 45.

35. Ibid.

36. Lowenfish and Lupien, *Imperfect Diamond*, 162.

37. Ibid.

38. *Gardella v. Chandler*, 172 F.2d 402 (2nd Cir. 1949), 409–10.

39. Thomas Ronan, "U.S. Appeals Court Orders Trial of Gardella Suit Against Baseball," *New York Times*, February 10, 1949, 39.

40. "Orderly in Hospital," *New York Times*, February 11, 1949, 30.

41. William H. Chafe, *The Unfinished Journey: America since World War II* (New York: Oxford University Press, 2007), 103.

42. "Game Key to American Way," *Sporting News*, February 2, 1949, 25, paperofrecord.hypernet.ca (accessed August 19, 2013).

43. "No Time for Squabbling," *Sporting News*, February 23, 1949, 14, paperofrecord.hypernet.ca (accessed August 19, 2013), and "Leniency to Jumpers Unjustified," *Sporting News*, March 2, 1949, 12, paperofrecord.hypernet.ca (accessed August 19, 2013).

44. "Organized Ball Has Nothing to Fear," *Sporting News*, February 16, 1949, 12, paperofrecord.hypernet.ca (accessed August 19, 2013).

45. "'Peonage at $100,000 Nice Work'—Chandler," *Sporting News*, February 16, 1949, 3, paperofrecord.hypernet.ca (accessed August 19, 2013).

46. Shirley Povich, "Serfdom? It's Wonderful," *Sporting News*, February 23, 1949, 14, paperofrecord.hypernet.ca (accessed August 19, 2013).

47. "Rep. Herlong (Fla.) Asks Gardella to Reconsider," *Sporting News*, February 23, 1949, 14, paperofrecord.hypernet.ca (accessed August 19, 2013).

48. Lee George, "Gardella Refused to Join 11 in Appeal, Says Owen," *Sporting News*, February 23, 1949, 20, paperofrecord.hypernet.ca (accessed August 19, 2013).

49. "Leniency to Jumpers Unjustified," *Sporting News*, March 2, 1949, 12, paperofrecord.hypernet.ca (accessed August 19, 2013).

50. Dan Daniel, "Chandler Sounds Rally-Call in Game's Defense," *Sporting News*, March 30, 1949, 7, paperofrecord.hypernet.ca (accessed August 19, 2013).

51. "Ban on Major Leaguers Who Jumped to Mexico Lifted by Chandler," *New York Times*, June 6, 1949, 24.

52. Marshall, *Baseball's Pivotal Era*, 244.

53. Gardella Council Query Chandler on World Series, All-Star Moneys," *Sporting News*, September 20, 1949, 2, paperofrecord.hypernet.ca (accessed August 19, 2013).

54. Ibid.

55. Ibid.

56. "Happy Bats 1.000," *Sporting News*, November 2, 1949, 10, paperofrecord. hypernet.ca (accessed August 19, 2013).

57. John A. Sprout, "Restraint of Trade: Application of Anti-Trust Laws to Baseball," *California Law Review* 37, no. 2 (1949): 323.

58. *Toolson v. New York Yankees*, 346 U.S. 356 (1953).

59. Allen, "Danny Gardella: Baseball's King of Laughter," and Marshall, *Baseball's Pivotal Era*, 247.

CHAPTER SEVEN: POWERLIFTING'S WATERSHED

1. Although they are in fact very different sports, powerlifting is often confused with Olympic weightlifting. In comparison to the "brute strength" events in powerlifting (squat, bench press, and deadlift), weightlifting features two "technique events" (the clean and jerk and the snatch). The lifts in weightlifting require greater speed and dexterity than their counterparts in powerlifting. Moreover, weightlifting, in contrast to powerlifting, is included on the Olympic program. It is governed by the International Weightlifting Federation and, at the national level within the United States, by USA Weightlifting.

2. Jan Todd, "Chaos Can Have Gentle Beginnings: The Early History of the Quest for Drug Testing in American Powerlifting: 1964–1984," *Iron Game History: The Journal of Physical Culture* 8, no. 3 (2004): 3.

3. For a study on the early history of powerlifting, see ibid. An exception to the relative lack of scholarship on the recent history of powerlifting is a chapter in a book sponsored by the Hastings Center for Bioethics: Jan Todd and Terry Todd, "Reflections on the 'Parallel Federation Solution' to the Problem of Drug Use in Sport: The Cautionary Tale of Powerlifting," in *Performance-Enhancing Technologies in Sports: Ethical, Conceptual, and Scientific Issues*, ed. Thomas H. Murray, Karen J. Maschke, and Angela A. Wasunna (Baltimore: Johns Hopkins University Press, 2009).

4. Its appeal and reconsideration upon remand required examination of the case by multiple courts. For clarity in these notes, we have divided them into [Case 1], [Case 2], and [Case 3]. The citations are *Frantz v. United States Powerlifting Federation* [Case 1], 1986 U.S. Dist. LEXIS 18174 (N.D. Ill. 1986); *Frantz v. United States Powerlifting Federation* [Case 2], 836 F.2d 1063 (7th Cir. Ill. 1987); *Frantz v. United States Powerlifting Federation* [Case 3], 1988 U.S. Dist. LEXIS 5694 (N.D. Ill. 1988).

5. Robert K. Merton, "The Unanticipated Consequences of Purposive Social Action," *American Sociological Review* 1, no. 6 (1936): 901.

6. J. Todd, "Chaos Can Have Gentle Beginnings," 3.

7. In the authors' home state, for example, 613 girls and 480 boys competed in their respective Texas State High School Championship meets in 2012. "2012 Meet Results," Texas High School Powerlifting Home Page, http://thspa.us (accessed September 1, 2012).

8. Glenn M. Wong, *Essentials of Sports Law,* 3rd ed. (Westport, CT: Praeger, 2002), 155.

9. While the IOC started testing for some performance-enhancing drugs during the 1968 Mexico City Olympic Games, it first tested for steroids in 1976. For a timeline of drug usage and drug testing in the Olympic movement, see Jan Todd and Terry Todd, "Significant Events in the History of Drug Testing and the Olympic Movement: 1960–1999," in *Doping in Elite Sport: The Politics of Drugs in the Olympic Movement*, ed. Wayne Wilson and Edward Derse (Champaign, IL: Human Kinetics, 2001).

10. IPF bylaws quoted in J. Todd, "Chaos Can Have Gentle Beginnings," 8. See also J. Todd and T. Todd, "Reflections on the 'Parallel Federation Solution' to the Problem of Drug Use in Sport," 53.

11. On this point, see John M. Hoberman, *Testosterone Dreams: Rejuvenation, Aphrodisia, Doping* (Berkeley: University of California Press, 2005), 249–60.

12. See Thomas M. Hunt, *Drug Games: The International Olympic Committee and the Politics of Doping, 1960–2008* (Austin: University of Texas Press, 2011).

13. For a list of reasons that International Sport Federations expanded their drug-testing programs, see Barrie Houlihan, "Anti-Doping Policy in Sport: The Politics of International Policy Co-Ordination," *Public Administration* 77, no. 2 (1999): 318–20.

14. Roger Gedney to Joe Zarella, May 8, 1981, Judy Gedney Papers, Stark Center for Physical Culture and Sports, University of Texas at Austin.

15. J. Todd, "Chaos Can Have Gentle Beginnings," 14.

16. "Brother Bennett, the Man behind the ADFPA Interviewed by Dr. Judd Biasiotto and Arny Ferrando of World Class Enterprises," *Powerlifting USA* (May 1987): 16.

17. Quoted in J. Todd and T. Todd, "Reflections on the 'Parallel Federation Solution' to the Problem of Drug Use in Sport," 55.

18. Roger Gedney to Conrad Cotter, August 4, 1982, Judy Gedney Papers, Stark Center for Physical Culture and Sports, University of Texas at Austin.

19. J. Todd, "Chaos Can Have Gentle Beginnings," 16.

20. Ibid., 17.

21. Nate Foster to Heinz Vierthaler, n.d., Judy Gedney Papers, Stark Center for Physical Culture and Sports, University of Texas at Austin.

22. On this point, see Andy Kerr, "Do We Need a New Set of Records?: The Question as Answered by Andy Kerr," *Powerlifting USA* (December 1987): 24–25.

23. Ernie Frantz, "Dear Fellow Lifter, Meet Promoter and Distributor," January 1983, Stark Center for Physical Culture and Sports, University of Texas at Austin.

24. "Proposal by John T. Black, Jr. to Ernie Frantz and Larry Pacifico of the American Powerlifting Federation on Behalf of the American International Professional Powerlifting Federation," n.d., Rader Collection, APF Folder, Stark Center for Physical Culture and Sports, University of Texas at Austin.

25. Roger Gedney to Conrad Cotter.

26. "Interview with Maris Sternberg by Eric Stone, 4/9/04," http://www.chicago powerlifting.com/MarisInterview.html (accessed March 22, 2005).

27. *Powerlifting USA* (November 1985): 31.

28. Judy Gedney to Ernie Frantz, March 4, 1985, Stark Center for Physical Culture and Sports, University of Texas at Austin.

29. Barrie Houlihan, *Sport and International Politics* (New York: Harvester Wheatsheaf, 1994), 56–57.

30. Quoted in J. Todd and T. Todd, "Reflections on the 'Parallel Federation Solution' to the Problem of Drug Use in Sport," 57.

31. Ernie Frantz to Conrad Cotter, February 4, 1980, Stark Center for Physical Culture and Sports, University of Texas at Austin.

32. Quoted in Hoberman, *Testosterone Dreams,* 251.

33. Ernie Frantz, "Proposal for APF/AMPF Meeting Submitted by Ernie Frantz, January 28, 1983." Rader Collection, APF folder, Stark Center for Physical Culture and Sports, University of Texas at Austin.

34. Quoted in J. Todd, "Chaos Can Have Gentle Beginnings," 17.

35. "On the A.P.F. Side," *Powerlifting USA* (November 1985): 31.

36. Ibid.

37. Frantz, "Dear Fellow Lifter, Meet Promoter and Distributor."

38. Reference to the letter is contained at Conrad Cotter, "Message from the President [September 1984]," *Powerlifting USA* (September 1984): 30.

39. Quoted in Conrad Cotter to Arnold Bostrom, July 1, 1984, Judy Gedney Papers, Stark Center for Physical Culture and Sports, University of Texas at Austin.

40. Cotter, "Message from the President," *Powerlifting USA* (September 1984).

41. "Ernie Frantz Talks about His Meet," *Powerlifting USA* (September 1984): 30.

42. Affidavit of Plaintiff Maris Sternberg, filed January 28, 1987, *Frantz v. United States Powerlifting Case Records*, Stark Center for Physical Culture and Sports, University of Texas at Austin.

43. Conrad Cotter, Minutes of the Executive Committee meeting held via conference call on June 8, 1984, at 10:00 P.M. C.D.T., Judy Gedney Papers, Stark Center for Physical Culture and Sports, University of Texas at Austin.

44. Cotter, "Message from the President" (September 1984).

45. Sherman Antitrust Act of 1890, 15 U.S.C.S. § 1, et seq.

46. Cotter, "Message from the President" (September 1984).

47. Cotter to Bostrom, July 1, 1984.

48. Emphasis added. [Illegible] Elmore, "Disciplinary Committee of the I.P.F. held in Dallas, USA, November, 1984," Judy Gedney Papers, Stark Center for Physical Culture and Sports, University of Texas at Austin.

49. "Interview with Maris Sternberg by Eric Stone, 4/9/04."

50. Elmore, "Disciplinary Committee of the I.P.F. held in Dallas, USA, November, 1984."

51. Ibid.

52. "Interview with Maris Sternberg by Eric Stone, 4/9/04."

53. Affidavit of Plaintiff Maris Sternberg.

54. Ibid.

55. Nate Foster to Heinz Vierthaler, n.d.

56. Ibid.

57. "Interview with Maris Sternberg by Eric Stone, 4/9/04."

58. On this point, see *Frantz v. United States Powerlifting Federation* [Case 1], 2.

59. "Interview with Maris Sternberg by Eric Stone, 4/9/04."

60. Ernie Frantz to Conrad Cotter.

61. Ibid.

62. Ibid.

63. Ernie Frantz to Judy Gedney, February 25, 1985, Judy Gedney Papers, Stark Center for Physical Culture and Sports, University of Texas at Austin.

64. Ibid.

65. Judy Gedney to Ernie Frantz, March 4, 1985, Stark Center for Physical Culture and Sports, University of Texas at Austin.

66. Ibid.

67. Ibid.

68. Ibid.

69. Gedney's handwritten notes are found in Ernie Frantz to Judy Gedney.

70. "Interview with Maris Sternberg by Eric Stone, 4/9/04."

71. Ibid.

72. The following legal document details the dates on which legal documents were filed with the courts: Stephen L. Sulzer to Honorable H. Stuart Cunningham, February 16, 1987, *Frantz v. United States Powerlifting Federation* File, Stark Center for Physical Culture and Sports, University of Texas at Austin.

73. *Frantz v. United States Powerlifting Federation* [Case 1], 4.

74. Ibid.

75. "Judgment" for *Frantz v. United States Powerlifting Federation,* February 4, 1987, *Frantz v. United States Powerlifting Federation* case records, Stark Center for Physical Culture and Sports, University of Texas at Austin.

76. *Frantz v. United States Powerlifting Federation* [Case 1], 6.

77. Ibid., 14.

78. *Frantz v. United States Powerlifting Federation* [Case 2], 1064.

79. Ibid.

80. Ibid.

81. Ibid. It is worth noting here that the case's historical significance in the law rests on this narrow issue of appropriate attorneys' fees. The case has been cited on these grounds in 110 cases. See, for example, *Bay State Towing Co. v. Barge American*, 899 F.2d 129 (1st Cir. Mass. 1990), 133; *Cross & Cross Properties, Ltd. v. Everett Allied Co.*, 886 F.2d 497 (2d Cir. N.Y. 1989), 505.

82. See *Frantz v. United States Powerlifting Federation* [Case 3], 3.

83. Ibid., 9.

84. Conrad Cotter, "Message from the U.S.P.F. President [August 1985]," *Powerlifting USA* (August 1985): 29.

85. Conrad Cotter, "Message from the President [May 1986]," *Powerlifting USA* (May 1986): 31.

86. Conrad Cotter, "Message from the U.S.P.F. President [October 1987]," *Powerlifting USA* (October 1987): 36.

87. Ibid.

88. Ibid.

89. Mike Lambert, "What's Going On With USA Powerlifting?" *Powerlifting USA* (April 1997): 6–7, 90–91.

90. Ernie Frantz, "Message from the President of the American Powerlifting Federation in Rebuttal to the article in March 1988 *Powerlifting USA* from Conrad Cotter over the Lawsuit between the U.S.P.F., the A.P.F. and the I.P.F.," *Powerlifting USA* (May 1988): 50.

91. Michael W. Overdeer to Andrew Cominos, February 20, 1997, Stark Center for Physical Culture and Sports, ADPFA Unification with USPF (The Downhill Slide) folder, University of Texas at Austin.

92. Ibid.

93. Ernie Frantz online interview by Eric Stone, November 25, 2003, http://www.chicagopowerlifting.com/ErnieFrantzInterview.html (accessed August 5, 2013).

94. Ernie Frantz to Conrad Cotter.

95. "Interview with Maris Sternberg by Eric Stone, 4/9/04."

96. Ernie Frantz online interview by Eric Stone, November 25, 2003, http://www.chicagopowerlifting.com/ErnieFrantzInterview.html (accessed August 5, 2013).

97. "Interview with Maris Sternberg by Eric Stone, 4/9/04."

98. Daniel Wagman, Lewis Curry, and David Cook, "An Investigation into Anabolic Androgenic Steroid Use by Elite U.S. Powerlifters," *Journal of Strength and Conditioning Research* 9, no. 3 (1995): 153.

99. Telephone interview of Judith Gedney by Jan Todd, May 6, 2005.

100. Ibid.

101. J. Todd, "Chaos Can Have Gentle Beginnings," 9–10.

102. John J. MacAloon, "Doping and Moral Authority: Sport Organizations Today," in *Doping in Elite Sports: The Politics of Drugs in the Olympic Movement,* ed. Wilson and Derse, 210.

103. Todd and Todd, "Reflections on the 'Parallel Federation Solution' to the Problem of Drug Use in Sport," 59.

Section III: The Impact of Sport on Law

1. 400 N.Y.S. 2d 267 (1977).

2. For the purposes of this essay, transsexual refers to individuals who have used medical means (hormones and/or surgery) to physically change their sex. Transgender refers to those individuals whose gender identity does not match their biological sex but who have not yet taken medical steps to change their body.

3. 419 U.S. 522 (1975).

4. 405 U.S. 438 (1972).

5. John Gaudiosi, "EA Sports Exec Says NFL Lockout Has Been Good for Its NCAA Football Franchise," *Forbes,* May 2, 2011.

Chapter Eight: Thirty-Five Years after *Richards v. USTA*

1. "IAAF Urges Caution Over Semenya Intersex Claims," *CNN.com,* September 11, 2009, http://www.cnn.com/2009/SPORT/09/11/athletics.semenya.gender.iaaf/index.html (accessed November 17, 2011).

2. Richard Williams, "Oscar Pistorius and Caster Semenya's Running Battle to Reach Starting Blocks," *The Guardian,* August 26, 2011, http://www.guardian.co.uk/sport/2011/aug/26/oscar-pistorius-caster-semenya-athletics (accessed December 13, 2011).

3. Jim Buzinski and Cyd Zeigler, "The Outsports Revolution," 2007, 156–57; Martin Blake, "Transsexual Set to Claim European Tour Card," *The Age,* November 3, 2004, http://www.theage.com.au/news/Golf/Transsexual-set-to-claim-European-tour-card/2004/11/02/1099362143207.html (accessed December 13, 2011).

4. "Has Transsexuality in Football Turned a Corner?" http://www.kickitout.org/1264.php (accessed December 13, 2011).

5. James Achenbach, "Ladies Tees? Long Drive Champ Used to Be a Man,"*Golfweek.com,* December 22, 2008, http://redout.org/ipb/index.php/topic/35374-wtf-ladies-long-drive-champ-used-to-be-a-man/ (accessed August 5, 2013).

6. Mike Fish, "A Level Playing Field? Transgender Athletes Pose New Questions about Competition," *SI.com,* June 24, 2003, http://sportsillustrated.cnn.com/inside_game/mike_fish/news/2003/06/24/fish_dumaresq/ (accessed November 17, 2011).

7. Stan Grossfeld, "After Years of Torment, Bates All-American Godsey Makes a Difficult Gender Self-Identification Decision," *Boston Globe,* March 3, 2006, http://www.boston.com/sports/colleges/articles/2006/03/03/addressing_issue/ (accessed December 13, 2011).

8. Frederick Dreier, "For Transgender Triathlete, a Top Finish in New York Is Secondary," *New York Times,* August 5, 2010, http://www.nytimes.com/2011/08/06/sports/for-transgender-triathlete-a-top-finish-is-secondary.html?_r=1 (accessed December 13, 2011).

9. Erik Brady, "Transgender male Kye Allums·on the Women's Team at GW," USA Today, November 4, 2010, http://www.usatoday.com/sports/collegewomens basketball/atlantic10/2010-11-03-kye-allums-george-washington-transgender_N. htm (accessed December 13, 2011).

10. Patrick Letellier, "*Transgender* News Update," *Lesbian News* 34, no. 3 (October 2008): 15.

11. Cyd Zeigler, "Video: ESPN Profiles Kye Allums," *Outsports,* http://outsports.com/jocktalkblog/2011/04/04/video-espn-profiles-kye-allums/ (accessed December 13, 2011).

12. Jim Morris, "Transgendered Racer Insulted; Second-Place Finisher Wears T-shirt '100 Per Cent Pure Woman Champ,'" *The Spectator (Hamilton, Ont.),* August 3, 2006.

13. Transgender Law Center, *Advancements in State and Federal Law Regarding Transgender Employees,* http://transgenderlawcenter.org/pdf/Advancements in State and Federal Law Regarding California Transgender Employees.pdf (accessed November 17, 2011).

14. Transgender Law Center, *Advancements in State and Federal Law Regarding Transgender Employees,* http://transgenderlawcenter.org/pdf/Advancements in State and Federal Law Regarding California Transgender Employees.pdf (accessed November 17, 2011).

15. Tarynn M. Witten and A. E. Eyler, "Hate Crimes and Violence Against the Transgendered," *Peace Review* 11, no. 3 (1999): 463–64.

16. Human Rights Campaign, "Transgender Population and Number of Transgender Employees," http://2fwww.hrc.org/issues/9598.htm (accessed November 17, 2011).

17. Witten and Eyler, "Hate Crimes," 463–64.

18. Tarynn M. Witten and Jeremy D. Kidd, "Transgender and Trans Sexual Identities: The Next Strange Fruit—Hate Crimes, Violence and Genocide Against the Global Trans-Communities," *Journal of Hate Studies* 6, no. 1 (2007/2008): 33.

19. National Collegiate Athletic Association, "Current NCAA Position Regarding Transgender Student-Athlete Participation and Resource List," May 18, 2007, http://www.athleticbusiness.com/articles/article.aspx?articleid=1817& zoneid=3 (accessed November 17, 2011).

20. Kay Brown, "20th Century Transgender History and Experience," *San Francisco; Harvey Milk Institute,* December 10, 1999, located on *Human Rights Campaign,* "How Do Transgender People Suffer from Discrimination?" http://www.ncavp.org/common/document_files/Reports/2008 HV Report smaller file.pdf (accessed November 17, 2011). Bloggers and activists have criticized the use of this incidence statistic as misleading. Daran, "Are Transgender People Over a Thousand

Times More Likely to Be Murdered than the Cisgendered?" *Feminist Critics,* 2008, http://www.feministcritics.org/blog/2008/08/24/are-transgender-people-over-a-thousand-times-more-likely-to-be-murdered-than-the-cisgendered/ (accessed December 13, 2011).

21. California Safe Schools Coalition, "Safe Place to Learn: Consequences of Harassment Based on Actual or Perceived Sexual Orientation and Gender Non-Conformity and Steps for Making Schools Safer," University of California, Davis (2004): 16, http://www.casafeschools.org/SafePlacetoLearnLow.pdf (accessed November 17, 2011). S. T. Russell, J. K. McGuire, R. Toomey, and C. R. Anderson, "Gender Non-conformity and School Safety: Documenting the Problem and Steps Schools Can Take," *California Safe Schools Coalition Research Brief No. 12.* San Francisco, CA: California Safe Schools Coalition, 2010, http://www.casafeschools.org/getfacts.html (accessed December 13, 2011).

22. Gay, Lesbian and Straight Education Network, "National School Climate Survey," 2001, http://www.glsen.org/binary-dataGLSEN_ATTACHMENTS/file/185-1.pdf (accessed August 10, 2009).

23. Jaime M. Grant et al., *Injustice at Every Turn: A Report of the National Transgender Discrimination Survey* (Washington, DC: National Center for Transgender Equality and National Gay and Lesbian Task Force, 2011), 11, http://www.thetaskforce.org/reports_and_research/ntds (accessed December 14, 2011).

24. Angela Lumpkin, "Sport as a Reflection of Society," *Phi Kappa Phi Forum* 88, no. 4 (2008): 34.

25. Jan Boxill, "Introduction: The Moral Significance of Sport," *Sports Ethics: An Anthology*, ed. Jan Boxill (Malden, MA: Blackwell Publishing, 2003), 1.

26. Pat Griffin, "Inclusion of Transgender Athletes on Sports Teams," *It Takes a Team! Women's Sports Foundation*, 2008, reprinted at http://www.transgenderlaw.org/resources/Griffinarticle.pdf (accessed August 17, 2013).

27. *Richards v. USTA*, 400 N.Y.S. 2d 267 (1977).

28. Judith S. Baughman ed., et al., "Introduction," *American Decades*, 7, *1960–1969* (Detroit: Gale, 2001), *Gale U.S. History in Context*, http://www.gale.cengage.com/InContext/hist_us.htm (accessed March 25, 2012).

29. Baughman, "Introduction"; Stephen Tuck, "Introduction: Reconsidering the 1970s–the 1960s to a Disco Beat?," *Journal of Contemporary History* 43, no. 4 (October 2008): 617–20.

30. Baughman, "Introduction."

31. Carol Brennan, ed., et al., "The Gay Rights Movement," *American Social Reform Movements Reference Library,* 1, *Almanac* (Detroit: UXL, 2007): 191–218, *Gale U.S. History in Context,* http://www.gale.cengage.com/InContext/hist_us.htm (accessed March 25, 2012).

32. Carol Andreas, Katherine Culkin, and Joan D. Mandle, "Women's Rights Movement," *Dictionary of American History*, ed. Stanley I. Kutler, 3rd ed., vol. 8 (New York: Charles Scribner's Sons, 2003), 512–19, *Gale U.S. History in Context* http://www.gale.cengage.com/InContext/hist_us.htm (accessed March 25, 2012).

33. Ibid., 191–218.

34. Donna Alvah, "Civil Rights Movement," *Dictionary of American History*, ed. Stanley I. Kutler, 3rd ed., vol. 2 (New York: Charles Scribner's Sons, 2003): 200–206.

35. Ibid.

36. Brennan et al., "The Gay Rights Movement."

37. Ibid.

38. Ibid.

39. Andreas, Culkin, and Mandle, "Women's Rights Movement."

40. Ibid.

41. Steven A. Riess, "Sports," *Dictionary of American History*, ed. Stanley I. Kutler, 3rd ed., 7 (New York: Charles Scribner's Sons, 2003): 507–12, *Gale U.S. History in Context* http://www.gale.cengage.com/InContext/hist_us.htm (accessed March 25, 2012).

42. Ibid.

43. Ami Walsh, "2 Black and White Photographs," *A Tour of Their Own Tennis* 35, no. 9 (November 1999): 30.

44. Ibid.

45. Lindsay Parks Pieper, "Mixed Doubles: Renée Richards and the Perpetuation of the Gender Binary in Athletics" (MA diss., Ohio State University, 2010).

46. *Boys Don't Cry*, directed by Kimberly Peirce, Fox Searchlight Pictures, 1999.

47. *Transamerica*, directed by Duncan Tucker, Weinstein Co., 2005.

48. Michael Giltz, "Second Set," *Advocate*, March 27, 2007, 47.

49. Renée Richards and John Ames, *Second Serve: The Renée Richards Story* (Briarcliff Manor, NY: Stein and Day Publishers, 1983), 1–19.

50. Ibid., 19–23.

51. Ibid., 39.

52. Giltz, "Second Set," 47.

53. Richards and Ames, *Second Serve*.

54. Ibid., 61–76.

55. Ibid., 117–50.

56. Ibid., 210.

57. Ibid., 259–70.

58. Ibid., 272.

59. Ibid., 301.

60. Ibid., 314–20.

61. Ibid., 324.

62. Ibid., 324–49.

63. Jill Pilgrim, David Martin, and Will Binder, "Far from the Finish Line: Transsexualism and Athletic Competition," *Fordham Intellectual Property, Media & Entertainment Law Journal* 13 (Winter 2003): 513.

64. *Richards*, 400 N.Y.S. 2d at 268.

65. Ibid.

66. Ibid.

67. N.Y. Exec. Law § 290(3); N.Y. Exec Law § 296(1)(a).

68. *Richards*, 400 N.Y.S. 2d at 268.

69. Ibid.

70. Ibid.

71. Ibid., 269.

72. Ibid., 269.

73. Ibid., 269.

74. Ibid., 270.

75. Ibid., 270–71.

76. Ibid., 271.

77. Ibid., 271–72.

78. Ibid., 272.

79. Ibid., 273.

80. Ibid., 268.

81. Ibid., 273.

82. Ibid., 273.

83. Renée Richards, interview with Lindsay Parks Pieper, July 9, 2009, oral interview for *Renée*, directed by Eric Drath, Live Star Entertainment, 2011.

84. Lindsay P. Pieper, "Gender Regulation: Renée Richards Revisited," *International Journal of the History of Sport* 29, no. 5 (2012): 675–90.

85. Ibid., 683.

86. Richards and Ames, *Second Serve*.

87. Renée Richards and John Ames, *No Way Renée: The Second Half of My Notorious Life* (New York: Simon and Schuster, 2007), 2–3.

88. Richards and Ames, *Second Serve,* 299–300.

89. Pieper, "Mixed Doubles," 71; *Renée*, directed by Drath.

90. Giltz, "Second Set," 47; Belinda Goldsmith, "Transsexual Pioneer Renée Richards Regrets Fame," *Reuters News*, February 18, 2007, http://www.nytimes.com/2007/02/01/garden/01renee.html (accessed August 1, 2013); *Renée*, directed by Drath; Pieper, "Mixed Doubles."

91. Pieper, "Mixed Doubles."

92. Ibid., 58–59.

93. Giltz, "Second Set," 48.

94. Sarah Netter, "Transgender Golfer Lana Lawless Sues LPGA for Right to Compete," *ABC News,* October 14, 2010, http://abcnews.go.com/US/transgender-golfer-lana-lawless-sues-lpga-compete/story?id=11881508 (accessed December 13, 2011); Douglas Robson, "Lana Lawless' Suit Puts Gender in Sports in Spotlight Again," *USA Today,* November 30, 2010, http://www.usatoday.com/sports/2010-11-29-1 ana-lawless-lpga-transgender_N.htm (accessed December 13, 2011).

95. "Joint Statement by Lana Lawless and the LPGA," *PRWEB*, May 3, 2011, http://www.prweb.com/releases/2011/5/prweb8374477.htm (accessed December 13, 2011).

96. 42 U.S.C. § 2000e-2(a).

97. *Ulane v. Eastern Airlines, Inc.*, 742 F. 2d 1081 (7th Cir. 1984), *cert. denied*, 471 U.S. 1017 (1985); Transgender Law Center, *Advancements in State and Federal Law.* Please refer to the section titled "Background."

98. *Price Waterhouse v. Hopkins*, 490 U.S. 228 (1989); *Schwenk v. Hartford,* 204 F3d 1187 (9th Cir. 2000); *Smith v. City of Salem, Ohio* 2004 WL 1745840 (6th Cir. August 5, 2004); *Schroer v. Billington*, 2009 U.S. Dist. LEXIS 43903 (D.D.C., April 28, 2009); Transgender Law Center, *Advancements in State and Federal Law.* Please refer to the section titled "Background."

99. Tanya A. DeVos, "Tenth Annual Review of Gender and Sexuality Law: Employment Law Chapter: Sexuality and Transgender Issues in Employment Law," *Georgetown Journal of Gender and Law* 10 (2000): 624.

100. US Const. amend. XIV, 1; Pilgrim, Martin, and Binder, "Far from the Finish Line," 540.

101. U.S. Const. amend. XIV, § 2.

102. 16B American Jurisprudence 2d Constitutional Law § 814.

103. Pilgrim, Martin, and Binder, "Far from the Finish Line," 495, 541–42; Erin E. Buzuvis, "Transgender Student Athletes and Sex Segregate Sport: Developing Policies of Inclusion for Intercollegiate and Interscholastic Athletics," *Seton Hall J. Sports & Entertainment Law* 21 (2011): 30.

104. Buzuvis, "Transgender Student Athletes," 31.

105. Ibid., 32; *Price Waterhouse v. Hopkins*, 490 U.S. 228 (1989).

106. Buzuvis, "Transgender Student Athletes," 32; *Glenn v. Bumby*, No. 1:08-CV-2360-RWS, 2010 WL 2674413, at 16 (M.D. Ga. July 2, 2010).

107. Buzuvis, "Transgender Student Athletes," 32.

108. 20 U.S.C. 1681-1688 (2000).

109. *Montgomery v. Indep. School Dist.*, 109 F. Supp. 2d 1083, 1090–1093 (D. Minn. 2000); *Theno v. Tonganoxie Unified School District No. 464*, 377 F. Supp. 2d 952, 964 (D. Kan. 2005).

110. Leena D. Phadke, "When Women Aren't Women and Men Aren't Men: The Problem of Transgender Sex Discrimination under Title IX," *University of Kansas Law Review* 54 (2006): 850; Boaz I. Green, "Discussion and Expression of Gender and Sexuality in Schools," *Georgetown Journal of Gender and Law* 5 (2004): 329, 335–36.

111. Women's Sports Foundation, "Participation of Transgender Athletes in Women's Sports: A Women's Sports Foundation Position Paper," 2008, http://www.womenssportsfoundation.org/en/sitecore/content/home/advocate/title-ix-and-issues/title-ix-positions/participation_of_transgender_athletes.aspx (accessed August 17, 2013).

112. DeVos, "Tenth Annual Review," 611.

113. Ibid.

114. National Gay and Lesbian Task Force, "State Nondiscrimination Laws in the US," May 21, 2014, http://www.thetaskforce.org/downloads/reports/issue_maps/non_discrimination_5_14_color.pdf (accessed May 26, 2014).

115. National Gay and Lesbian Task Force, "Jurisdictions with Explicitly Transgender-Inclusive Nondiscrimination Laws," June 11, 2012, http://www.thetaskforce.org/reports_and_research/all_jurisdictions (accessed August 1, 2012). A growing number of states have enacted legislation explicitly prohibiting discrimination based on gender identity/expression: California, Colorado, Connecticut, Hawaii, Illinois, Iowa, Maine, Massachusetts, Minnesota, New Jersey, New Mexico, Nevada, Oregon, Rhode Island, Vermont, Washington, and the District of Columbia.

116. National Gay and Lesbian Task Force, "Jurisdictions with Explicitly Transgender-Inclusive Nondiscrimination Laws."

117. Human Rights Campaign, "State Hate Crimes Laws," June 19, 2013, http://hrc-assets.s3-website-us-east-1.amazonaws.com//files/assets/resources/hate_crimes_laws_022014.pdf (accessed May 26, 2014).

118. Buzuvis, "Transgender Student Athletes," 33; D.C. Code § 2-1402.41 (2010) (education); see also Iowa Code Ann. § 216.9 (West 2010) (education); Maine Revised Statutes Annotated title 5, § 4601 (2010) (education). Several

additional states are currently pursuing comparable laws. Many educational institutions themselves prohibit discrimination on the basis of gender identity and expression. *Transgender Law & Policy Institute*, http://www.transgenderlaw.org/college/index.htm#policies (accessed December 14, 2011) (identifying 416 colleges and universities that do so).

119. Philip M. Berkowitz, "Employment Law Post-Summer Roundup: Court Rulings, Legislative Proposals," *New York Law Journal*, September 13, 2007, 5.

120. Declaratory Ruling on Behalf of John/Jane Doe (Conn. Human Rights Commission 2000); *Lie v. Sky Publishing Corp.*, 15 *Massachusetts Law Reporter* 412, 2002 WL 31492397 (Mass. Super. 2002); *Enriquez v. West Jersey Health Systems*, 342 N.J. Super. 501, 777 A.2d 365 (N.J. Super.), *cert. denied,* 170 N.J. 211, 785 A.2d 439 (N.J. 2001); *Maffei v. Kolaeton Industry, Inc.*, 626 N.Y.S. 2d 391 (N.Y. Sup. Ct. 1995); *Rentos v. OCE-Office Systems*, 1996 U.S. Dist. LEXIS 19060 (S.D.N.Y. 1996); Transgender Law Center, *"Advancements in State and Federal Law.* Please refer to the section titled "Background."

121. See Americans with Disabilities Act of 1990, 42 U.S.C.A. § 12101-02; *Smith v. City of Jacksonville Corr. Inst.*, Fla. Human Relations Commission, No. 88-5451 (1992); Enriquez v. W. Jersey Health Systems, 777 A.2d 365, 376 (N.J. 2001).

122. *Summer v. Iowa Civil Rights Commission*, 337 N.W.2d 470, 477 (Iowa 1983).

123. Interesting questions arise concerning who gets to create the definitions of male and female athletes and who creates the criteria to determine eligibility. Authors have addressed these questions and the history of defining gender in sports. See Lindsay P. Pieper, "Policing Womanhood: The International Olympic Committee, Sex Testing and the Maintenance of White Hetero-Femininity, 1968–2000" (PhD diss., Ohio State University, 2013); Sarah Teetzel, "Rules and Reform: Eligibility, Gender Differences, and the Olympic Games." *Sport in Society* 14, no. 3 (2011): 386–98.

124. "Pat Griffin's comment," on "Washington Interscholastic Activities Association Policy on Transgender High School Athletes," *Pat Griffin LBGT Sport Blog*, June 10, 2008, http://ittakesateam.blogspot.com/2008/06/washington-state-adopts-policy-on.html (accessed November 17, 2011).

125. International Olympic Committee Medical Commission, "Statement of the Stockholm Consensus on Sex Reassignment in Sports," October 28, 2003, http://www.olympic.org/Documents/Reports/EN/en_report_905.pdf (accessed June 10, 2013).

126. Ibid.

127. United States Golf Association, "Gender Policy for the United States Golf Association," 2005, http://www.usga.org/championships/transgendered/ (accessed August 14, 2013); *USA Track & Field*, "Policy on Transgender and Transsexual Athletes," February 27, 2005, http://www.usatf.org/about/policies/transgender AndTranssexualAthletes/ (accessed November 17, 2011).

128. Griffin, "Inclusion of Transgender Athletes."

129. Buzuvis, "Transgender Student Athletes," 22.

130. Keith Daniel, "Transgender Policy," *The FA.com*, March 7, 2007, http://www.thefa.com/TheFA/WhoWeAre/NewsAndFeatures/2007/TransgenderTranssexual (accessed December 13, 2007).

131. Griffin, "Inclusion of Transgender Athletes"; World Out Games, "Gender Identity Policy," *Gay and Lesbian International Sport Association*, 2009, http://woga2013.org/?PageId=105 (accessed November 17, 2011).

132. "Current NCAA Position Regarding Transgender Student-Athlete Participation & Resource List," *Transgender Law & Policy Institute*, http://www.transgenderlaw.org/resources/NCAA_Policy.pdf (accessed December 13, 2011).

133. Griffin, "Inclusion of Transgender Athletes."

134. Marta Lawrence, "Transgender Policy Approved," *National Collegiate Athletic Association,* September 13, 2011, http://www.ncaa.org/wps/wcm/connect/public/NCAA/Resources/Latest+News/2011/September/Transgender+policy+approved (accessed December 13, 2011).

135. Athletic Management, "Tackling Transgender Issues," February/March 2008, http://www.athleticmanagement.com/2008/03/04/tackling_transgender_issues/index.php. (accessed November 17, 2011).

136. Laura Onstot, "Shoulder Pads, Pom-Poms, and the Angry Inch," *Seattle Weekly*, October 16, 2007.

137. "Pat Griffin's Comment"; *Washington Interscholastic Activities Association Handbook*, "Student Standards for Interscholastic Eligibility," Washington Interscholastic Activities Association, 2008, 40–41, http://www.wiaa.com/ConDocs/Con951/Handbook%20(Web).pdf (accessed November 17, 2011); Washington Interscholastic Athletic Association, 2010–2011 Official Handbook 18.15.0, http://www.wiaa.com/ConDocs/Con358/Eligibility.pdf; Buzuvis, "Transgender Student Athletes," 26.

138. Buzuvis, "Transgender Student Athletes," 26.

139. Searches for policies on transgender eligibility from the National Football League, National Basketball League, Major League Soccer, Major League Baseball, National Hockey League, Women's Professional Soccer, Women's National Basketball League, National Pro Fastpitch (women's softball), and NASCAR revealed no results.

140. "Monica Roberts Comment," on "Transgender Athletes Get Into Game," *TransGriot Blog*, June 24, 2007, http://transgriot.blogspot.com/2007/06/transgender-athletes-get-into-game.html (accessed November 17, 2011); Rona Marech, "Debate Rages on the Fairness of New Inclusion Rule," *San Francisco Chronicle*, June 14, 2004, http://www.sfgate.com/cgi-bin/article.cgi?file=/c/a/2004/06/14/MNGNM75MUK1.DTL#ixzz0OYsEb8Pn (accessed November 17, 2011); "Pat Griffin's Comment."

141. Shawn M. Crincoli, "You Can Only Race if You Can't Win? The Curious Cases of Oscar Pistorius & Caster Semenya," *Texas Review of Entertainment and Sports Law* 12 (2011): 176.

142. *Romer v. Evans*, 517 U.S. 620, 635 (1996).

143. DeVos, "Tenth Annual Review," 610.

144. Ibid., 624; National Gay and Lesbian Task Force, "Transgender-Inclusive Nondiscrimination Laws."

145. Refer to notes 4–14 and text of introduction.

146. Dean Spade, "Elimination of Bias: Transformation," *Los Angeles Lawyer* 31 (2008): 34.

147. Dean Spade, "Intersections of Transgender Lives and the Law: Trans Law & Politics on a Neoliberal Landscape," *Temple Political & Civil Rights Law Review* 18 (2009): 355.

148. H.R. 1397: *Employment Non-Discrimination Act of 2011*, http://thomas. loc.gov/cgi-bin/bdquery/D?d112:2:./temp/~bdxjek:@@@L&summ2=m&l/home/ LegislativeData.php?n=BSS;c=112| (accessed December 14, 2011).

149. Pat Griffin and Helen Carroll, "On the Team: Equal Opportunity for Transgender Student-Athletes" (National Center for Lesbian Rights and It Takes A Team!, an Initiative of Women's Sports Foundation, 2009), 22–23.

150. Ibid., 24–26.

151. Ibid., 28.

152. Buzuvis, "Transgender Student Athletes," 35–50.

153. Ibid., 56–58.

154. Women's Sports Foundation, "Participation of Transgender Athletes in Women's Sports."

155. Ibid., 3; Griffin and Carroll, "On the Team," 31–32.

156. Ironically, Richards herself has indicated she regrets fighting for the opportunity to play and has not supported subsequent trans athletes who have continued the battle. Pieper, "Gender Regulation: Renée Richards Revisited," 675–90.

Chapter Nine: "Clean Up the Abuses"

1. *Ballplayer: Pelotero*, directed by Ross Finkel, Jon Paley, and Trevor Martin, Makuhari Media in association with Guagua Productions and Endeavor Films, 2011.

2. Nick Carfado, "MLB Officials React to Bobby Valentine Documentary," *Boston Globe*, July 10, 2012, http://www.boston.com/sports/baseball/redsox/extras/ extra_bases/2012/07/mlb_officials_r.html (accessed June 17, 2013).

3. See Arturo J. Marcano and David P. Fidler, "The Globalization of Baseball: Major League Baseball and the Mistreatment of Latin American Baseball Talent," *Indiana Journal of Global Legal Studies* 6 (1999): 511–77; *Stealing Lives: The Globalization of Baseball and the Tragic Story of Alexis Quiroz* (Bloomington: Indiana University Press, 2002); "Worldwide Draft," BaseballGuru.com, 2003, http:// baseballguru.com/articles/analysismarcano01.html (accessed June 17, 2013); "Baseball's Exploitation of Latin Talent," *North American Congress of Latin America Report on the Americas* (March/April 2004), http://www.nacla.org (accessed June 17, 2013); "Fighting Baseball Doping in Latin America: A Critical Analysis of Major League Baseball's Drug Prevention and Treatment Program in the Dominican Republic and Venezuela," *University of Miami International and Comparative Law Review* 15 (2007): 107–201; "Global Baseball: Latin America," in *The Cambridge Companion to Baseball,* ed. Leonard Cassuto and Stephen Partridge (Cambridge: Cambridge University Press, 2011), 171–84; and *"Ballplayer: Pelotero*—Major League Baseball, Human Rights, and the Globalization of Baseball," American Society of International Law Insight, August 22, 2012, http://www.asil.org/ insights120822.cfm (accessed June 17, 2013).

4. Yogi Berra, *The Yogi Book* (New York: Workman Publishing, 1998), 45.

5. See Brian Z. Tamanaha, *On the Rule of Law: History, Politics, Theory* (Cambridge: Cambridge University Press, 2004).

6. Jane Stromseth, David Wippman, and Rosa Brooks, *Can Might Make Rights? Building the Rule of Law after Military Interventions* (Cambridge: Cambridge University Press, 2006), 310.

7. See in this volume Samuel O. Regalado, "*Clay, aka Ali v. U.S.* (1971): Muhammad Ali, Precedent, and the Burger Court"; Sarah K. Fields, "Odd Bedfellows: Spencer Haywood and Justice William O. Douglas"; and Richard C. Crepeau, "The *Flood* Case (1972)."

8. All quotes and facts related to *Ballplayer: Pelotero* are taken from the documentary film.

9. As of May 2014, Sanó was still with the Minnesota Twins and considered one of its top prospects, but he had "Tommy John" surgery in March 2014 on his right elbow. Enrique Rojas, "Miguel Sanó: Surgery 'Went Well,'" ESPN.com, March 13, 2014, http://espn.go.com/mlb/story/_/id/10601611/miguel-sano-minnesota-twins-optimistic-return-surgery (accessed May 24, 2014).

10. During the 2013 season, Batista played rookie ball for the Houston Astros in the Gulf Coast League and Class A (Advanced) minor league ball for the Astros' affiliate the Lancaster JetHawks in the California League. As of May 2014, Batista was playing for the Douglas Diablos of the independent Pecos League. Jean Batista, Baseball Reference.com, http://www.baseball-reference.com/minors/player.cgi?id=batist002jea (accessed May 24, 2014).

11. Joe Morgenstern, "Ballplayer: Pelotero," *Wall Street Journal*, July 12, 2012, http://online.wsj.com/article/SB10001424052702303740704577521240098800540.html (accessed June 17, 2013).

12. Neil Genzlinger, "Baseball Dreams and Schemes: '*Ballplayer: Pelotero,'* Baseball Scouting in the Dominican Republic," *New York Times*, July 12, 2012, http://movies.nytimes.com/2012/07/13/movies/ballplayer-pelotero-baseball-scouting-in-the-dominican-republic.html (accessed June 17, 2013).

13. Kenneth Turan, "*Ballplayer: Pelotero* Takes a Damning Look at System," *Los Angeles Times*, July 12, 2012, http://www.latimes.com/entertainment/movies/moviesnow/la-et-mn-ballplayer-pelotero–20120713,0,7544531.story (accessed June 17, 2013).

14. Frank Scheck, "*Ballplayer: Pelotero*: Film Review," *Hollywood Reporter*, July 12, 2012, http://www.hollywoodreporter.com/review/ballplayer-pelotero-film-review-348545 (accessed June 17, 2013).

15. V. A. Musetto, "*Ballplayer: Pelotero*—Movie Review," *New York Post*, July 12, 2012, http://www.nypost.com/p/entertainment/movies/beisbol_doc_hits_solid_triple_yaAwoeqVAvXOFMegJTo4CP (accessed June 17, 2013).

16. Peter Hartlaub, "*Ballplayer: Pelotero* Review: Dominican Hopefuls," *San Francisco Chronicle*, July 12, 2012, http://www.sfgate.com/movies/article/Ballplayer-Pelotero-review-Dominican-hopefuls-3702990.php (accessed June 17, 2013).

17. Chuck Bowen, "*Ballplayer: Pelotero*," *Slant Magazine*, July 11, 2012, http://www.slantmagazine.com/film/review/ballplayer-pelotero/6390 (accessed June 17, 2013).

18. Andrew O'Heihir, "Inside the Secret World of Dominican Baseball," Salon.com, July 10, 2012, http://www.salon.com/2012/07/10/inside_the_secret_world_of_dominican_baseball/ (accessed June 17, 2013).

19. Under international human rights law, persons under eighteen years of age are considered children who require heightened care and protection. See Convention on the Rights of the Child, November 20, 1989, 1577 *United Nations Treaty Series* 3. For our arguments that MLB's operations in Latin American

countries violated the human rights of children, see Marcano and Fidler, "The Globalization of Baseball: Major League Baseball and the Mistreatment of Latin American Baseball Talent," 511–77 and *Stealing Lives,* especially, 171–82.

20. Stromseth, Wippman, and Brooks, *Can Might Make Rights?,* 78–79.

21. Marcano and Fidler, *Stealing Lives,* especially 30–49 (describing the MLB free agency system in Latin America).

22. Memorandum from Sandy Alderson to Commissioner Selig and Bob DuPuy concerning the Dominican Republic Committee, September 23, 2009 [Alderson Report], 1.

23. Ibid.

24. Rob Ruck, "Baseball's Recruitment Abuses," *Americas Quarterly*, July 14, 2011, http://americasquarterly.org/node/2745 (accessed June 17, 2013).

25. Melissa Segura, "Drafted at 13, How One Player Changed International Signing Rules," Sports Illustrated.com, July 2, 2012, http://sportsillustrated.cnn.com/2012/writers/melissa_segura/07/02/jimy-kelly/index.html (accessed June 17, 2013).

26. On MLB teams' violations of the age rule at this time, see Marcano and Fidler, *Stealing Lives,* 31–36.

27. See ibid., 41–44, on the contract translation issue and 181 on the requirement for teams to provide Spanish–language versions of contracts.

28. Marcano and Fidler, "Global Baseball: Latin America," 178–79.

29. For description and analysis, see Marcano and Fidler, "Fighting Baseball Doping in Latin America."

30. Alderson Report, 7.

31. Melissa Segura, "When Signing a Dominican Prospect, It's Buyer Beware," Sports Illustrated.com, March 3, 2009, http://sportsillustrated.cnn.com/2009/writers/melissa_segura/03/02/dr.investigators/ (accessed June 17, 2013).

32. Ibid.

33. Marcano and Fidler, "Global Baseball: Latin America," 179–80.

34. Jonathan Mahler, "From Jackie Robinson to Dead Silence," *New York Times*, June 18, 2011, D1.

35. The list includes problems with use of performance-enhancing drugs, which was not an issue in *Ballplayer: Pelotero*. For a recent exposé of this continuing problem with MLB operations in Latin America, see Nick Purdon, "Baseball Dreams," The National (Canadian Broadcasting Corporation), May 20, 2013, http://www.cbc.ca/player/News/TV%20Shows/The%20National/ID/2386426775/ (accessed June 17, 2013). *Ballplayer: Pelotero* also did not address problems with MLB facilities in the Dominican Republic having certified trainers on staff to deal with player health issues. On this problem, see Ian Gordon, "Inside Major League Baseball's Dominican Sweatshop System," *Mother Jones,* March 4, 2013, http://www.motherjones.com/politics/2013/03/baseball-dominican-system-yewri-guillen (accessed June 17, 2013) (reporting on the death from a treatable disease of a Dominican prospect at the Washington Nationals' Dominican academy).

36. Alderson Report, 1.

37. William B. Gould IV, *Bargaining with Baseball: Labor Relations in an Age of Prosperous Turmoil* (Jefferson, NC: McFarland, 2011), 258.

38. Alderson Report, 8.

39. Steve Fainaru, "The Business of Building Ballplayers," *Washington Post,* June

17, 2001, A01 (reporting on abuses associated with MLB's use of *buscones*).

40. Alderson Report, 2.

41. Ibid., 8.

42. Mike Ozanian, "The Business of Baseball 2012," Forbes.com, March 21, 2012, http://www.forbes.com/sites/mikeozanian/2012/03/21/the-business-of-baseball-2012/ (accessed June 17, 2013).

43. Fainaru, "The Business of Building Ballplayers," A01 (noting in connection with *buscones* that MLB "decries the abuses but effectively created the system that fosters them").

44. Ibid., 10.

45. Quoted in Jeff Passan, "Alderson Addresses Dominican Corruption," Yahoo! Sports, April 22, 2010, http://sports.yahoo.com/mlb/news?slug=jp-dominican042210 (accessed June 17, 2013).

46. Melissa Segura, "MLB Fires Top Latin American Exec Ronaldo Peralta," Sports Illustrated.com, March 10, 2010, http://sportsillustrated.cnn.com/2010/baseball/mlb/03/10/mlb.exec.ousted/index.html (accessed June 17, 2013).

47. Alderson Report, 13.

48. Quoted in ESPN, "MLB Addresses Identity Fraud Problem," *Outside the Lines*, March 8, 2012, http://espn.go.com/video/clip?id=7659920 (accessed June 17, 2013).

49. Quoted in Jesse Sanchez, "Venezuela Next Target for Clean–Up: MLB Pushing for Guidelines to be Followed in Latin America," MLB.com, May 13, 2010, http://mlb.mlb.com/news/article.jsp?ymd=20100513&content_id=10017300&vkey=news_mlb&fext=.jsp&c_id=mlb (accessed June 17, 2013).

50. Quoted in Passan, "Alderson Addresses Dominican Corruption."

51. Alderson Report, 12.

52. Marcano and Fidler, "Global Baseball: Latin America," 182.

53. Basic Agreement 2012–2016 between Major League Baseball and the Major League Baseball Players Association, December 12, 2011.

54. Basic Agreement 2003–2006 between Major League Baseball and the Major League Baseball Players Association, September 22, 2002, 202–4.

55. Basic Agreement 2012–2016, Attachment 46: International Amateur Talent, 265–76.

56. For example, for exceeding its signing bonus limit during the 2012 signing season, the Tampa Bay Rays "will be the first team to face the harshest penalties for exceeding their bonus pool[.]" Ben Badler, "International Review: Tampa Bay Rays," Baseball America.com, February 11, 2013, http://www.baseballamerica.com/today/prospects/international-affairs/2013/2614691.html (accessed June 17, 2013).

57. Basic Agreement 2012–2016, 265.

58. Ibid., 275.

59. Ben Badler, "MLB Slashes Money for International Players While Draft Bonus Pools Rise," Baseball America.com, April 14, 2014, http://www.baseballamerica.com/international/mlb-slashes-money-for-international-players-while-draft-bonus-pools-rise/ (accessed May 24, 2014).

60. Jesse Sanchez, "Allotment for International Signings Vital to Clubs," MLB.com, April 30, 2013, http://mlb.mlb.com/news/article.jsp?ymd=20130430&content_id=46192310&vkey=news_mlb&c_id=mlb (accessed June 17, 2013).

61. Ben Badler, "Trainer Frustration Grows Over Possible International Draft,"

Baseball America.com, May 30, 2013, http://www.baseballamerica.com/international/trainer-frustration-grows-over-possible-international-draft/ (accessed June 17, 2013).

62. Quoted in Ben Badler, "International Draft Raises Job Security Concerns Among Scouts," Baseball America.com, May 28, 2013, http://www.baseballamerica.com/international/international-draft-raises-job-security-concerns-among-scouts/ (accessed June 17, 2013).

63. MLBPA, News Release: MLBPA and Commissioner's Office End International Draft Discussions, May 31, 2013, http://mlb.mlb.com/pa/releases/releases.jsp?content=053113 (accessed June 17, 2013).

64. MLB, Statement on International Draft, May 31, 2013, http://mlb.mlb.com/news/article.jsp?ymd=20130531&content_id=49190958&vkey=pr_mlb&c_id=mlb (accessed June 17, 2013).

65. MLBPA, News Release.

66. Ben Badler, "Latin American Stars Sign Petition Opposing International Draft," Baseball America.com, May 29, 2013, www.baseballamerica.com/international/latin-american-stars-sign-petition-opposing-international-draft/ (accessed June 17, 2013).

67. Badler, "Trainer Frustration Grows Over Possible International Draft."

68. Ibid. The only Latin American on the International Talent Committee is Stan Javier, who is the MLBPA's special assistant for player services (Dominican Republic).

69. See, e.g., Segura, "Drafted at 13, How One Player Changed International Signing Rules" (noting in early July 2012 that the International Talent Committee had not reached any decision about the signing age issue).

70. See, e.g., Gordon, "Inside Major League Baseball's Dominican Sweatshop System" (reporting that, two years after the death of a Dominican prospect from a treatable disease at the academy of the Washington Nationals, "21 of MLB's 30 teams lack certified trainers in the Dominican Republic, including the Nationals"). On the continued lack of consistent standards at MLB academies in the Dominican Republic, see Badler, "Trainer Frustration Grows Over Possible International Draft" (quoting a Dominican baseball trainer stating that "[t]here are academies here that are good academies, and there are academies that suck").

71. Basic Agreement 2012–2016, 276.

72. Samuel O. Regalado, "'Latin Players on the Cheap': Professional Baseball Recruitment in Latin America and the Neocolonialist Tradition," Indiana Journal of Global Legal Studies 8 (2000): 9.

73. Marcano and Fidler, Stealing Lives, 194.

CHAPTER TEN: "A MATTER OF BASIC FAIRNESS"

It is my pleasure to acknowledge and thank Sarah Fields, Irvin Nathan, Greg Pfitzer, Sam Regalado, Susan Taylor, and two anonymous reviewers for their suggestions and support.

1. Mike Wise, "Nets Take a Big Chance and Select O'Bannon," New York Times, June 29, 1995, B13.

2. Malcolm Moran, "Wizardry Is Alive and Well in Westwood," New York Times, April 4, 1995, B9.

3. Gene Wojciechowski, "Wooden You Just Know It?" *Los Angeles Times*, April 8, 1995, C1; Wise, "Nets Take a Big Chance and Select O'Bannon," B13.

4. Dave Sheinin, "Ed O'Bannon Has Gone From the Hardwood to the Sales Floor," *Washington Post,* June 14, 2009, http://www.washingtonpost.com/ wp-dyn/content/article/2009/06/11/AR2009061103332.html (accessed July 2, 2012).

5. See http://www.basketball-reference.com/players/o/obanned01.html.

6. Sheinin, "Ed O'Bannon Has Gone From the Hardwood to the Sales Floor."

7. Ibid.

8. Mark Yost, *Varsity Green: A Behind-the-Scenes Look at Culture and Corruption in College Athletics* (Stanford: Stanford University Press, 2010), 65. According to the CLC website, collegiate licensed merchandise generates an estimated $4 billion annually; see http://www. clc.com/clcweb/publishing.nsf/Content/history.html. Michael McCann, "O'Bannon settles with EA Sports and CLC in class action, NCAA still remaining," *Sports Illustrated*, September 26, 2013, http://sportsillustrated. cnn.com/college-football/news/20130926/mccann-obannon-ea-clc-settlement/ (accessed May 29, 2014). Tom Farrey, "Players, game makers settle for $40M," May 31, 2014, http://espn.go.com/espn/otl/story/_/id/11010455/college-athletes-reach-40-million-settlement-ea-sports-ncaa-licensing-arm (accessed June 6, 2014).

9. In re NCAA Student-Athlete Name & Likeness Licensing Litigation, Case No. 4:09-cv-01967-CW, Northern District of California.

10. Michael McCann, "NCAA Faces Unspecified Damages, Changes in Latest Antitrust Case," July 21, 2009, http://sportsillustrated.cnn.com/2009/ writers/michael_mccann/07/21/ncaa/index.html#ixzz21KY7aJJe (accessed July 19, 2012).

11. Pete Thamel, "N.C.A.A. Fails to Stop Licensing Lawsuit," *New York Times*, February 8, 2010, B14.

12. Frank Deford, "Lawsuit against NCAA could lead to end of amateurism," March 11, 2010, http://sportsillustrated.cnn.com/2010/writers/frank_deford/03/10/NCAA-amateurism-lawsuit/index.html (accessed July 10, 2012).

13. See Ronald A. Smith, *Pay for Play: A History of Big-Time College Athletic Reform* (Urbana: University of Illinois Press, 2010).

14. In re NCAA Student-Athlete Name & Likeness Licensing Litigation, United States District Court, Northern District of California, Case No. C 09-01967 CW, March 10, 2010, 7.

15. Quoted in Wetzel, "Making NCAA Pay?"

16. Tom Farrey, "Change in compensation sought," August 31, 2012, http://espn.go.com/college-sports/story/_/id/8324732/new-motion-lawsuit-ncaa-change-how-athletes-compensated (accessed July 12, 2013).

17. The history of the term "student-athlete" is fascinating. Briefly, Walter Byers, the NCAA's first executive director, coined the phrase as a way to avoid workers' compensation claims from injured athletes in the 1950s. See Walter Byers (with Charles Hammer), *Unsportsmanlike Conduct: Exploiting College Athletes* (Ann Arbor: University of Michigan Press, [1995] 1998), 69. Taylor Branch describes the phrase as a legal "shield, and the organization continues to invoke it as both a legalistic defense and a noble ideal. Indeed, such is the term's rhetorical power that it is increasingly used as a sort of reflexive mantra against charges of rabid hypocrisy." Branch, "The Shame of College Sports," 89.

18. Dan Fitzgerald, "Calling a Foul," *Connecticut Law Tribune*, April 18, 2011, 1–2.

19. *Frontline*, "Money and March Madness," March 29, 2011, http://www. pbs. org/wgbh/pages/frontline/money-and-march-madness/etc/transcript.html#ixzz21 b5MpsrH (accessed July 22, 2012). For another version of this narrative, see Dan Wetzel, "Making NCAA Pay?" July 21, 2009, http://rivals.yahoo.com/ncaa/ basketball/news?slug=dw-ncaasuit072109 (accessed July 22, 2012).

20. Quoted in Libby Sander, "Ed O'Bannon Takes Aim at the NCAA," *Chronicle of Higher Education*, July 26, 2010, http://chronicle.com/blogs/players/ed-obannon-takes-aim-at-the-ncaa/25737 (accessed July 22, 2012).

21. Sander, "Ed O'Bannon Takes Aim at the NCAA"; Sam Laird, "Shoe Marketer Who Enriched N.C.A.A. Takes on His Creation," *New York Times*, March 12, 2011, A27.

22. Sander, "Ed O'Bannon Takes Aim at the NCAA."

23. Laird, "Shoe Marketer Who Enriched N.C.A.A. Takes on His Creation," A27.

24. Wetzel, "Making NCAA Pay?"

25. Ibid.

26. Yost, *Varsity Green*, 68.

27. Quoted in Wetzel, "Making NCAA Pay?"

28. In October 2012, Jon King "was fired by Hausfeld for undisclosed reasons," Tom Farrey of ESPN reports, "after serving as one of the lead lawyers in developing the case for the plaintiffs." Tom Farrey, "NCAA athletes can pursue TV money," January 29, 2013, http://espn.go.com/espn/otl/story/_/id/8895337/judge-rules-ncaa-athletes-legally-pursue-television-money (accessed July 12, 2013).

29. "Hausfeld LLP Files Lawsuit Against the NCAA on Behalf of Former Student Athletes," July 21, 2009, http://www.hausfeldllp.com/pages/inthenews/ 253/hausfeld-llp-files-lawsuit-against-the-ncaa-on-behalf-of-former-student-athletes- (accessed July 22, 2012).

30. Andrew B. Carrabis, "Strange Bedfellows: How the NCAA and EA Sports May Have Violated Antitrust and Right of Publicity Laws to Make a Profit at the Exploitation of Intercollegiate Amateurism," *Barry Law Review* 15 (Fall 2010): 18.

31. See http://www.ukathletics.com/doc_lib/compliance0809_sa_statement. pdf. The NCAA's current version (for the Academic Year 2010–11) of Form 08-3a is Form 10-3a. The current language is exactly the same as the former. See http:// grfx.cstv.com/photos/schools/beth/genrel/auto_pdf/StudentAthleteStatement. pdf?DB_OEM_ID=23910.

32. 2011–12 NCAA Division I Manual, 71. See http://ncaapublications.com/ p-4224-2011-2012-ncaa-division-i-manual.aspx.

33. In re NCAA Student-Athlete Name & Likeness Licensing Litigation, 8.

34. Ibid., 83.

35. Quoted in Karen Gullo, "Ex-Celtics Star Bill Russell Sues NCAA, Electronic Arts Over Image Use," October 6, 2011, http://mobile.bloomberg.com/news/ 2011-10-06/ex-celtics-star-bill-russell-sues-ncaa-for-antitrust-in-licensing-dispute (accessed August 1, 2012).

36. Gullo, "Ex-Celtics Star Bill Russell Sues NCAA, Electronic Arts Over Image Use."

37. Scott R. Chandler, "Whose Right Is It Anyway?: How Recent Cases and Controversies Have Blurred the Lines Between First Amendment Protection and an Athlete's Right of Publicity," *Marquette Sports Law Review* 21 (Fall 2010): 331.

38. Chandler, "Whose Right Is It Anyway?" 330–31.

39. In re NCAA Student-Athlete Name & Likeness Licensing Litigation, 2.

40. Katie Thomas, "College Stars See Themselves in Video Games, and Pause to Sue," *New York Times*, July 4, 2009, A1. Later, Judge Wilken separated the *O'Bannon* and *Keller* suits; the Keller "trial is set for March 2015." Mark Koba, "NCAA v. O'Bannon: 'Likely the players will win,'" CNBC, May 28, 2014, http://www.cnbc.com/id/101707534 (accessed May 29, 2014).

41. See Sheldon W. Halpern, "The Right of Publicity: Maturation of an Independent Right Protecting the Associative Value of Personality," *Hastings Law Journal* 46 (March 1995): 853, 856–59.

42. Marlen Garcia, "Judge approves ex-UCLA star Ed O'Bannon's lawsuit against NCAA," *USA Today*, February 9, 2010, http://www.usatoday.com/sports/college/2010-02-08-judge-approves-ncaa-suit_N.htm (accessed July 22, 2012).

43. Quoted in ibid.

44. Quoted in ibid.

45. In re NCAA Student-Athlete Name & Likeness Licensing Litigation, 7.

46. See Paul C. Weiler, Gary R. Roberts, Roger I. Abrams, and Stephen F. Ross, eds., *Sports and the Law: Text, Cases, and Problems*, 4th ed. (St. Paul, MN: West, 2011), 873.

47. In re NCAA Student-Athlete Name & Likeness Licensing Litigation, 49.

48. See "Revenue," January 17, 2012, http://www.ncaa.org/wps/ wcm/connect/public/NCAA/Finances/Revenue (accessed July 27, 2012).

49. In re NCAA Student-Athlete Name & Likeness Licensing Litigation, 54. "There is nothing unenforceable or even wrong about adhesion contracts," explains the *Gale Encyclopedia of American Law* (2011). "This does not mean, however, that all adhesion contracts are valid. Many adhesion contracts are unconscionable; they are so unfair to the weaker party that a court will refuse to enforce them." *Gale Encyclopedia of American Law*, 3rd ed. (Detroit: Gale Cengage Learning, 2011), 97.

50. In re NCAA Student-Athlete Name & Likeness Licensing Litigation, 82.

51. Ibid., 88.

52. Ibid., 91.

53. Ibid., 59.

54. Electronic Arts Inc. Fiscal Year 2011 Proxy Statement and Annual Report, June 10 2011, http://investor.ea.com/annual-proxy-2011/images/Electronic_Arts-2011.pdf (accessed July 27, 2012).

55. Julia Brighton, "The NCAA and the Right of Publicity: How the O'Bannon/Keller Case May Finally Level the Playing Field," *Hastings Communications and Entertainment Law Journal* 33 (Winter 2011): 278.

56. "Cardinals Stop 49ers in Nick of Time," *New York Times*, November 11, 2008, B17.

57. In re NCAA Student-Athlete Name & Likeness Licensing Litigation, 97.

58. Ibid., 97–131.

59. The complaint contends that there is a $4 billion annual market for collegiate licensed merchandise. Ibid., 93.

60. Ibid., 135.

61. Ibid., 136.

62. Marlen Garcia, "Judge dismisses video game maker EA from ex-players'

suit against NCAA," *USA Today*, May 5, 2011, http://content.usatoday.com/communities/campusrivalry/post/2011/05/judge-dismisses-video-game-maker-ea-from-ex-players-suit-against-ncaa/1#.UBJCjByk3zV (accessed July 26, 2012).

63. Quoted in Karen Gullo, "Electronic Arts Must Face Former Student Athletes' Antitrust Claims," July 28, 2011, http://www.bloomberg.com/news/2011-07-28/electronic-arts-must-face-ex-athletes-antitrust-claims-over-use-of-images.html (accessed July 26, 2012).

64. Quoted in Gullo, "Electronic Arts Must Face Former Student Athletes' Antitrust Claims."

65. Christian Dennie, "Changing the Game: The Litigation That May Be the Catalyst for Change in Intercollegiate Athletics," *Syracuse Law Review* 62 (2012): 22.

66. Smith, *Pay for Play*, 139.

67. Kirk Johnson, "Assistant Coaches Win N.C.A.A. Suit; $66 Million Award," *New York Times*, May 5, 1998, A1.

68. Johnson, "Assistant Coaches Win N.C.A.A. Suit; $66 Million Award," A1; "NCAA to Pay Coaches $54.5M," February 11, 2009, http://www.cbsnews.com/stories/1999/03/09/sports/main38197.shtml (accessed July 27, 2012).

69. Andrew Zimbalist, *Circling the Bases: Essays on the Challenges and Prospects of the Sports Industry* (Philadelphia: Temple University Press, 2011), 44.

70. For more on the NCAA and antitrust litigation, see Weiler, Roberts, Abrams, and Ross, *Sports and the Law*, 871–924.

71. For more on this issue, see Amanda Pintaro, "Is the NCAA Fulfilling Its Tax-Exempt Status?" *Illinois Business Law Journal*, February 21, 2010, http://www.law.illinois.edu/bljournal/post/2010/02/21/Is-the-NCAA-Fulfilling-its-Tax-Exempt-Status.aspx (accessed June 5, 2013).

72. 2011–12 NCAA Division I Manual, 1.

73. According to Taylor Branch, "In 2010, despite the faltering economy, a single college athletic league, the football-crazed Southeastern Conference (SEC), became the first to crack the billion-dollar barrier in athletic receipts. The Big Ten pursued closely at $905 million. That money comes from a combination of ticket sales, concession sales, merchandise, licensing fees, and other sources—but the great bulk of it comes from television contracts." Branch, "The Shame of College Sports," 82.

74. Since 1972, athletic scholarships "have been awarded on a one-year basis. The net result is that athletes are under great financial pressure to do whatever it takes to retain their scholarship, even if the training schedule and other athletic demands make it difficult for them to get a good education or elect a demanding major." Derek Bok, *Universities in the Marketplace: The Commercialization of Higher Education* (Princeton, NJ: Princeton University Press, 2003), 131; also see Zimbalist, *The Bottom Line*, 252.

75. "Scholarship shortfall study reveals college athletes pay to play," March 26, 2009, http://www.ncpanow.org/releases_advisories?id=0009 (accessed August 1, 2012).

76. Robert A. McCormick and Amy Christian McCormick, "The Myth of the Student-Athlete: The College Athlete as Employee," *Washington Law Review* 81 (2006): 71.

77. 2011–12 NCAA Division I Manual, 4.

78. Wallace I. Renfro, "2009 NCAA State of the Association," http://www.ncaa.org/wps/wcm/connect/public/NCAA/About+the+NCAA/Who+We+Are/Myles+Brand+Legacy/Legacy+of+Leadership/2009+NCAA+State+of+the+Association (accessed August 1, 2012).

79. Mary Catherine Moore, "There Is No 'I' In NCAA: Why College Sports Video Games Do Not Violate College Athletes' Rights of Publicity Such to Entitle Them to Compensation for Use of Their Likenesses," *Journal of Intellectual Property Law* 18 (Fall 2010): 273.

80. Brighton, "The NCAA and the Right of Publicity," 276.

81. Kristal S. Stippich and Kadence A. Otto, "Carrying a Good Joke Too Far? An Analysis of the Enforceability of Student-Athlete Consent to Use of Name and Likeness," *Journal of Legal Aspects of Sport* 20 (Summer 2010): 172.

82. Andrew B. Carrabis, "Strange Bedfellows: How the NCAA and EA Sports May Have Violated Antitrust and Right of Publicity Laws to Make a Profit at the Exploitation of Intercollegiate Amateurism," *Barry Law Review* 15 (Fall 2010): 39.

83. John K. Tokarz, "Involuntary Servants: The NCAA's Abridgement of Student-Athletes' Economic Rights in Perpetuity Violates the Thirteenth Amendment," *Wisconsin Law Review* (2010): 1505, 1519.

84. Ibid., 1521.

85. Ibid., 1536, 1535.

86. Jeffrey J. R. Sundram, "The Downside of Success: How Increased Commercialism Could Cost the NCAA Its Biggest Antitrust Defense," *Tulane Law Review* 85 (December 2010): 570.

87. For some of the other relevant articles, see Christian Dennie, "Tebow Drops Back to Pass: Videogames Have Crossed the Line, But Does the Right of Publicity Protect a Student-Athlete's Likeness When Balanced Against the First Amendment?" *Arkansas Law Review* 62 (2009): 645–81; Leslie E. Wong, "Our Blood, Our Sweat, Their Profit: Ed O'Bannon Takes on the NCAA for Infringing on the Former Student-Athlete's Right of Publicity," *Texas Tech Law Review* 42 (Summer 2010): 1069–1107; William D. Holthaus Jr., "*Ed O'Bannon v. NCAA*: Do Former NCAA Athletes Have a Case Against the NCAA for Its Use of Their Likenesses?" *Saint Louis University Law Journal* 55 (Fall 2010): 369–93; Beth A. Cianfrone and Thomas A. Baker III, "The Use of Student-Athlete Likenesses in Sport Video Games: An Application of the Right of Publicity," *Journal of Legal Aspects of Sport* 20 (Winter 2010): 35–74; James J. S. Holmes and Kanika D. Corley, "Defining Liability for Likeness of Athlete Avatars in Video Games," *Los Angeles Lawyer* 34 (May 2011): 17–21; Krista Correa, "All Your Faces Belong to Us: Protecting Celebrity Images in Hyper-Realistic Video Games," *Hastings Communications and Entertainment Law Journal* 34 (Fall 2011): 93–126; Brian Welch, "Unconscionable Amateurism: How the NCAA Violates Antitrust by Forcing Athletes to Sign Away Their Image Rights," *John Marshall Law Review* 44 (Winter 2011): 533–58.

88. John Brueggemann, *Rich, Free, and Miserable: The Failure of Success in America* (Lanham, MD: Rowman & Littlefield Publishers, 2010), 1.

89. Bok, Universities in the Marketplace, x.

90. Ibid., 35.

91. Ronald A. Smith, *Sports and Freedom: The Rise of Big-Time College Athletics* (New York: Oxford University Press, [1988] 1990), ix.

92. Zimbalist, *The Bottom Line*, 240.

93. Branch, "The Shame of College Sports," 82.

94. Wetzel, "Making NCAA Pay?"

95. 2011–12 NCAA Division I Manual, 4.

96. Quoted in "Hausfeld LLP Files Lawsuit Against the NCAA on Behalf of Former Student Athletes," July 21, 2009, http://www.hausfeldllp.com/pages/press_releases/252/hausfeld-llp-files-lawsuit-against-the-ncaa-on-behalf-of-former-student-athletes- (accessed August 9, 2012).

97. Quoted in "'Corrupt' College Sports System in Danger of Collapse," August 31, 2011, http://herald-review.com/sports/college/c7b796dc-d244-11e0-a6eb-001cc4c03286.html (accessed August 9, 2012).

98. Deford, "NCAA: Show Me the Money!"

99. Ronald Smith writes, "Most of the problems that existed with the first intercollegiate contests at the beginning of the railroad era were still in existence a century and a half later." Smith, *Pay for Play*, 208.

100. Deford, "NCAA: Show Me the Money!"

101. Michael McCann, "O'Bannon expands NCAA lawsuit," September 1, 2012, http://sportsillustrated.cnn.com/2012/writers/michael_mccann/09/01/obannon-ncaa-lawsuit/index.html#ixzz2ZKRthFWJ (accessed July 12, 2013).

102. "Judge lets class-action efforts in O'Bannon case go on," *USA Today*, January 30, 2012, http://www.usatoday.com/story/sports/ncaaf/2013/01/30/ncaa-obannon-players-lawsuit-name-and-likeness/1877031/ (accessed July 12, 2013).

103. Quoted in "Student-athlete likeness lawsuit timeline," September 1, 2012, http://www.ncaa.org/wps/wcm/connect/public/ncaa/resources/ latest+news/2012/september/student+athlete+likeness+lawsuit+timeline (accessed July 12, 2013).

104. "Judge lets class-action efforts in O'Bannon case go on," *USA Today*, January 30, 2012, http://www.usatoday.com/story/sports/ncaaf/2013/01/30/ncaa-obannon-players-lawsuit-name-and-likeness/1877031/ (accessed July 12, 2013).

105. Jon Solomon, "Ed O'Bannon hearing: Judge wants current player added to suit and amended complaint," June 21, 2013, http://www.al.com/sports/index.ssf/2013/06/ ed_obannon_hearing_judge_wants.html (accessed July 12, 2013); Jon Solomon, "Ed O'Bannon lawyer asks NCAA to agree in writing not to hurt current player added to suit," July 8, 2012, http://www.al.com/sports/index.ssf/2013/07/ed_obannon_lawyer_asks_ncaa_to.html (accessed July 12, 2013).

106. Quoted in Solomon, "Ed O'Bannon hearing."

107. The six student-athletes are Jake Fischer and Jake Smith of the University of Arizona, Darius Robinson of Clemson University, Chase Garnham of Vanderbilt University, and Moses Alipate and Victor Keise of the University of Minnesota. Erik Brady and Steve Berkowitz, "Six Active Players Join O'Bannon Lawsuit against NCAA," *USA Today*, July 18, 2013, http://www.usatoday.com/story/sports/college/2013/07/18/ncaa-ed-obannon-lawsuit-active-players-arizona-clemson/2564375/ (accessed July 18, 2013).

108. Quoted in Tom Farrey, "6 Current Players Join NCAA Lawsuit," July 18, 2013, http://espn.go.com/espn/otl/story/_/id/9491249/six-current-football-players-join-ed-obannon-ncaa-lawsuit (accessed July 18, 2013).

109. Quoted in Farrey, "6 Current Players Join NCAA Lawsuit."

110. Rachel Bachman and Mike Sielski, "NCAA Won't Renew Deal With EA

Sports," *Wall Street Journal,* July 17, 2013, http://online.wsj.com/article/SB1000142 4127887324448104578612013170068062.html (accessed July 18, 2013).

111. Lester Munson, "Events Ratchet Up NCAA Pressure," July 19, 2013, http://espn.go.com/espn/otl/story/_/id/9491666/latest-developments-ncaa-electronic-arts-lawsuit-significantly-change-case (accessed July 22, 2013).

112. Brent Schrotenboer, "EA Sports Re-ups on College Football after NCAA Snub," *USA Today*, July 19, 2013, http://www.usatoday.com/story/sports/ncaaf/2013/07/19/ ea-sports-college-football-contract-renewed/2570119/ (accessed July 22, 2013).

113. Ibid.

114. Joe Nocera, "The Lawsuit and the N.C.A.A.," *New York Times*, June 21, 2013, http://www.nytimes.com/2013/06/22/opinion/nocera-the-lawsuit-and-the-ncaa.html (accessed July 12, 2013).

115. Ibid.

116. Sarah K. Fields, "Law and Shame: The Legal Implications of Athletic Scandals," paper presented at the 2013 North American Society for Sport History annual conference.

117. Quoted in Greg Bishop, "Lawsuit Named for O'Bannon Has Other Critical Participants," *New York Times*, June 19, 2013, http://www. nytimes.com/2013/06/20/sports/ lawsuit-named-for-obannon-has-other-critical-participants.html?pagewanted=all&_r=0 (accessed July 12, 2013).

Chapter Eleven: Epilogue

1. "Roberts: 'My job is to call balls and strikes and not pitch or bat,'" CNN, September 12, 2005. http://articles.cnn.com/2005-09-12/politics/roberts.statement_1_judicial-role-judges-judicial-oath?_s=PM:POLITICS (accessed August 6, 2005).

2. Allen Guttman, *From Ritual to Record: The Nature of Modern Sports* (New York: Columbia University Press, 1978), 97.

3. Peter Lattman, "Justice Blackmun's Lengthy Ode to Baseball," The Wall Street Journal "Law Blog" (October 27, 2006). http://blogs.wsj.com/law/2006/10/27/justice-blackmuns-lengthy-ode-to-baseball/ (accessed August 8, 2012).

4. Adam Liptak, "This Bench Belongs in a Dugout," *New York Times*, May 31, 2010. http://www.nytimes.com/2010/06/01/us/01bar.html (accessed August 11, 2010).

5. Peter Levine, *American Sport: A Documentary History* (Englewood Cliffs, NJ: Prentice-Hall, 1989), xi.

6. See Lydia Jessup, "Olympic Profile: Caster Semenya," *Global Post*, July 24, 2012, http://www.globalpost.com/dispatch/globalpost-blogs/world-at-play/120710/olympic-profile-caster-semenya (accessed August 21, 2012), and Ken Borland, "Caster Semenya Denies Allegations She Lost Olympic 800 Metres on Purpose," *National Post*, August 14, 2012, http://sports.nationalpost.com/2012/08/14/caster-semenya-says-allegations-she-lost-olympic-800-metres-on-purpose-are-untrue/ (accessed August 21, 2012).

Thoughts Regarding Scholarly Methods

1. Gilbert H. Montague, "Antitrust Laws and the Federal Trade Commission, 1914–1927," *Columbia Law Review* 27 (1927): 650–78.

2. Frederic A. Johnson, "Baseball Law," *United States Law Review* 73 (1939): 252–70. Johnson practiced what he preached and represented Danny Gardella in his lawsuit against baseball.

3. This list is just a sample of some of the US-based sport law journals available in 2014. Most issues after 1982 are available through the Lexis-Nexis and Westlaw databases. Older issues are often available through HeinOnline. Be aware as well that many of these journals change names over time. See *DePaul Journal of Sports Law and Contemporary Problems*; *Entertainment and Sports Lawyer*; *Entertainment & Sports Law Journal*; *Florida Entertainment, Art, and Sport Law Journal*; *Fordham Intellectual Property, Media, & Entertainment Law Journal*; *International Sports Journal*; *International Sports Law Journal*; *International Sports Law Review*; *Legal Issues in Collegiate Athletics*; *Marquette Sports Law Review*; *Seton Hall Journal of Sports and Entertainment Law*; *The Sports Lawyer*; *The Sports Lawyer Journal*; *Texas Review of Entertainment & Sports Law*; *University of Miami Entertainment and Sports Law Review*; *Villanova Sports and Entertainment Law Journal*; and *Virginia Sports and Entertainment Law Journal*. For links to these and other journals along with name changes, see "Law Library: Sports Law Journals," Cleveland-Marshall College of Law.com, https://www.law.csuohio.edu/lawlibrary/guides/sportsjournals (accessed August 8, 2013).

4. Deborah L. Brake, *Getting into the Game: Title IX and the Women's Sports Revolution* (New York: New York University Press, 2010).

5. Roger I. Abrams, *Sports Justice: The Law and Business of Sport* (Boston: Northeastern University Press, 2010).

6. andre douglas pond cummings and Anne Marie Lofaso, *Reversing Field: Examining Commercialization, Labor, Gender, and Race in 21st-Century Sports Law* (Morgantown: West Virginia University Press, 2010).

7. Lorne W. Sawula, "Canadian Governmental Intervention in Sport: Why 1970, Why Not Before?," NASSH Conference Proceedings 1973, http://library.la84.org/SportsLibrary/NASSH_Proceedings/NP1973/NP1973l.pdf (accessed August 8, 2013). A version of that conference paper was published as Lorne W. Sawula, "Why 1970, Why Not Before?" *Canadian Journal of the History of Sport and Physical Education* 4, no. 2 (1973): 43–58.

8. Al-Tony Gilmore, "Jack Johnson and White Women: The National Impact," *Journal of Negro History* 58 (1973): 18–38.

9. J. Thomas Jable, "Pennsylvania's Early Blue Laws: A Quaker Experiment in the Suppression of Sport and Amusements, 1682–1740," *Journal of Sport History* 1 (1974): 107–21.

10. John Marshall Carter, "Sports, Crime, and Peasants in Thirteenth-Century England," *Canadian Journal of Sport History* 17, no. 2 (1986): 28–57.

11. R. C. Watson and John C. MacLellan, "Smitting to Spitting: 80 Years of Ice-Hockey in Canadian Courts," *Canadian Journal of Sport History* 17, no. 2 (1986): 10–27.

12. Kevin B. Wamsley, "State Formation and Institutionalized Racism: Gambling Laws in Nineteenth and Early Twentieth Century Canada," *Sport History Review* 29 (1998): 77–85.

13. Sarah K. Fields, *Female Gladiators: Gender, Law, and Contact Sport in America* (Urbana: University of Illinois Press, 2005).

14. Thomas M. Hunt, *Drug Games: The International Olympic Committee and the Politics of Doping, 1986–2000* (Austin: University of Texas Press, 2011).

15. Ying Wushanley, *Playing Nice and Losing: The Struggle for Control of Women's Intercollegiate Athletics, 1960–2000* (Syracuse, NY: Syracuse University Press, 2004).

16. *Fern Kellmeyer v. National Education Association* was filed in the U.S. District Court in the South District of Florida on January 17, 1973. As Wushanley describes, the case was settled before it went to court.

17. Ronald A. Smith, *Pay for Play: A History of Big-Time College Athletic Reform* (Urbana: University of Illinois Press, 2011).

18. Wilbert Leonard, *Sociological Perspective of Sport* (New York: McMillan, 1993).

19. Jay Johnson and Margery Holman, *Making the Team* (Toronto: Canadian Scholarly Press, 1993).

20. Ross Coomber, *Drugs and Drug Use in Society* (New York: New York University Press, 1994).

21. Verner Møller, *The Ethics of Doping and Anti-Doping: Redeeming the Soul of Sport?* (New York: Routledge, 2010).

22. Glenn M. Wong, *The Essentials of Sports Law*, 4th ed. (Westport, CT: Praeger Publishing, 2010). A search of amazon.com or any other library catalog with the search term "sports law" gives dozens of references.

23. See Legal Information Institute at Cornell University Law School, http://www.law.cornell.edu (accessed August 11, 2013).

Contributors

Ron Briley is an instructor at Sandia Preparatory School and author of *The Baseball Film in Postwar America: A Critical Study, 1948–1962.*

Richard Crepeau, PhD, is a Professor of History at the University of Central Florida and the author of *Baseball: America's Diamond Mind, 1919–1941.*

Anne L. DeMartini, JD, is an Assistant Professor of Sport Management at Flagler College.

David P. Fidler, JD, is the James Louis Calamaras Professor of Law at Indiana University and coauthor with Arturo J. Marcano Guevara of *Stealing Lives: The Globalization of Baseball and Tragic Story of Alex Quiroz.*

Sarah K. Fields, JD, PhD, is an Associate Professor of Communication at the University of Colorado, Denver, and author of *Female Gladiators: Gender, Law, and Contact Sport in America.*

Steven P. Gietschier, PhD, is University Curator and Assistant Professor of History at Lindenwood University.

Thomas M. Hunt, JD, PhD, is an Assistant Professor of Kinesiology and Health Education at the University of Texas and author of *Drug Games: The International Olympic Committee and the Politics of Doping.*

Arturo J. Marcano Guevara, LLM, is a Toronto lawyer and served as international legal adviser to the Venezuelan Baseball Players Association. He is coauthor with David P. Fidler, of *Stealing Lives: The Globalization of Baseball and Tragic Story of Alex Quiroz.*

Daniel A. Nathan, PhD, is an Associate Professor of American Studies at Skidmore College. He is the author of *Saying It's So: A Cultural History of the Black Sox Scandal.*

Samuel O. Regalado, PhD, is a Professor of History at California State University, Stanislaus. He is author of *Nikkei Baseball: From Immigration to Internment to the Major Leagues.*

Janice S. Todd, PhD, is a Professor of Kinesiology and Health Education at the University of Texas and codirector of the H. J. Lutcher Stark Center for Physical Culture and Sports. She is the author of *Physical Culture and the Body Beautiful: Purposive Exercise in the Lives of American Women.*

Index

A

Abdul-Jabbar, Kareem, 16, 21
abortion cases, 2, 38
Abrams, Roger I., 162
advocacy for transgender athletes, 112–13
Advocates for Informed Choice, 111
Afghanistan War, 17
age and identity fraud, 125
Alcindor, Lew. *See* Abdul-Jabbar, Kareem
Alderson, Sandy, 121
Alderson Report, 121–27, 132, 158–59
Aleman, Miguel, 66
Alexander, Charles, 39
Ali, Muhammad, 43, 149, 156, 166; celebrity
    of, 12; convicted of draft evasion, 5, 11;
    legacy of, 17; legal team of, 14; refusal to
    be inducted, 3–5; retirement of, 16; sport-
    writers on, 4–5; Supreme Court victory of,
    15; suspension of, 5; symbolism as a black
    athlete, 9–10; at the United States Armed
    Forces Examining and Entrance Station, 3.
    See also Clay v. United States
Allen, Maury, 59
Allums, Kye, 98
amateurism. *See In re: NCAA Student-Athlete
    Name & Likeness Licensing Litigation*
Ambrose, Stephen, 45
American Basketball Association, 21–22, 156
American Civil Liberties Union of Washington,
    111
American Drug Free Powerlifting Association
    (ADFPA), 78, 88–89
American League, 60
American Legion, 5
American Masters Powerlifting Federation, 81
American Powerlifting Federation (APF), 76,
    78–79; antitrust laws and, 80–83
American Psychiatric Association, 93
American Sociological Review, 76
Americans with Disabilities Act (ADA), 110
American University, 47
antitrust law, 34, 37, 38, 43, 67, 136; estab-
    lishment, 53; exemption from, 55, 60–61;
    language, 53–54; Mexican League and,
    57–58, 63, 64–66, 70; powerlifting and,
    84–91; publicity and likenesses and, 141;
    rule of reason and, 54–55; sports league
    organization and, 55–56; vagueness, 54
"Antitrust Laws and the Federal Trade
    Commission, 1914–1927," 161
Arizona Diamondbacks, 119

Arizona State University, 141
armed forces: conscientious objector status
    and, 4, 6–8, 13–15, 156; history of the
    draft and, 6–7; recruiting procedures, 3–4
Armstrong, Scott, 11, 15, 38, 39
Arver, Joseph F., 16
Association of Intercollegiate Athletics for
    Women (AIAW), 101
athletes: amateurism, 135, 136, 159–60;
    antitrust laws and, 34, 37, 38; in the
    armed forces, 3–4; black, 4, 9–10 (*See
    also* Ali, Muhammad); careers in law,
    161; civil rights movement and, 14, 75,
    100–101; drug testing of, 75, 76, 77–80;
    female, 77–78, 83–84, 93, 97, 100–104,
    157–58, 162–63; free agency, 40, 41, 90;
    gay, 94; Latin American, 94–95, 115–33,
    158–59; Olympic, 2, 9–10; organizational
    sponsorship of, 87–88; players associations,
    31, 35, 40, 48–62, 127–31; reserve clause
    and, 58–62; sportive nationalism and, 80;
    transgender, 93, 97–114
Autobiography of Malcolm X, 15

B

Bagger, Mianne, 97
Baki, 10
Baldwin, Tammy, 94
Ballplayer: Pelotero, 115, 128, 132; Alderson
    Report and, 121–27; reactions to, 119–21;
    subject matter, 117–19
Baltimore Federal League, 33
Barr body test, 103–5
baseball. *See* Major League Baseball (MLB)
Baseball Encyclopedia, 39
basketball: women's, 98. *See also Haywood v.
    National Basketball Association*
Baskir, Lawrence M., 6, 8–9, 16
Batista, Jean Carlos, 117–19, 120–21
Berg, Moe, 39
Bergman, Lowell, 137
Berra, Yogi, 115
Bettman, Gary, 161
biking, 98
Birmingham, Joe, 62
Bishop, Edmund, 78, 88
Black, Hugo, 1, 11, 12–13, 50
black athletes, 4, 9–10; civil rights movement
    and, 14, 75; in college, 21
Blackmun, Harry, 1, 11, 12, 27, 37, 38, 39,
    155; nomination of, 49–50

Dominican Republic: Alderson Report and, 121–27, 158–59; documentary on baseball prospects from, 115–17; Miguel Angel Sanó and Jean Carlos Batista of, 117–19

Douglas, William O., 1, 11, 12, 19, 37, 50; early life of, 24–25; *Haywood v. National Basketball Association* decision and, 19–20, 28–30; judicial career of, 25–26; retirement of, 30

draft, military: conscientious objectors to, 4, 6–8, 13, 14–15, 156; ending of, 16–17; evasion, 5, 10–11; history of, 6–7, 16; peacetime, 7

Drug Games: The International Olympic Committee and the Politics of Doping, 1960–2008, 162

Drugs and Drug Use in Society, 163

drug testing, 75, 76, 77–80, 88

Dumaresq, Michelle, 98

Duquette, Jerold J., 61

E

Early, Gerald, 4

EA Sports, 94, 135–36, 137, 140–44, 152. *See also In re: NCAA Student-Athlete Name & Likeness Licensing Litigation; O'Bannon v. NCAA*

Easterbrook, Frank, 86–87

Eastland, James, 47

Education Amendments Act, 101, 109

Edwards, Harry, 9–10, 17

Ehrlichman, John, 50–51

Eisenhower, Dwight, 11, 44, 45, 49

Eisenstadt v. Baird, 93

Equal Pay Act, 101

Equal Protection Clause, 108–9

Eskridge, Chauncey, 14

Essentials of Sports Law, The, 163

Ethics of Doping and Anti-Doping: Redeeming the Soul of Sport, The, 163

Evert, Chris, 101

F

Fair Play: Journal of Sport, Philosophy, Ethics and Law, 163

farm clubs, 68

Federal Baseball Club v. National League, 33, 34–35, 60–61, 72

Federal Bureau of Investigation, 10

Federal League, 60, 67

Federal Rules of Civil Procedure, 86

Feller, Bob, 64

female athletes, 162–63; civil rights movement and, 100–101; gender testing of, 97, 103–4, 157–58; growth in number of, 101; in powerlifting, 77–78, 83–84; in tennis history, 101–2; Title IX, Educational

Amendments Act and, 101. *See also* transgender athletes

Female Gladiators: Gender, Law, and Contact Sport in America, 162

Ferguson, Warren J., 27–28

Fields, Sarah K., 162

First Amendment rights, 140–41

Fischer, Jake, 152

Fitton, Tony, 82

Fitzgerald, Dan, 137, 138

Flood, Curt, 33, 40, 43, 58, 59, 60, 68, 149, 156, 157. *See also Flood v. Kuhn*

Flood v. Kuhn, 1, 27, 43, 72, 149, 155, 156–57, 165; decision, 37–38; *Federal Baseball Club v. National League* and, 33, 34–35; filing of, 36–37; historical significance of, 33, 39–41; lower court preliminary injunction denied and, 35–36; precedent affecting, 33–34; *Toolson v. New York Yankees* and, 33–34, 35, 36, 38

Florida State League, 70

Flynn, Neil, 41

Folley, Zora, 16

Football Association, 111

Ford, Gerald, 26, 30

Foreman, George, 16

Fortas, Abe, 26, 43–48

"Fortas of the Supreme Court: A Question of Ethics," 48

Foster, Nate, 83

Foxx, Jimmie, 39

Frank, Jerome N., 68, 70

Frantz, Diane, 83

Frantz, Ernie, 78–80, 82, 89; women powerlifters and, 83–84

Frantz v. United States Powerlifting, 76, 88, 158

free agency, 40, 41, 90

Friday, Herschel, 50

Friedman, Lawrence, 54

Frontline, 137

Frostburg State University, 40

G

gambling, 54, 59

Gardella, Danny, 34, 57–58, 157; background of, 62–63; challenge of the baseball establishment, 66–72; legacy of, 59, 72–73; in the Mexican League, 64–66

Gay and Lesbian International Sport Association, 111

Gay Games Federation, 111

Gayo, Rene, 117–18

Gedney, Judy, 89–90

Gedney, Roger, 78, 79, 84

gender identity. *See* transgender athletes

General Association of International Sports Federations (GAISF), 77

George Mason University, 155